IMAGES
of America

MILTON
AND THE
NEW HAMPSHIRE FARM MUSEUM

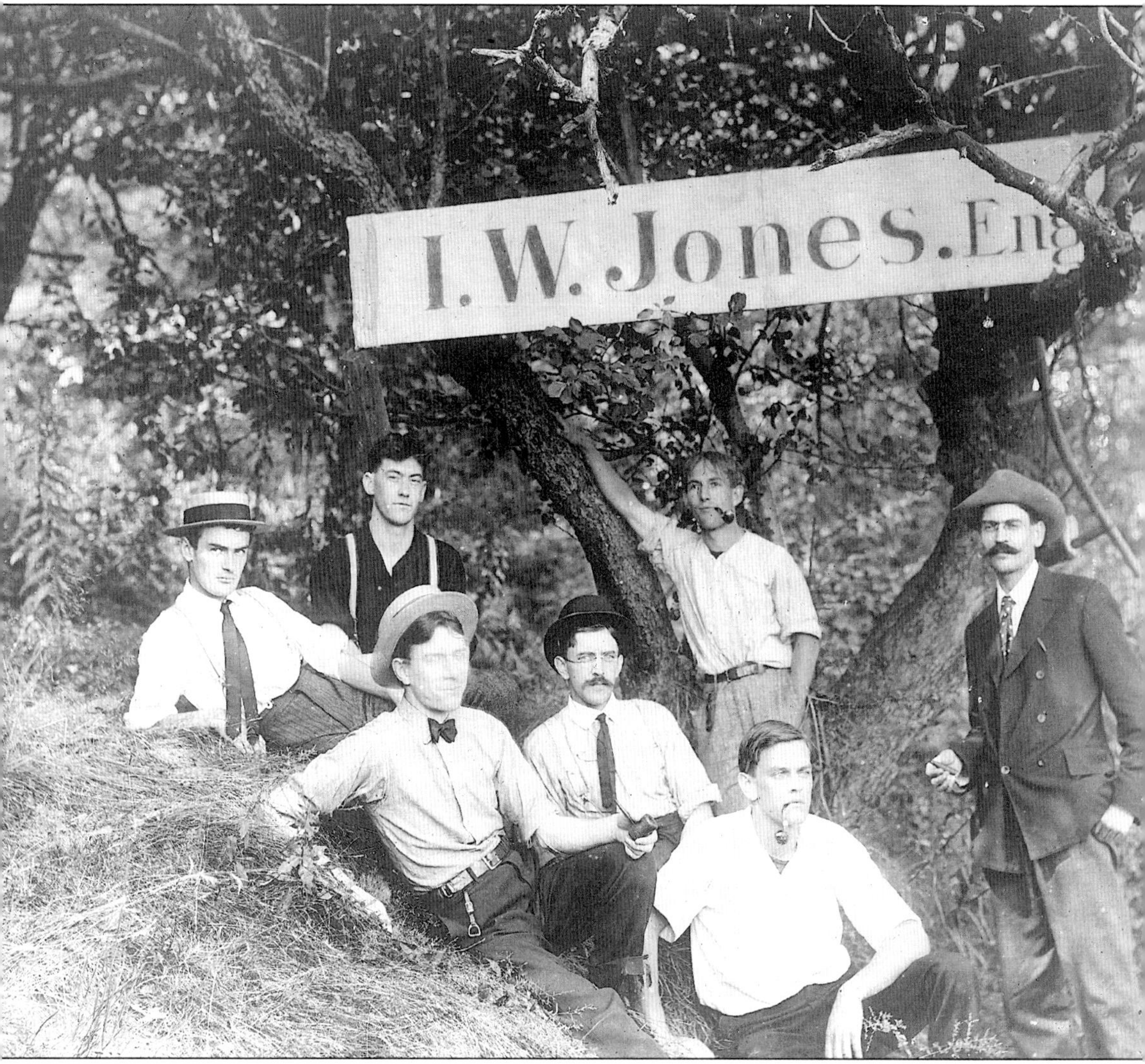

I.W. Jones. This bucolic scene shows a group of men relaxing for a c. 1905 photograph. The "Eng." on the sign suggests the word "engineer." The men could possibly be members of a surveying crew.

IMAGES
of America

MILTON
AND THE
NEW HAMPSHIRE FARM MUSEUM

Sarah Ricker

ARCADIA
PUBLISHING

ISBN 978-0-7385-6402-9

Published by Arcadia Publishing
Charleston SC, Chicago IL, Portsmouth NH, San Francisco CA

Printed in the United States of America

Library of Congress Catalog Card Number: 2008939741

For all general information contact Arcadia Publishing at:
Telephone 843-853-2070
Fax 843-853-0044
E-mail sales@arcadiapublishing.com
For customer service and orders:
Toll-Free 1-888-313-2665

Visit us on the Internet at www.arcadiapublishing.com

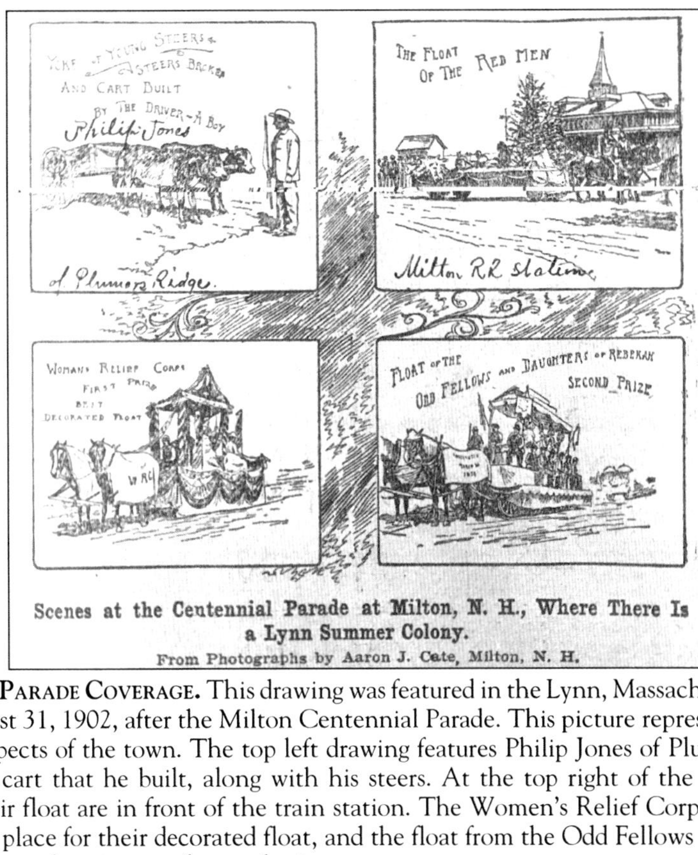

Scenes at the Centennial Parade at Milton, N. H., Where There Is a Lynn Summer Colony.
From Photographs by Aaron J. Cate, Milton, N. H.

CENTENNIAL PARADE COVERAGE. This drawing was featured in the Lynn, Massachusetts, *Evening Star* on August 31, 1902, after the Milton Centennial Parade. This picture represents the many important aspects of the town. The top left drawing features Philip Jones of Plummer's Ridge, showing the cart that he built, along with his steers. At the top right of the page, the Red Men and their float are in front of the train station. The Women's Relief Corps is featured as winning first place for their decorated float, and the float from the Odd Fellows and Daughters of Rebekah were the winners of second prize.

Contents

ACKNOWLEDGMENTS

This book is dedicated to my professor, mentor, and friend, Dr. Patricia O'Malley, who teaches history at Bradford College. Over the past four years she has watched me grow and change my mind about what I want to do with the rest of my life. She has been supportive, when just about every month I would walk into her office with a new career idea, history being the only link between all the different careers. Now, as I graduate college, I know what I want to do, and I owe her many thanks for being part of that decision. Thank you.

I would also like to thank the following people, who have been very generous with letting me borrow the family photographs that made this book possible: the New Hampshire Farm Museum, the Milton Historical Society, Nute Library, Jake Bordeau, Vicki Dawson, Bonnie Dunton, Isabelle Eldridge, John and Judy Gilman, Barbara Loiselle, Donald Stowe and family, and Martha Verrel. I would also like to take this opportunity to thank my parents, William and Mary Ricker, and my sister Emily for being helpful and supportive while I have been working on this project.

Introduction

This is the story of a little part of southeast New Hampshire. It is a story told through old photographs that have been lovingly saved for generations. It is the story of Milton, New Hampshire, and its immediate neighbor, Milton Mills. The photographs recapture a past of farms and orchards, ice houses and paper mills, shoe shops and blanket mills. We can walk through the center of the old town with its still familiar sights, and visit the schoolrooms that our grandparents knew in their childhood. We can stroll the banks of the Salmon Falls River and delight in the natural beauty of the Flume. The past continues into the present because the old photographs have frozen those moments and places and people in time. With a turn of the page, we can be transported back to long ago.

This is the story, too, of the Jones family and its farm and orchards on Plummer's Ridge. A detailed photographic archive recaptures that special place and time in our local history. Today, the New Hampshire Farm Museum graces that land and has recreated agricultural life in the 19th century for the scholar as well as the casual visitor.

Milton was originally the Northeast Parish of Rochester. In 1802, the residents in that far corner separated themselves from their mother-town and established their own place. Their complaint with Rochester was one of distance, especially the distance required to go to church services. Church in the town of Rochester was held on Rochester Hill, a good distance for a family to travel from Milton, especially in the winter, even with a horse and buggy. All residents, however, whether they could attend church or not, were expected to help support the local minister and the church through taxation. The people living in the Northeast Parish resolved the issue by inviting minister Ruben Nayson to serve them. The first services were held in the home of Elijah Horn in 1802.

It was also in Lt. Elijah Horn's house on Plummer's Ridge that the first official town meeting was held. The date was August 30, 1802, and the first piece of business was to grant Horn a license to have a public tavern, or meetinghouse. With a public place to gather, the parish could now request to become a town.

This book is also a photographic and historical visit to Milton Mills, which like Milton, is directly on the Maine state border. Milton Mills was once known as Shapleigh Mills. In the past it has had several sawmills, a woolen mill, and a distillery. The distillery was owned and operated by Stephen Watson, who made his whiskey from potatoes.

The Salmon Falls River has shaped much of the history of Milton and Milton Mills since the Colonial era. The first dam was built by Samuel Palmer in 1784. The present dam is on the same location. Sawmills were built on each side of the river. The ice industry flourished there until the late 1920s. At one point there were five ice houses: the Lynn, Boston, Metropolitan, Porter, and Downing ice companies. The Porter and Downing companies burned to the ground. The other three were either torn down or fell down due to neglect.

The Salmon Falls River was also the center of a series of law suits in the 1820s. The Great Falls Manufacturing Company sued over and again to have the right to use the waterpower of the river to power its machinery. The suits failed. How different Milton's history would have been had they succeeded!

Many important people have come from Milton and its environs, but two deserve special mention. The first is Lewis W. Nute. He was born on February 17, 1820, and may be Milton's most significant resident from the past. He moved to Boston at age 20 to become a clerk in a shoe factory. Thirteen years later, on May 1, 1853, he bought part ownership of the company, which became known as Potter, Elder and Nute. After his death, he willed $125,000 to build and support a public high school in Milton and $30,000 to build and support a chapel in West Milton.

The second person is Robert Edmond Jones. His is a national reputation, for he perfected the use of Technicolor in films. He first used the technique in the movie *Becky Sharp*. In 1974, when his sister Elizabeth Jones was ill and decided to auction off the family furniture, people came from all over the country to try to buy an item related to Robert Jones. He was an influential man known for his great love of the theatre, as well as his home in Milton.

Milton and its immediate neighbors might have become a significant industrial place if a few things in the past had been different. But it did not, and all the rest, as they say, is history. People love this town for what it is. Few want to change it. It was, and is, a small town that cares about all the people who call it home. This book is my tribute to my home town.

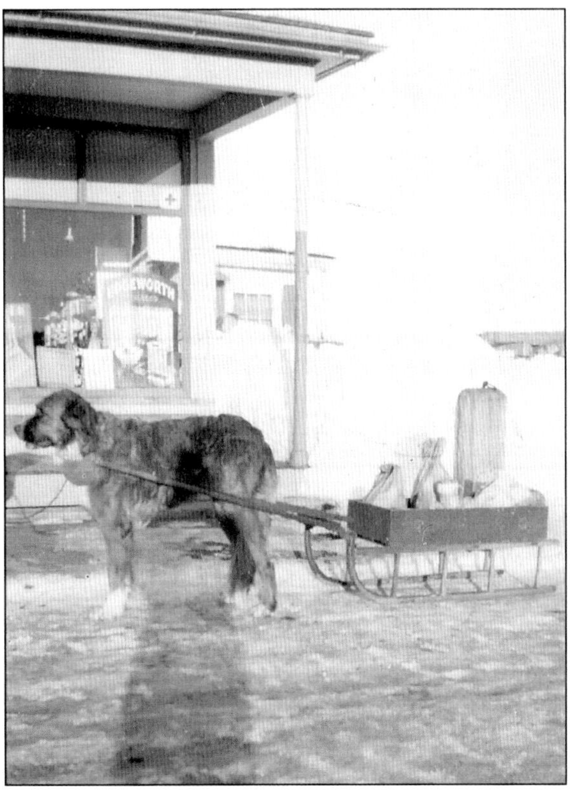

The Jones Family's Beloved Saint Bernard. Animals were a very important part of the Jones family. Dogs and cats were not the only animals considered pets, but also the sheep and the chickens. Here the family Saint Bernard is pulling a small sled of groceries.

One

West Milton

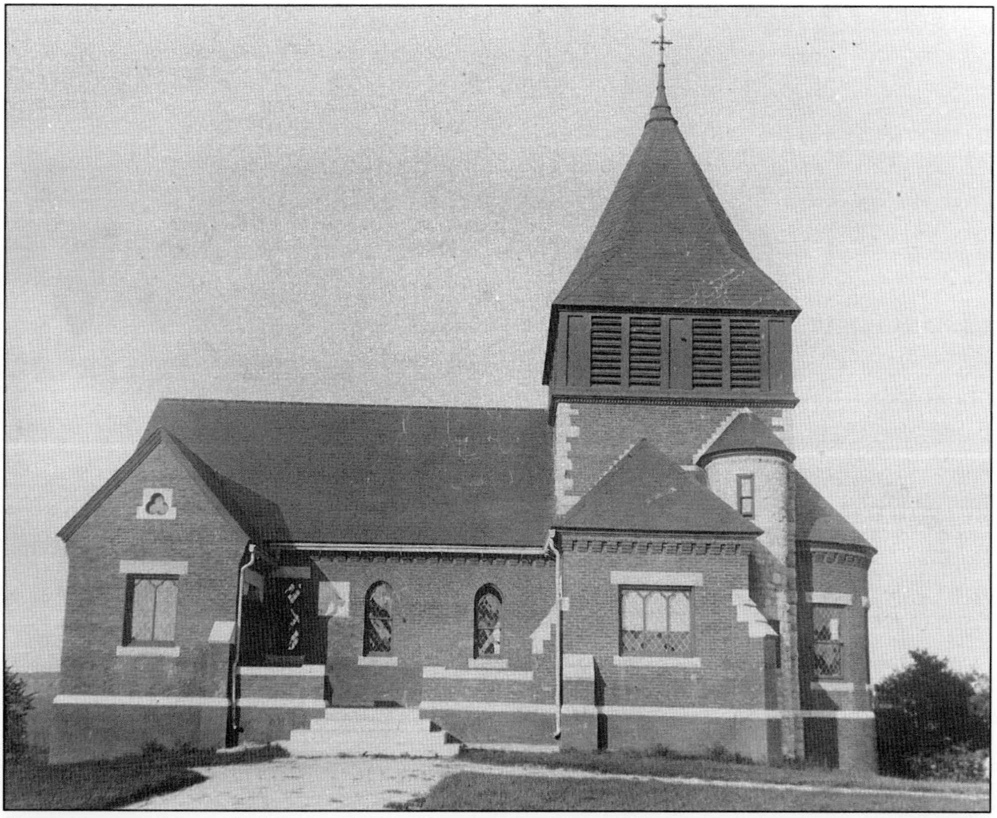

Nute Chapel. Lewis W. Nute left the money to build this chapel upon his death in 1888. The building is located on Governor's Road and is constructed in the late 19th-century architectural style known as Richardsonian Romanesque, after the great architect of Boston's Trinity Church, Henry Hobson Richardson. The chapel was dedicated on October 23, 1890. Nute provided $10,000 for construction and left another $30,000 in a trust to maintain it.

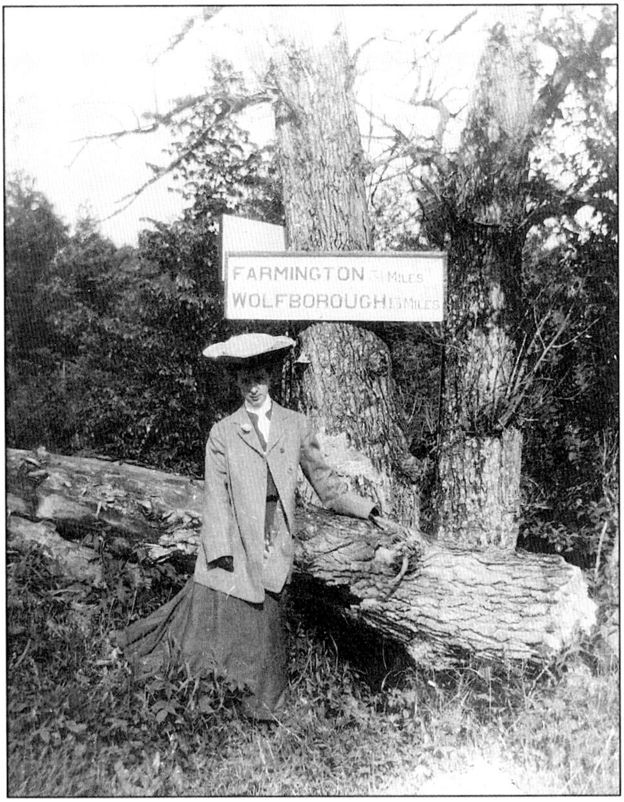

AT THE CROSSROADS. This photo is from a scrapbook kept by one of the girls from the Plummer family. The album dates from about 1902. The young lady stands in front of a sign reading "Farmington 3 miles, Wolfborough 15 miles." The location is at the intersection of Governor's Road and what is presently Route 75.

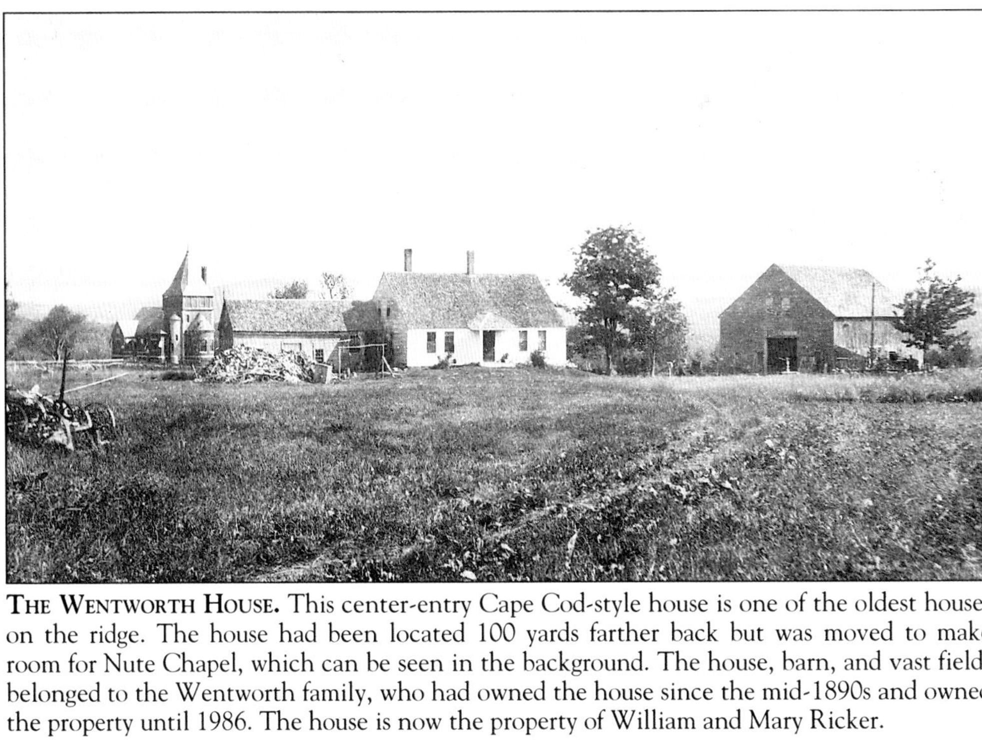

THE WENTWORTH HOUSE. This center-entry Cape Cod-style house is one of the oldest houses on the ridge. The house had been located 100 yards farther back but was moved to make room for Nute Chapel, which can be seen in the background. The house, barn, and vast fields belonged to the Wentworth family, who had owned the house since the mid-1890s and owned the property until 1986. The house is now the property of William and Mary Ricker.

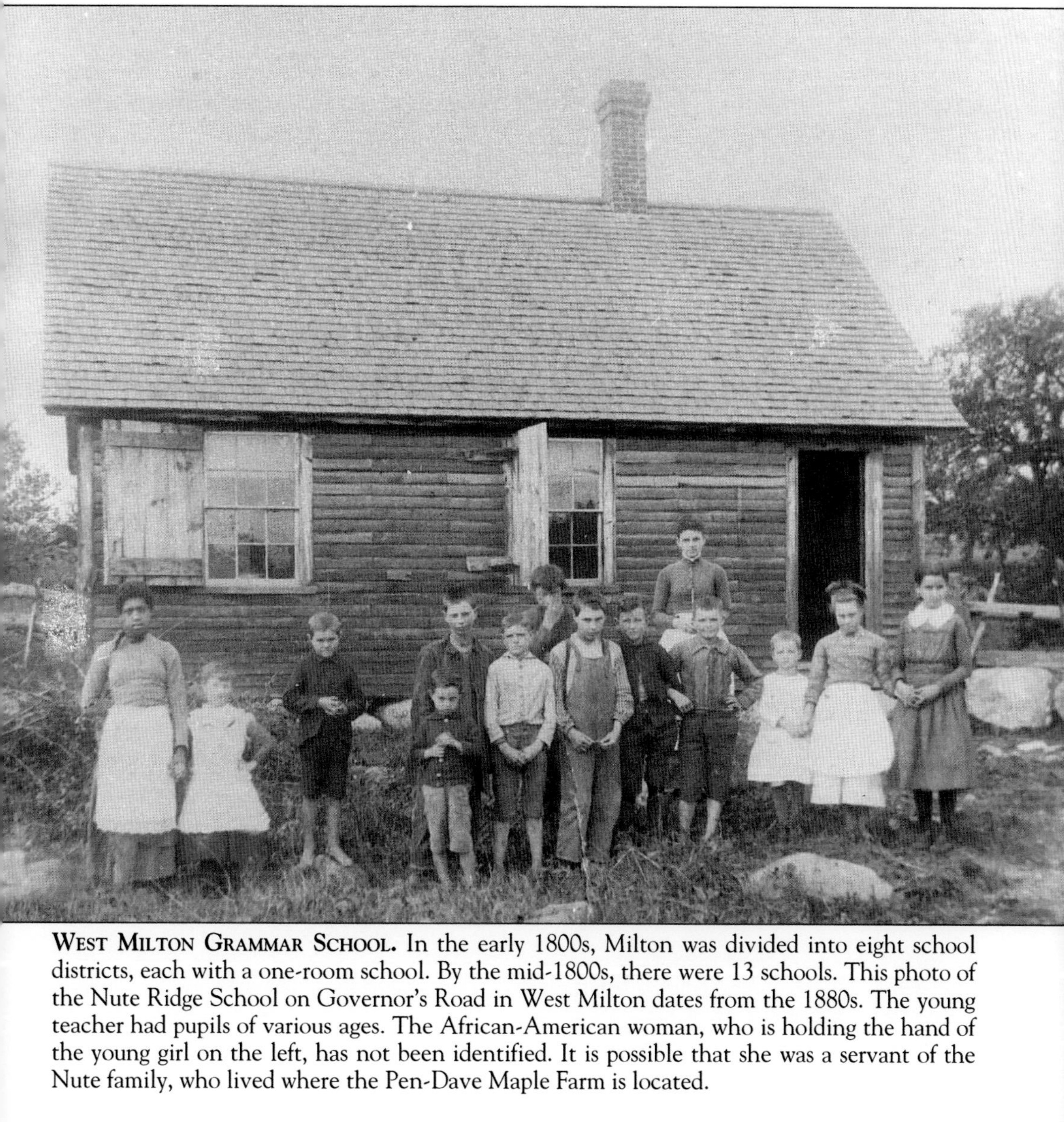

West Milton Grammar School. In the early 1800s, Milton was divided into eight school districts, each with a one-room school. By the mid-1800s, there were 13 schools. This photo of the Nute Ridge School on Governor's Road in West Milton dates from the 1880s. The young teacher had pupils of various ages. The African-American woman, who is holding the hand of the young girl on the left, has not been identified. It is possible that she was a servant of the Nute family, who lived where the Pen-Dave Maple Farm is located.

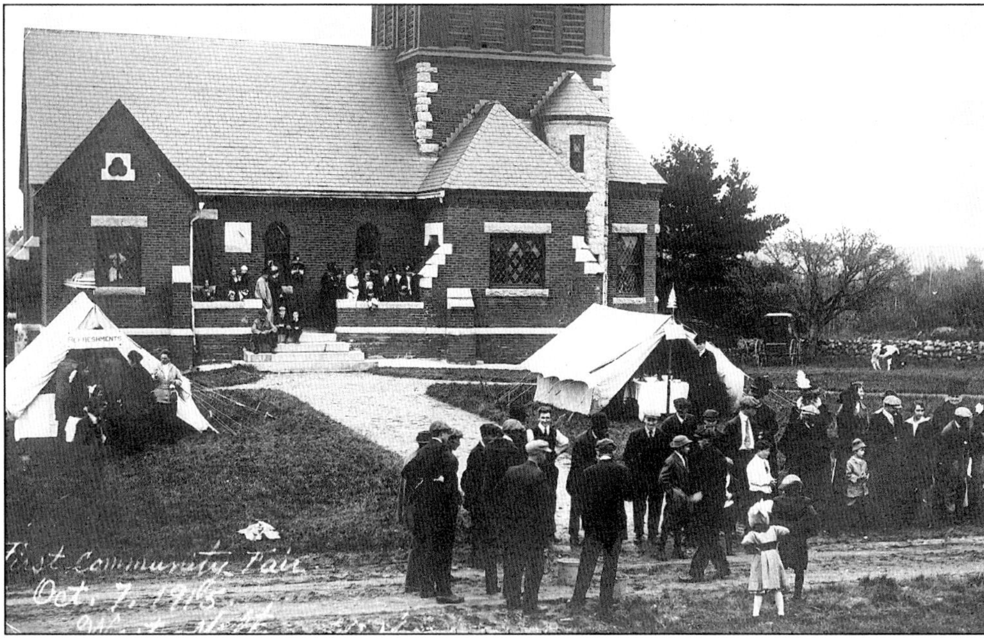

First Community Fair. On October 7, 1915, the residents of West Milton gathered for a harvest-time fair on the grounds outside Nute Chapel. The little tents held displays of arts and crafts and refreshments. As with all New England harvest fairs, it was a time for socializing with neighbors. The chapel's location in the center of West Milton was ideal for a community gathering.

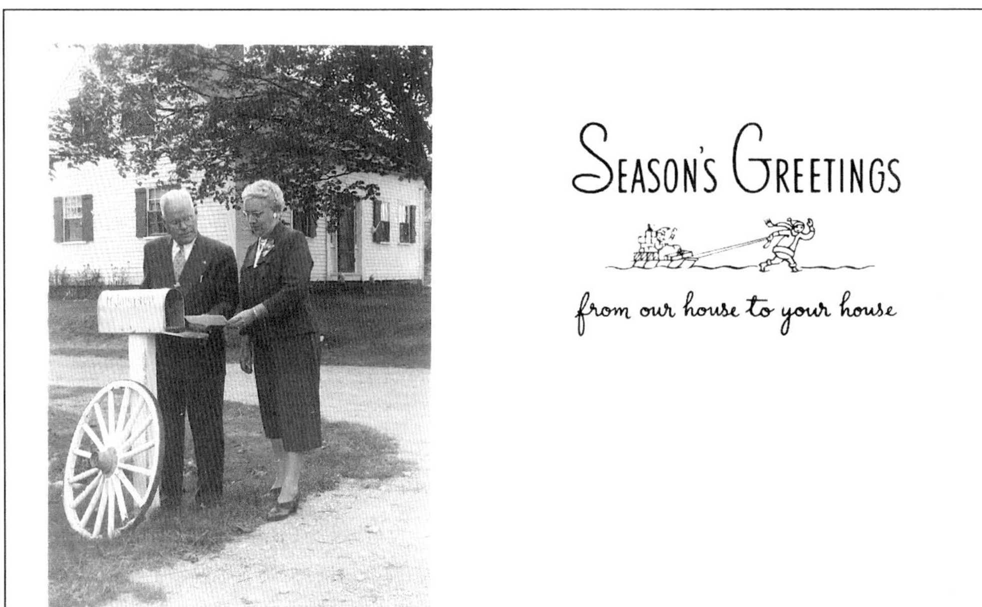

The Johnson House. Henry and Grace Johnson owned this two-bay Cape Cod house on the north side of Governor's Road. The photograph was taken c. 1930. Henry and Grace, shown at the mailbox, liked it so much that they used it as their Christmas card that year.

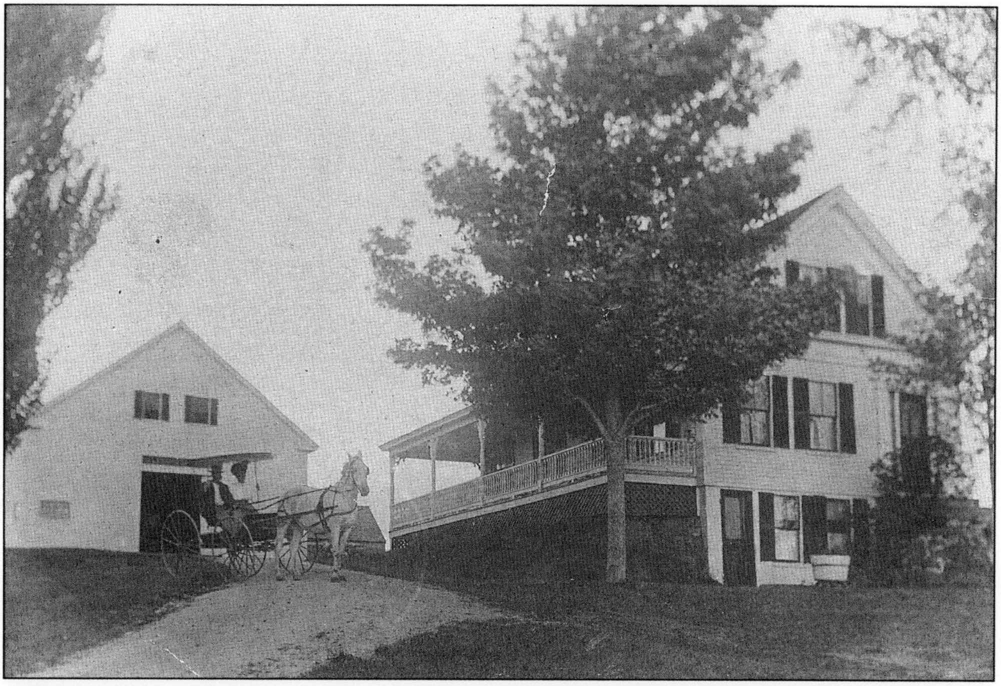

Garland Farm. This Greek Revival home was built in the early 1800s, when this style of architecture became popular in the United States. Coming down the driveway is a horse and buggy, probably pulling Mr. Garland and his wife, out for a Sunday drive.

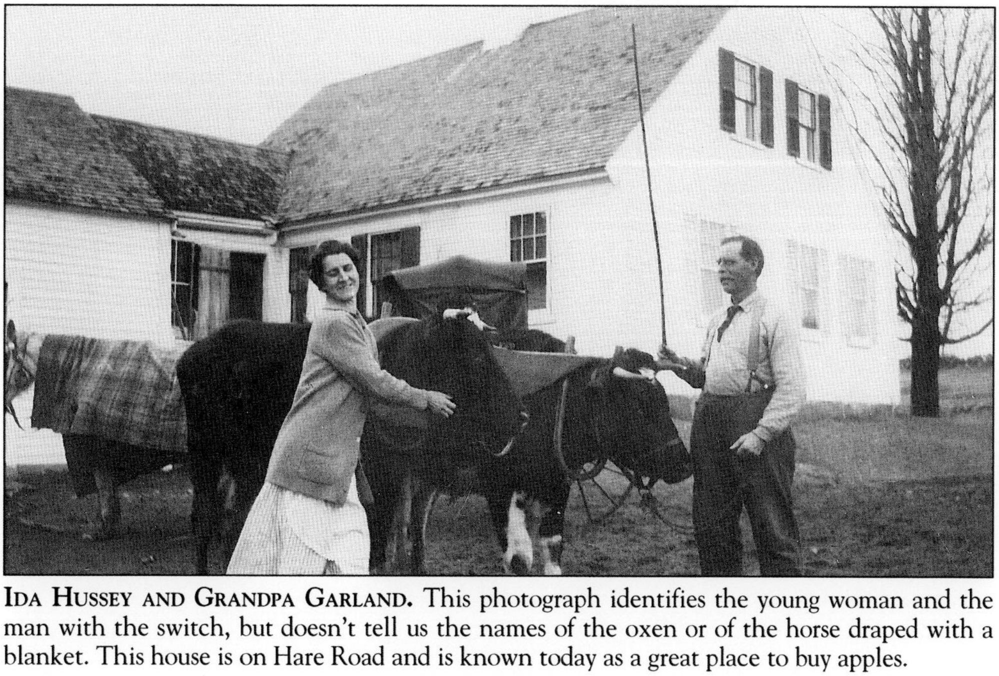

Ida Hussey and Grandpa Garland. This photograph identifies the young woman and the man with the switch, but doesn't tell us the names of the oxen or of the horse draped with a blanket. This house is on Hare Road and is known today as a great place to buy apples.

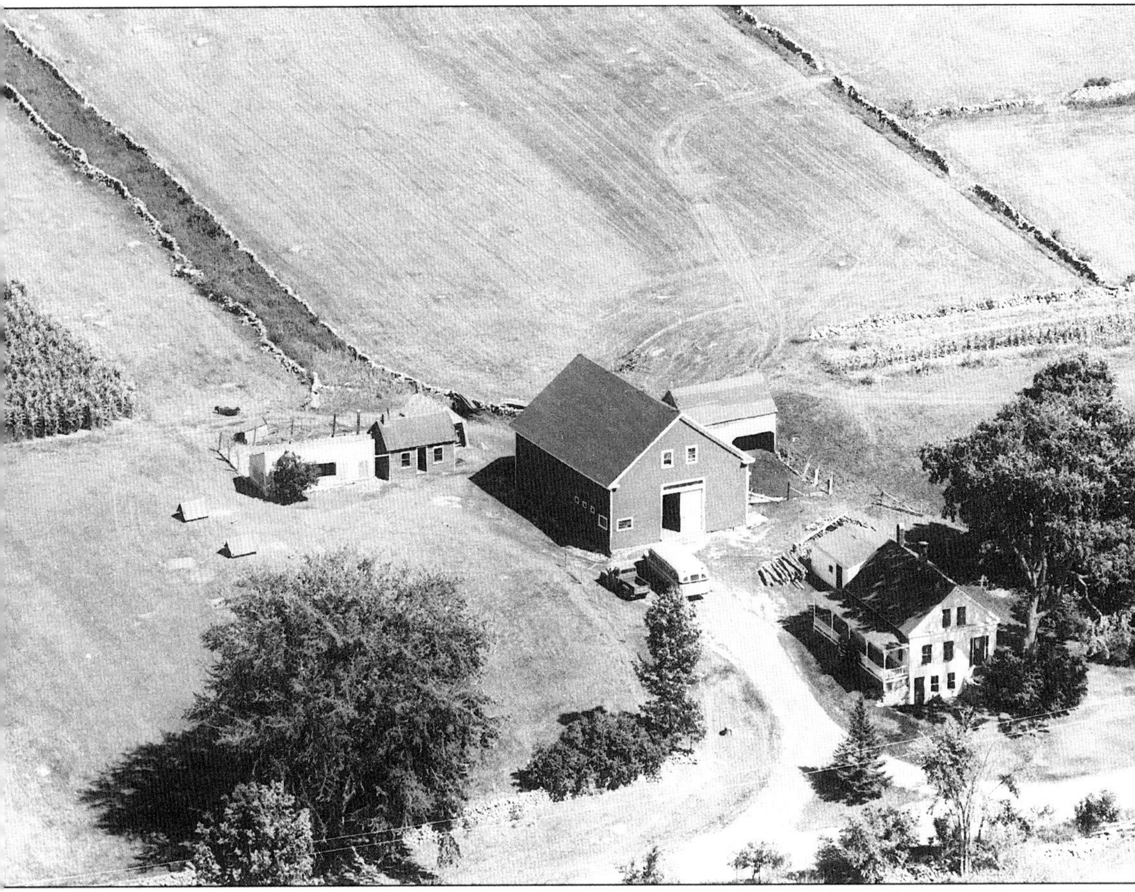

AERIAL VIEW OF THE GARLAND FARM. This aerial photo was taken in the mid-20th century and shows few changes from the previous view. The most significant changes are the color of the barn and the school bus parked in front of it.

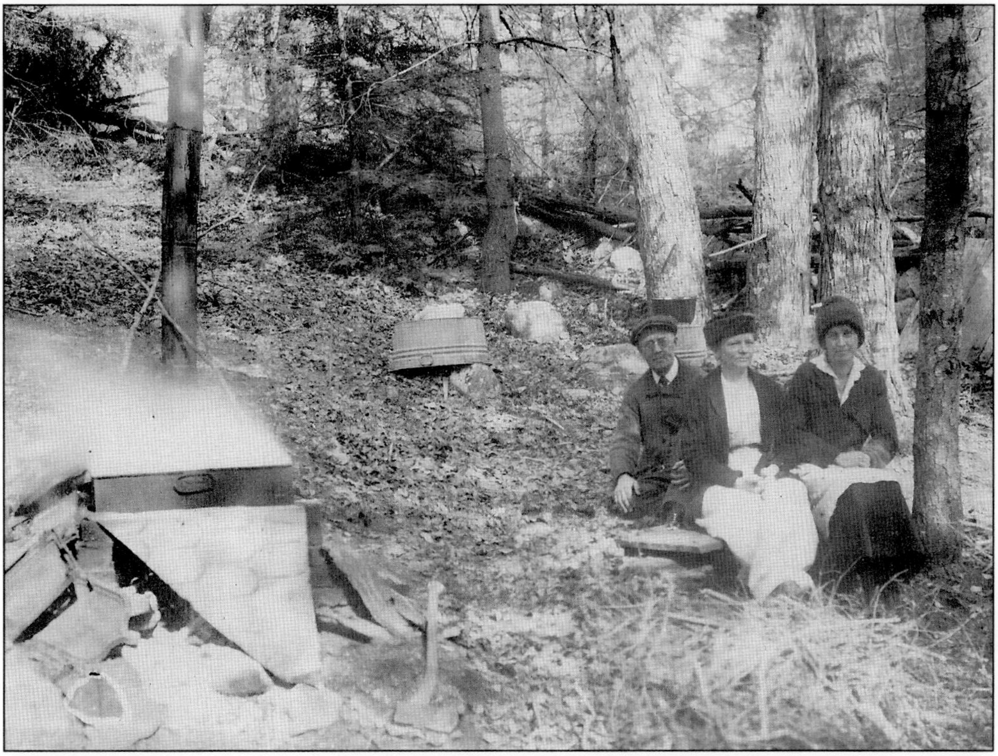

The Gilman Pasture. Members of the Gilman family sit in the overgrown pasture on their land. This was located off of what was formerly known as Ray Nute Road. It appears that the Gilman family have decided to have a summer cookout in their pasture.

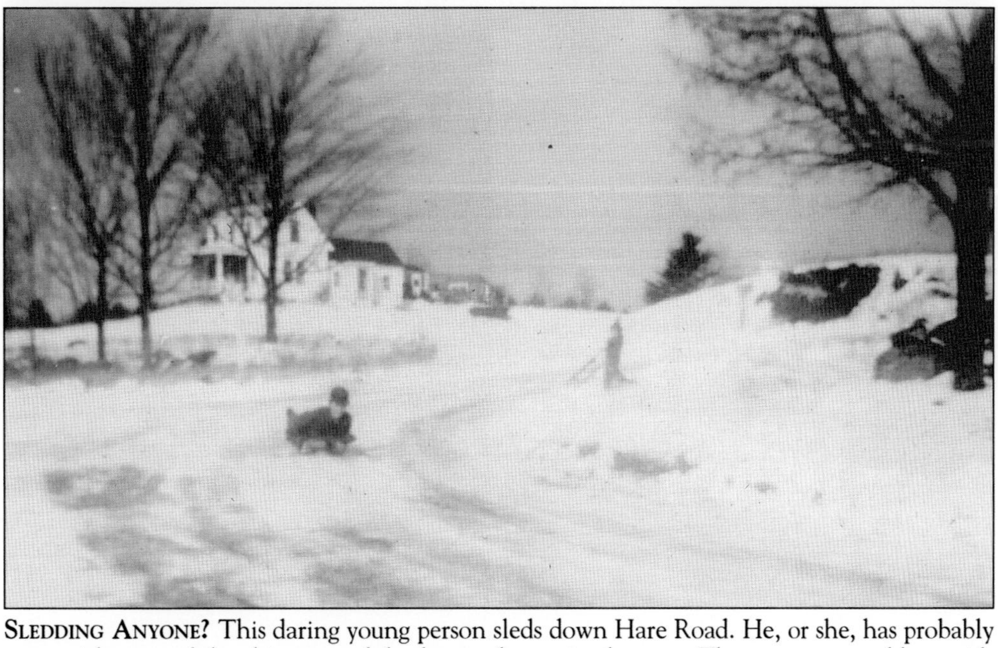

Sledding Anyone? This daring young person sleds down Hare Road. He, or she, has probably come right out of the driveway of the house shown in the rear. There was no problem with traffic interfering with a good run on the sled!

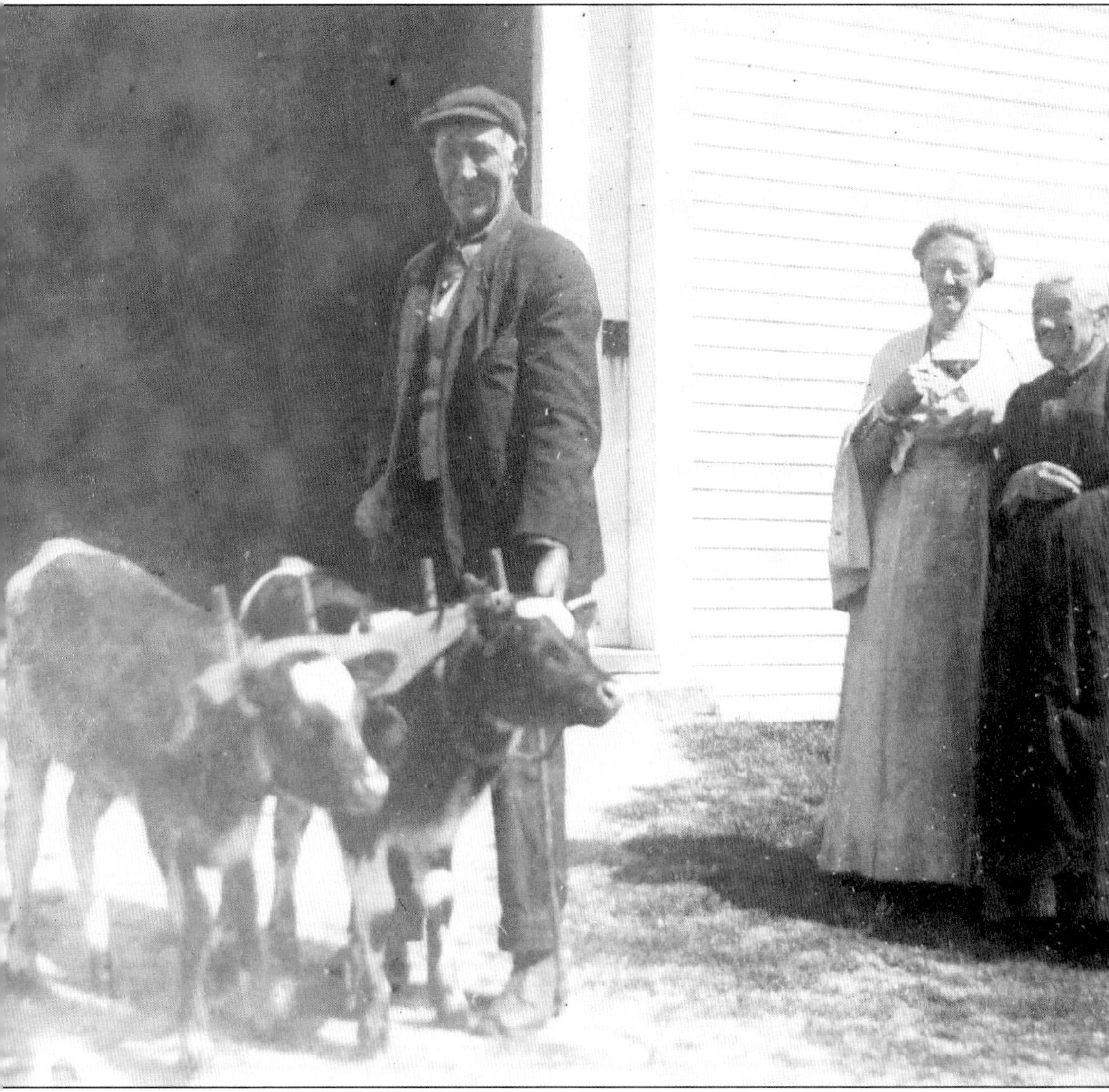

THE NEW CALVES. A young pair of bull calves are being broken into the yoke at an early age. The man and woman stand in front of the Garland Farm barn in a photo that dates from the early 1900s. The farm is owned by John and Judy Gilman.

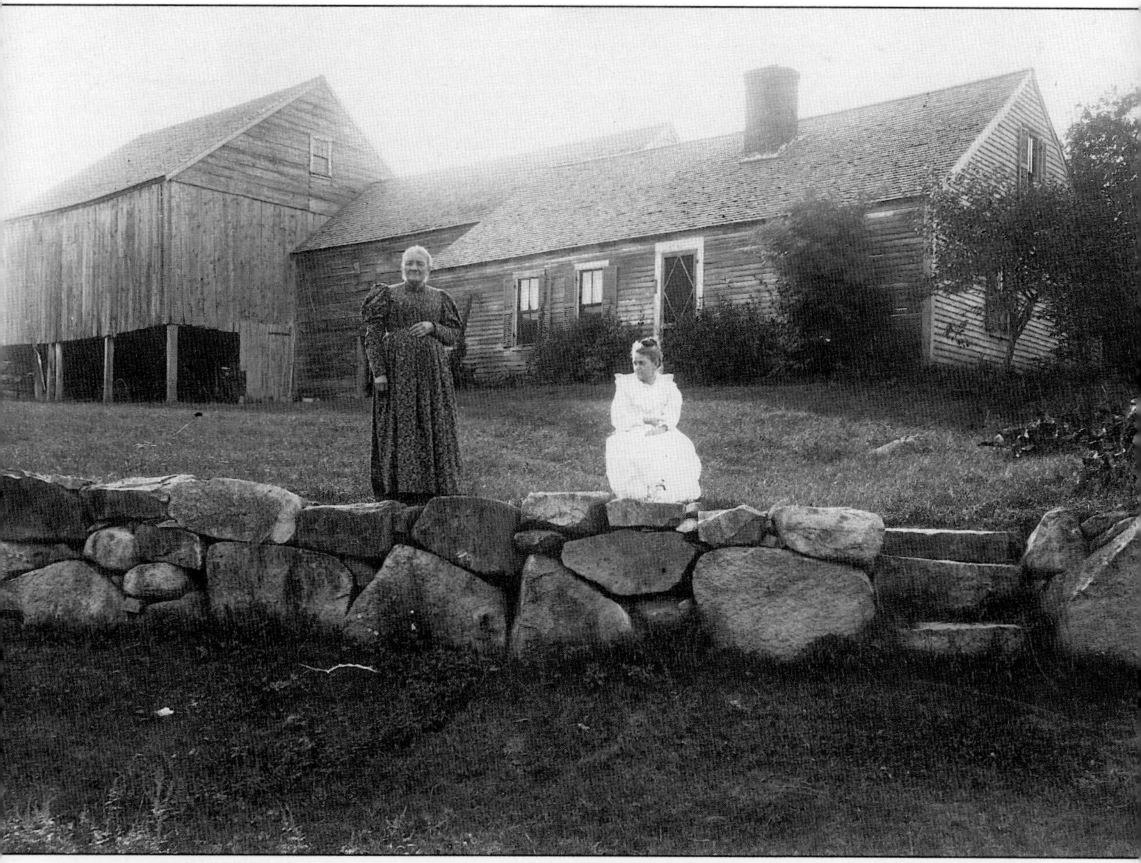

Goodall Home. The back of this photo was simply marked with a name: Almarette Goodall. This beautiful old Cape is still standing in West Milton. The woman on the left is Almarette; the other woman is unknown. This photo was taken in the late 1800s.

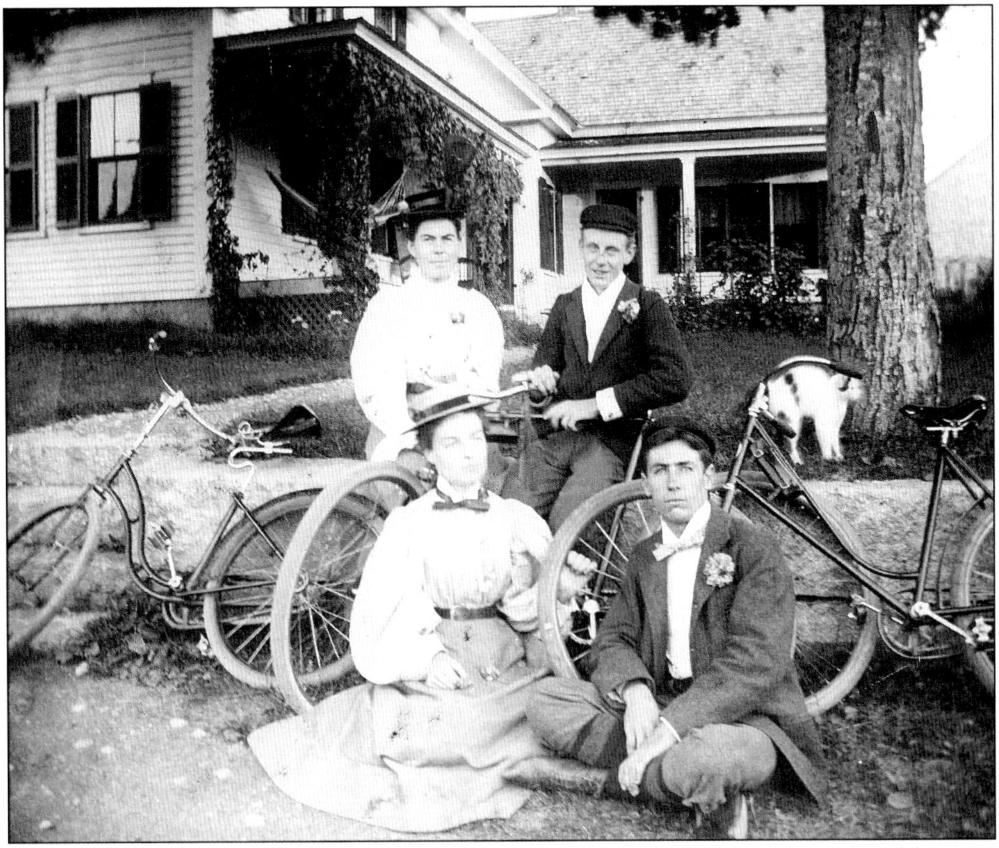

A Great Day for Cycling. These four young cyclists were taking part in the latest athletic fad of the 1890s—bicycle riding. The "leg o' mutton" sleeves on the women's dresses and the straw boaters date this picture to the mid-1890s. The building is the Scates House in South Milton. Only a few photos of South Milton were available for inclusion in this book.

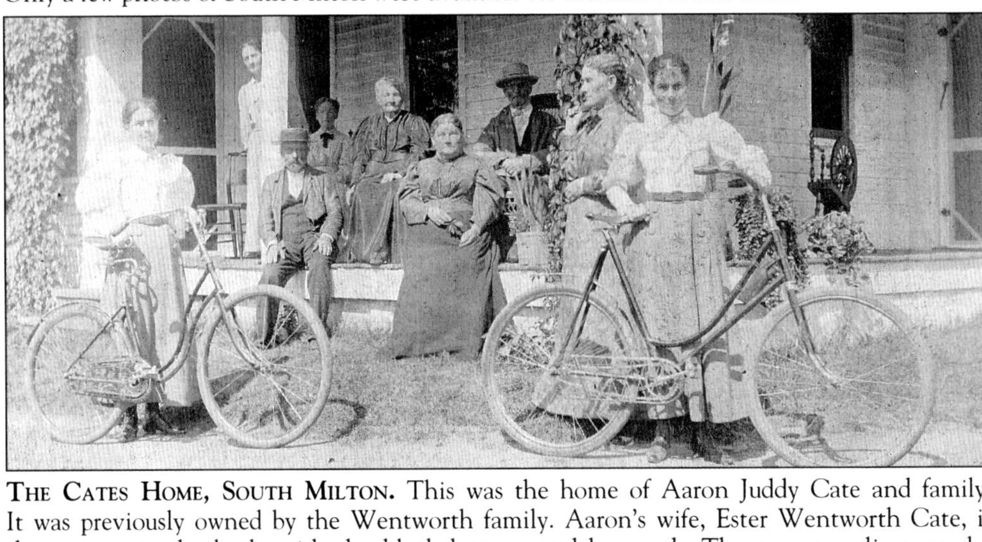

The Cates Home, South Milton. This was the home of Aaron Juddy Cate and family. It was previously owned by the Wentworth family. Aaron's wife, Ester Wentworth Cate, is the woman in the back, with the black bow around her neck. The young cyclists are the Clements twins.

Two

Nute High School and Grammar School

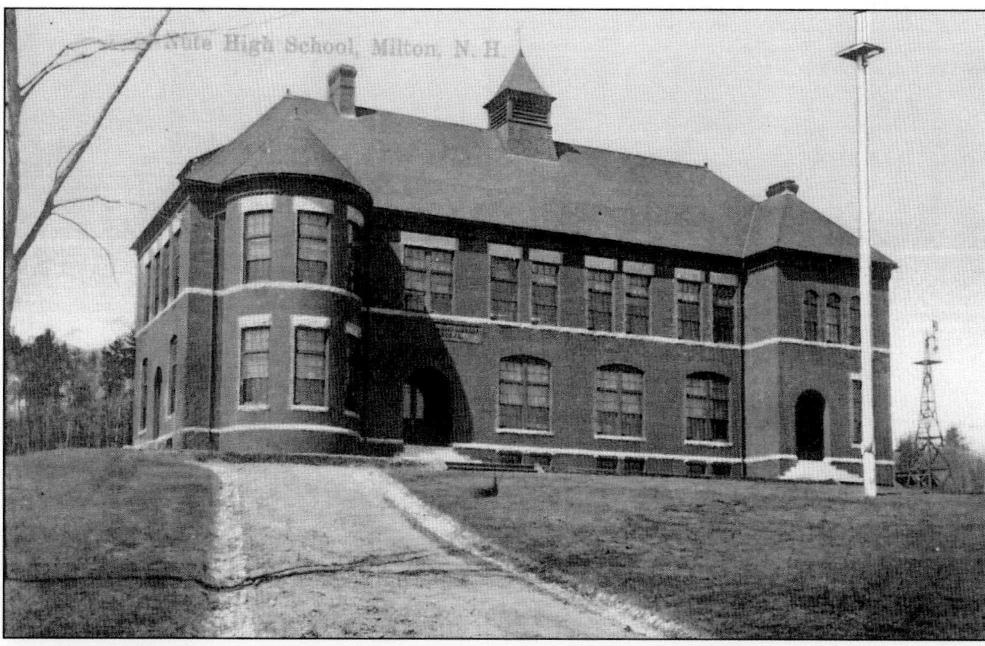

Nute High School. The high school was built in the Richardsonian Romanesque style, which was very popular in New England in the 1890s. The school was named after Lewis W. Nute. In December of 1853, while living in Boston, Nute bought the business of Potter, Elder and Nute. Upon his death, he willed $125,000 to build and support a public high school.

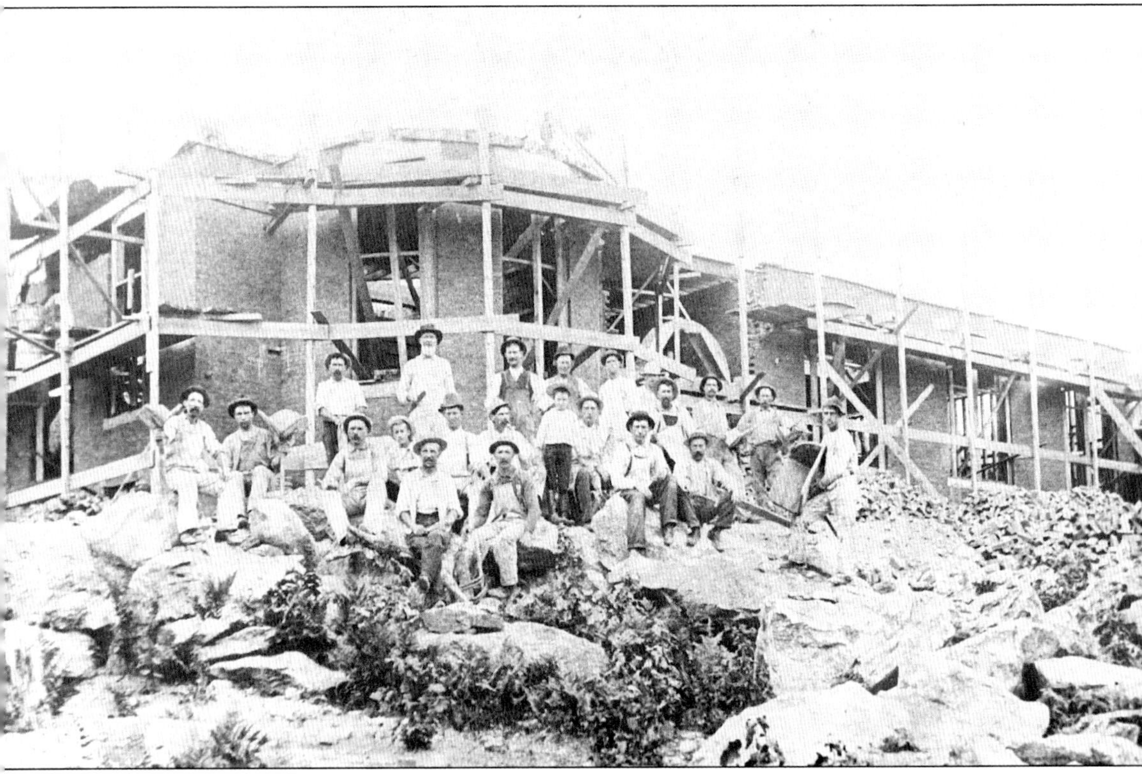

THE BUILDING OF NUTE HIGH SCHOOL. The construction workers of the high school took a break for this photo to be taken. They posed with the hods, some still filled with the cement they used to lay the bricks on the facade. Near the center of the picture is a little boy who probably came to see his father being photographed, and joined in. The school opened on September 8, 1891, with 54 scholars, but wasn't completed until 1892.

LEWIS WOSTER NUTE. The Nute name is known and heard all over the town of Milton. Lewis W. Nute was a great man who cared about the welfare of the children of Milton. He wanted the children to have a fair chance in life, and knew with the proper education, it would be possible. He gave to the town what he earned as a shoe manufacturer in Massachusetts, giving generously to the building of the school and the Chapel on Nute's Ridge.

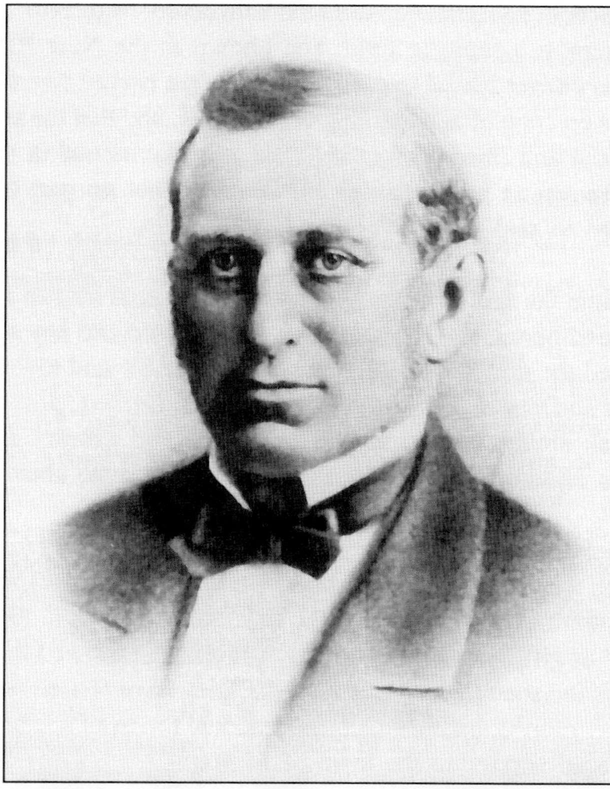

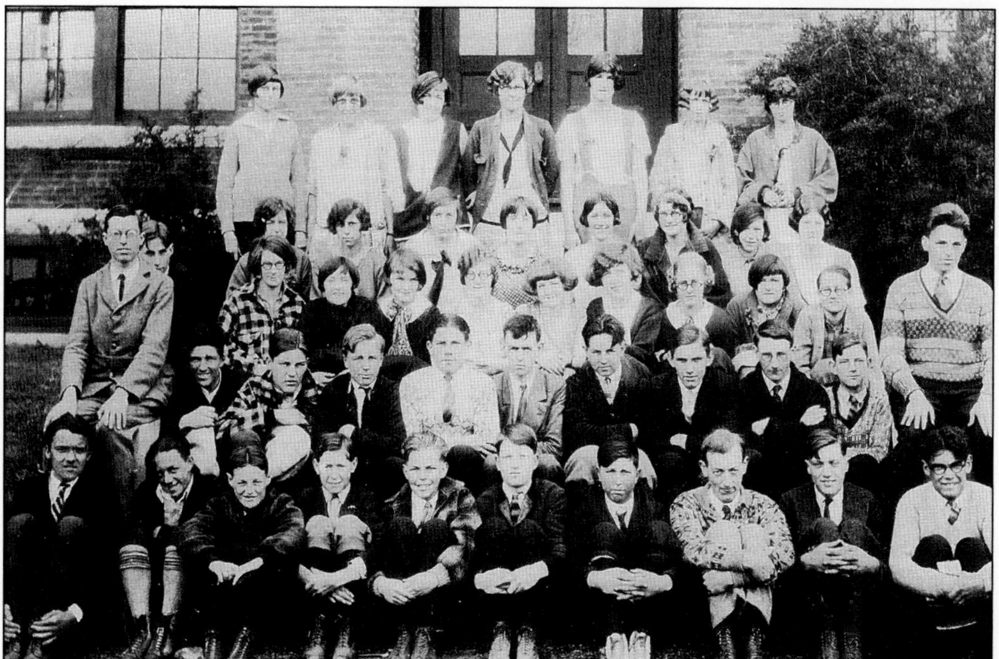

GRADES 9–12. The entire student body of Nute High School gathers for this photograph. It was taken in the mid to late 1920s, judging by the look of the clothing and hairstyles.

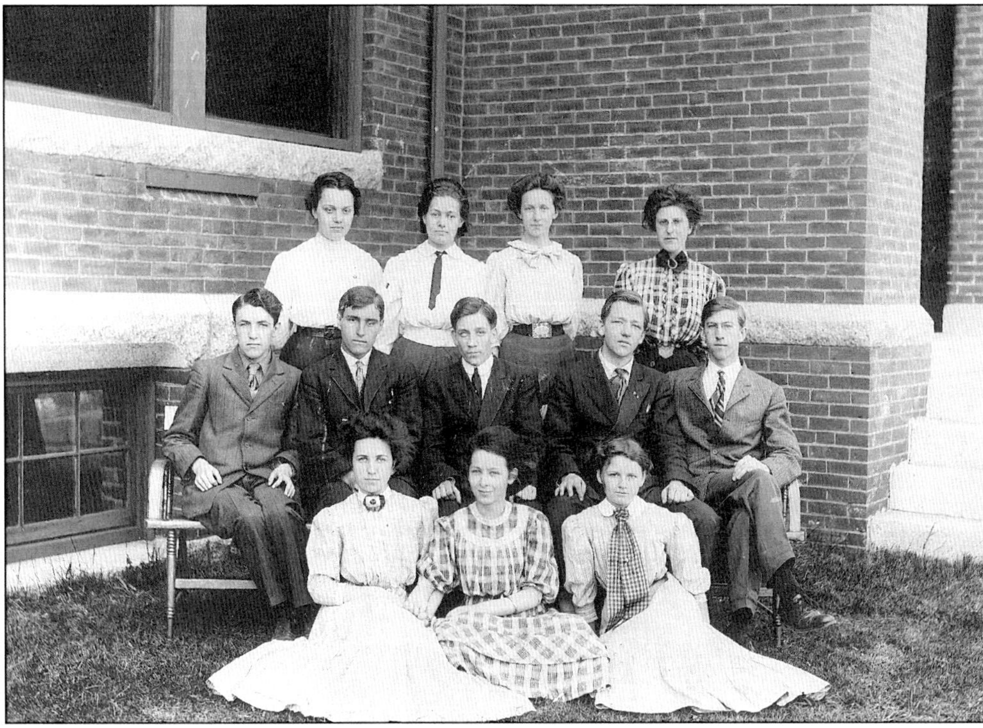

Class of 1909. Nute graduated 12 scholars in 1909. Clara Columbus is in the center of the front row, while Mary Jones is on the right end of the back row. This photo was taken in front of the high school. Plaid became a very popular fabric for women's dresses at the end of the 19th century.

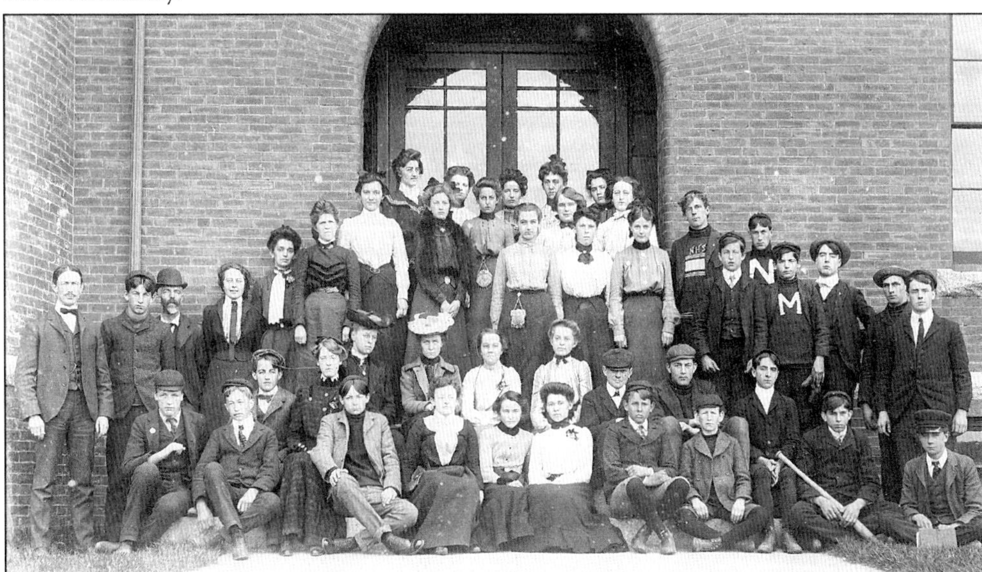

High School, Faculty, and Students. In this 1901 photo, it seems obvious that the girls were trying their hardest to look older and more sophisticated. The boys, on the other hand, seem bored or eager to get back to the baseball field. Note that the boys on the right are wearing their letter sweaters.

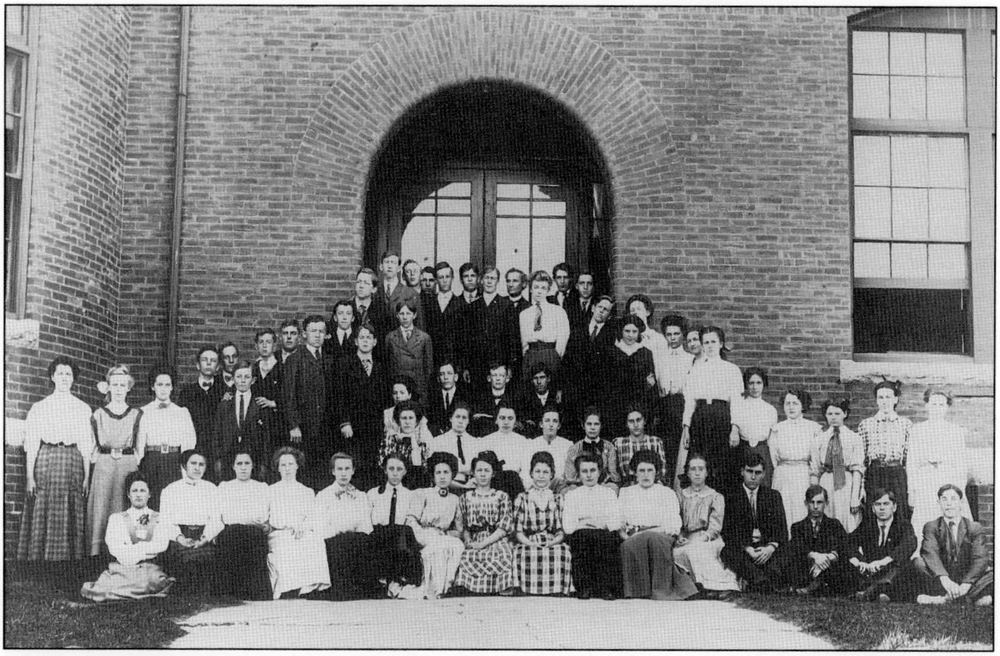

Entire School. This was the entire high school, grades 9–12, in 1909. Mary C. Jones is sitting in the second row on the left.

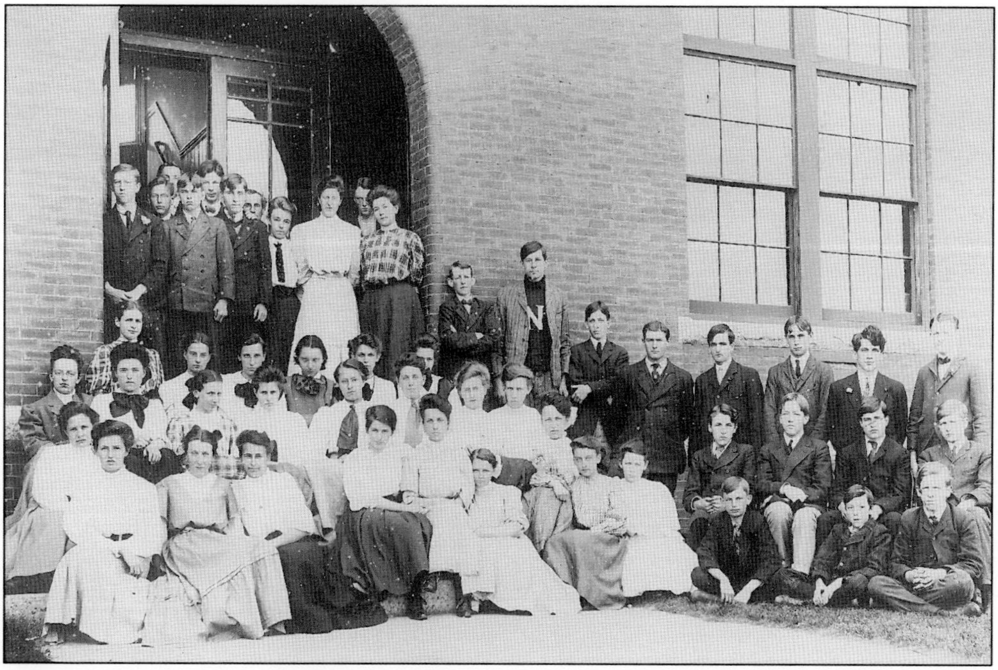

Mary C. Jones. Perhaps by this time, Mary C. Jones had become a teacher at Nute. She is in this photograph, standing on the top step, dressed in white. There may also have been a baseball game after school; one of the boys is wearing his letter sweater.

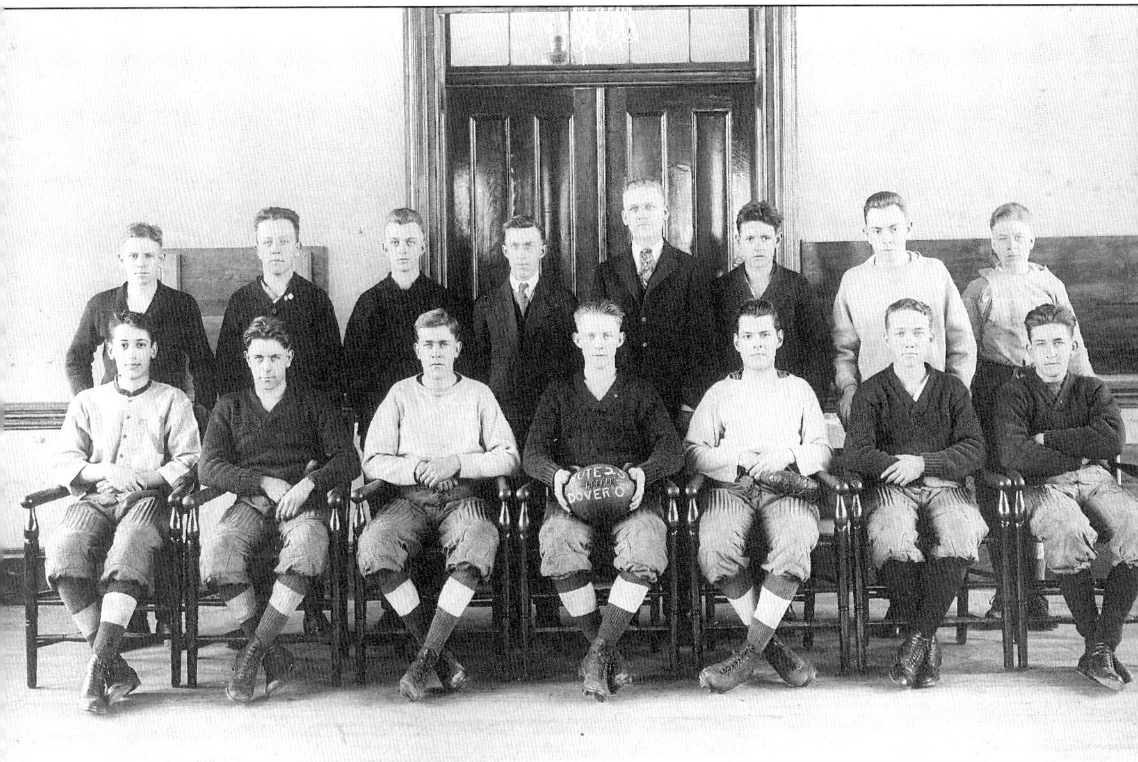

NUTE FOOTBALL TEAM. This 1910 photograph reads: "Nute 25 Dover 0." The gymnasium was located on the second floor of the high school and remained there for many years. The man in the center rear is probably the coach.

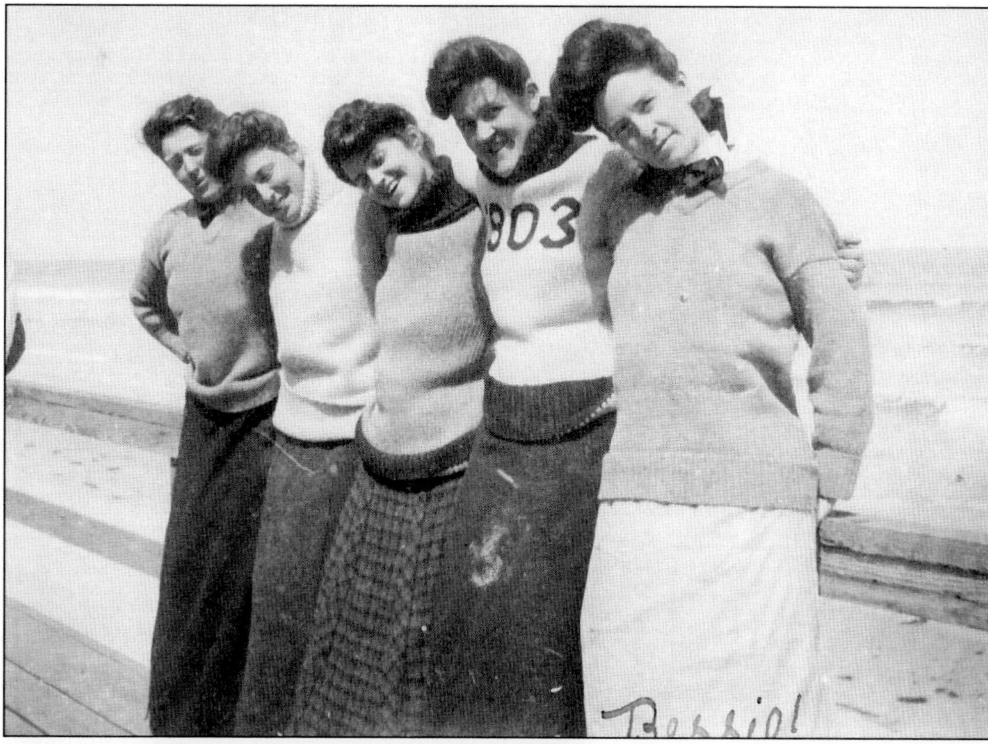

A Day at the Beach. This was photograph was taken *c.* 1903, according to the date on the girls' sweaters. It was probably a visit to Hampton Beach. The girls look happy, even though there seems to be a strong breeze off the ocean.

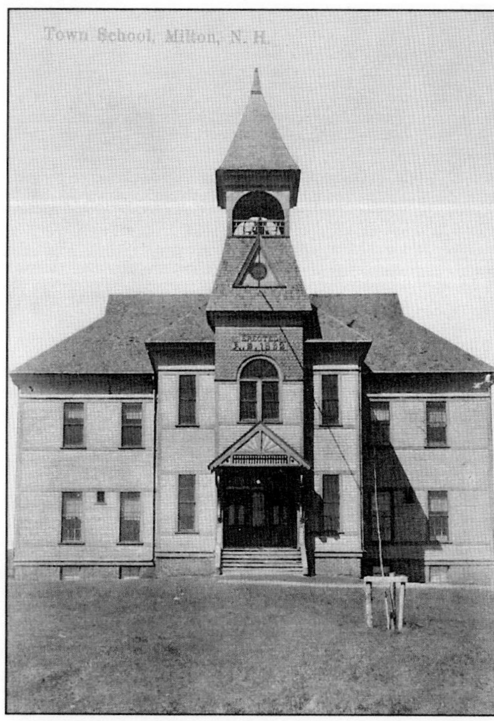

Milton Grammar School. The school was built in 1882, in the Victorian Stick style, which made use of decorative shingles and raised horizontal and vertical boards. After it burned in 1914, it was rebuilt and renamed the Milton Elementary School.

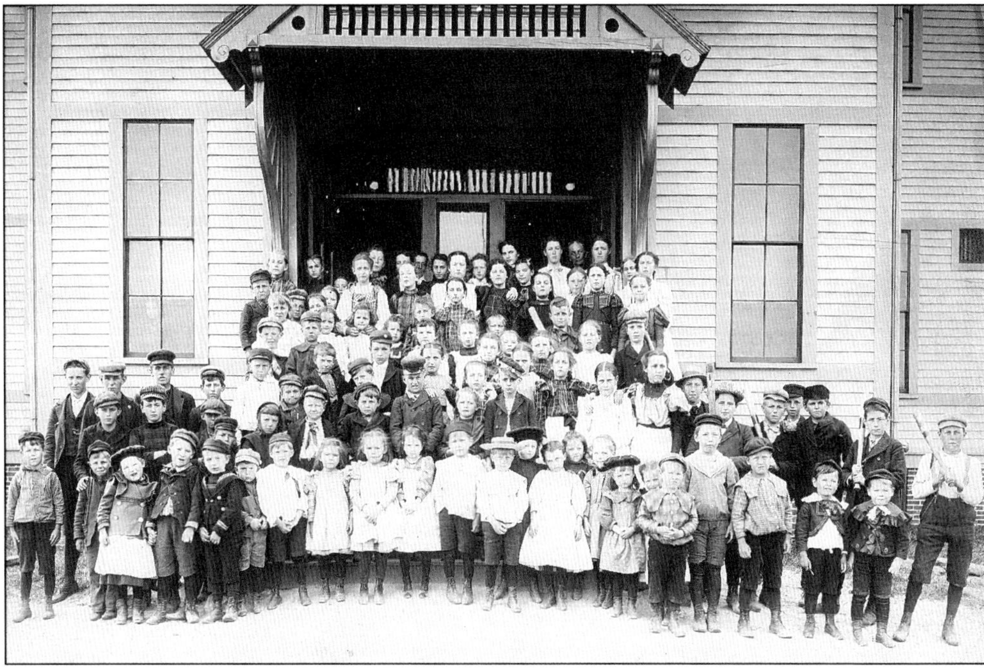

Grammar School Students. This photo was taken in 1898 on the front steps of the school. Laura Ella Jones is in the fifth row, on the far right side. Note how elaborately some of the children are dressed, especially the little boys in the front row at right. Five of the young lads have their baseball bats on display.

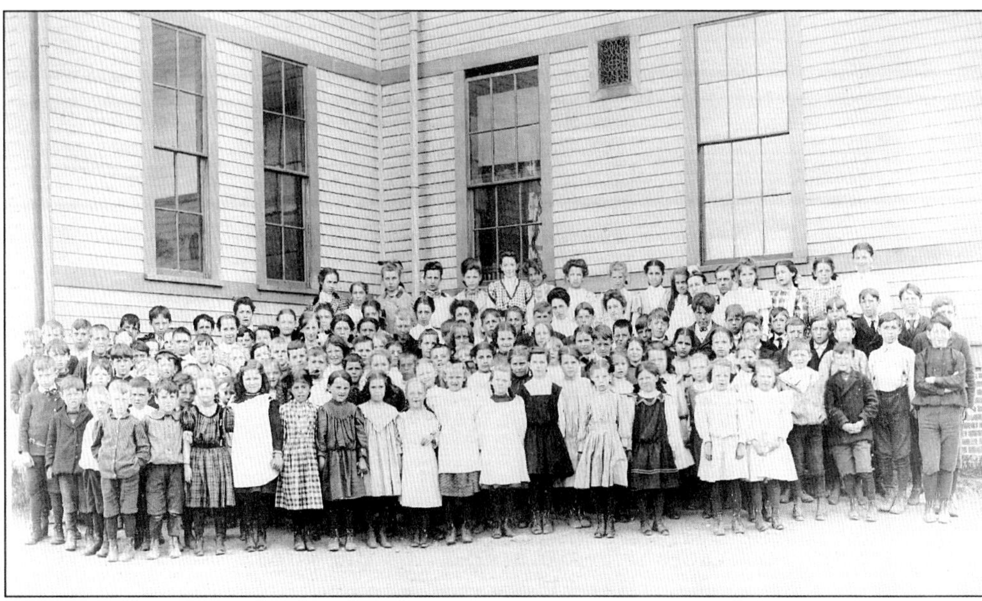

Entire Grammar School. This photo was taken c. 1905, during a time when it was very popular for young girls to wear plaid.

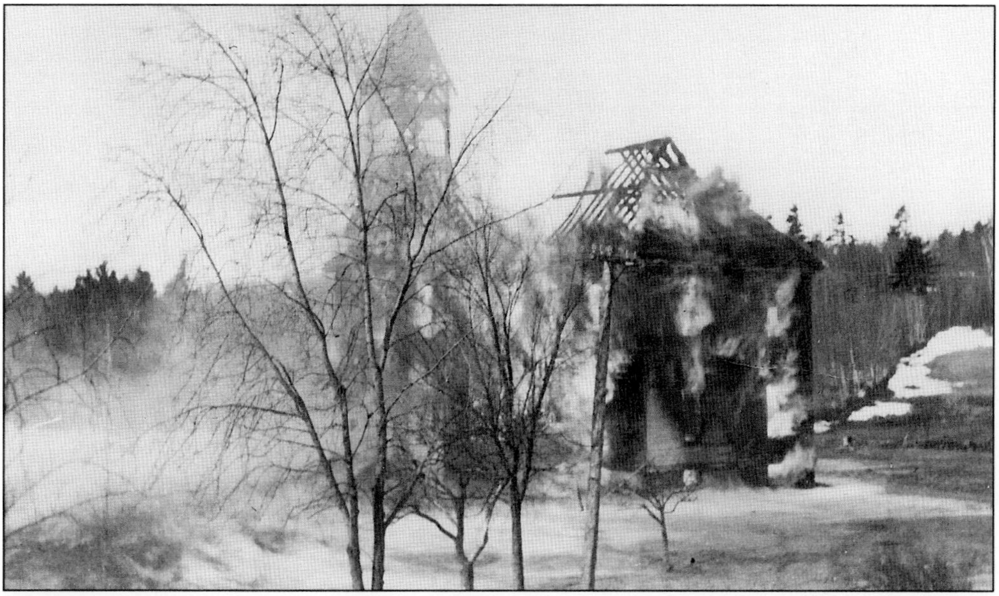

Burning of the Grammar School. In 1914, the Grammar School burned to the ground. At this point during the fire, the roof and tower had not yet fallen. Notice the snow in the background.

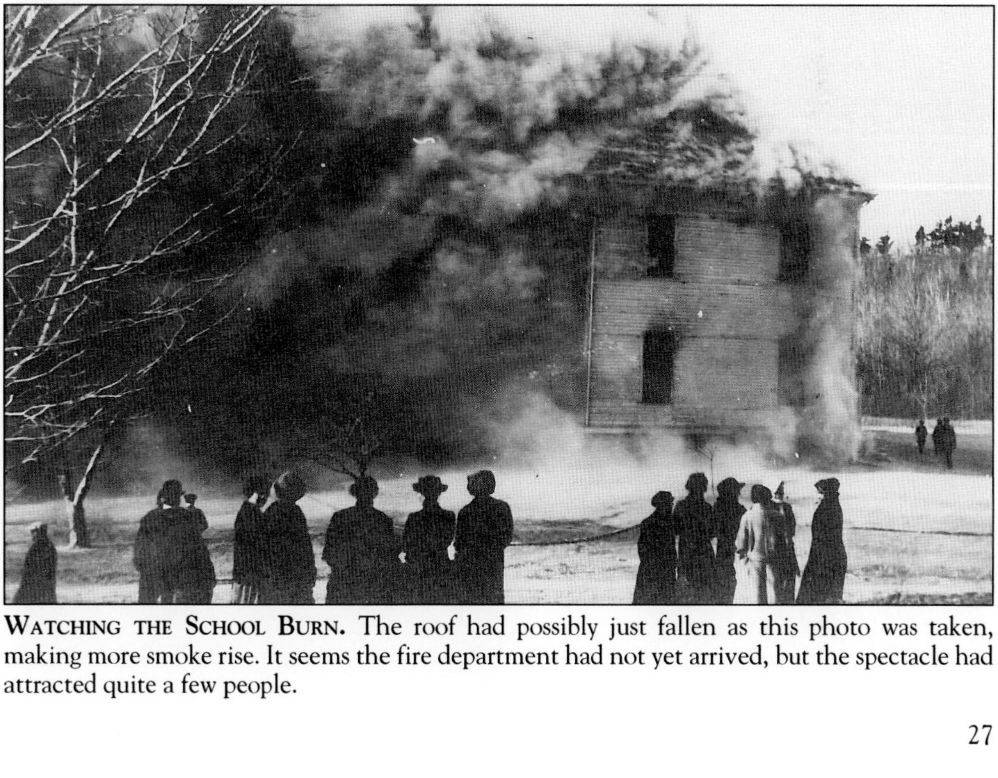

Watching the School Burn. The roof had possibly just fallen as this photo was taken, making more smoke rise. It seems the fire department had not yet arrived, but the spectacle had attracted quite a few people.

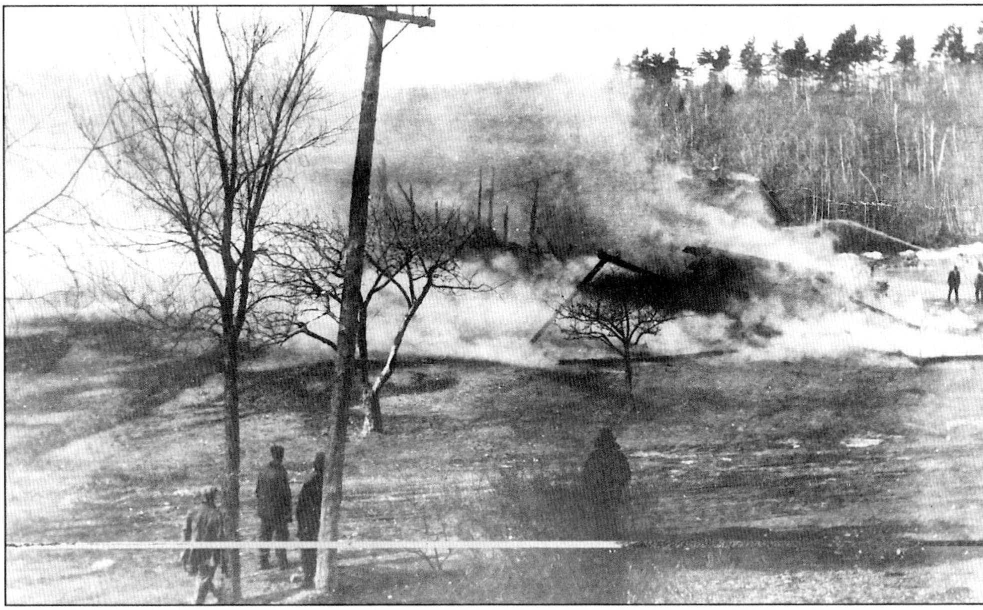

GRAMMAR SCHOOL FALLING. This is the last stage of the burning of the Grammar School. Finally, the fire department has shown up; they are shown on the right, spraying water on the burning building.

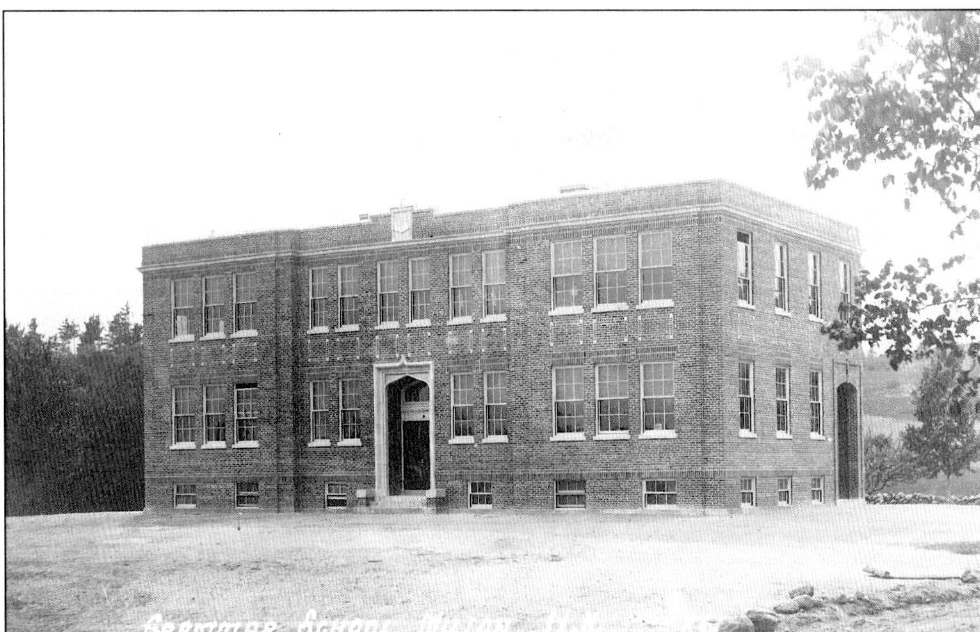

THE NEW ELEMENTARY SCHOOL. This was built the same year the Grammar School burned (1914). The architecture is Colonial Revival style, which was a very popular building style for schools at the time.

Three

Central Milton

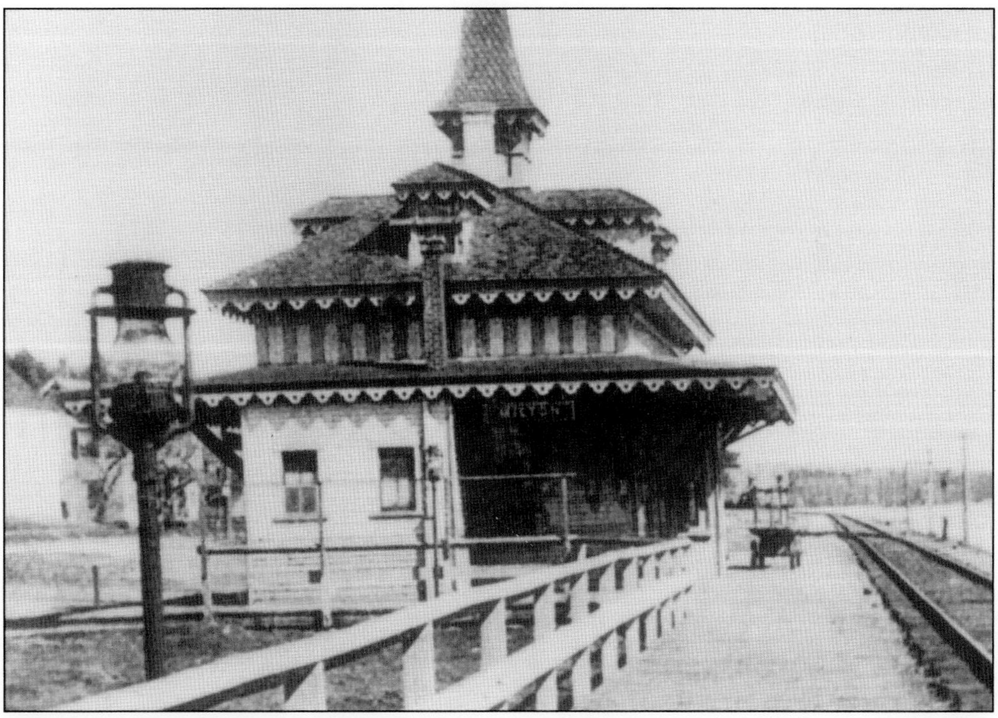

Boston and Maine Train Station. The center of Milton was the true heart of the town. Here were the stores, a Congregational and a Baptist church, the post office, and the hotels where the transient ice cutters lived. Here, too, was the dam that provided the power for the mills in the area. The B&M Train Station was built in 1873, about the time Milton began shipping ice to Boston.

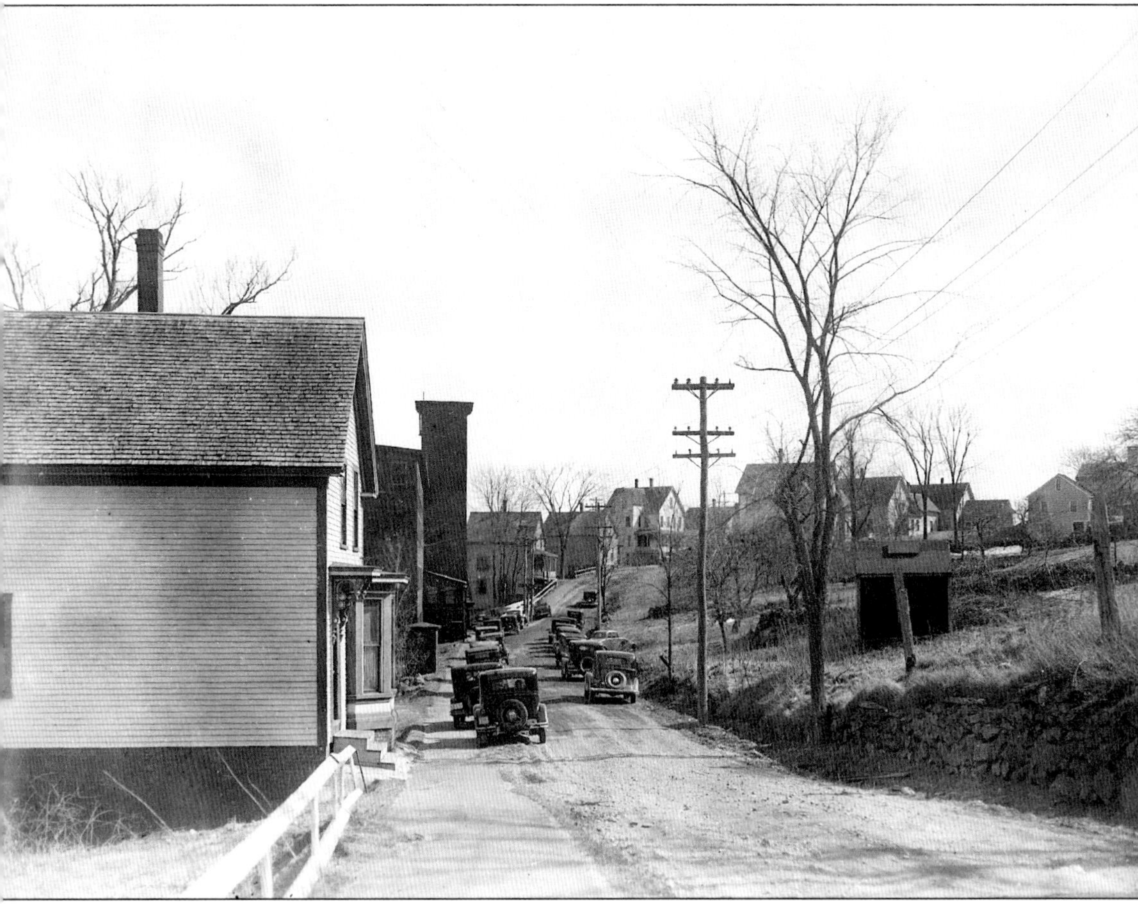

CHARLES STREET. Charles Street begins at the Sacred Heart Church and runs north, parallel to Route 125. Also, parallel to Charles Street is the Milton Leather Board Company; the road to this factory is only accessible by Charles Street. It doesn't seem possible that Milton needed a one-way street in the 1930s, but each car in this photo is facing the same direction, regardless of the side of the street it is parked on.

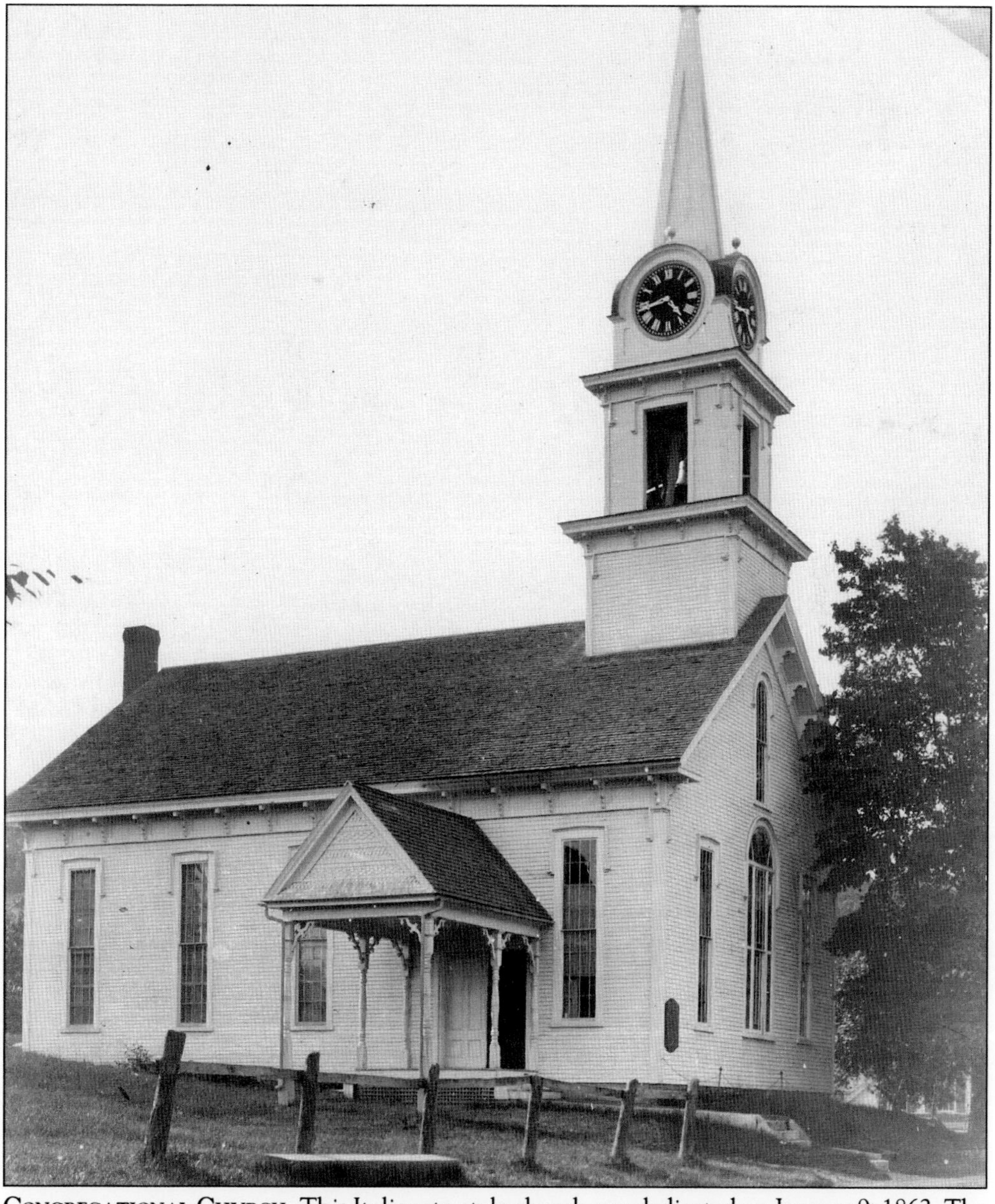

Congregational Church. This Italianate-style church was dedicated on January 9, 1862. The Congregational Church congregation has a long history. It was first known as "The First Church of Christ," and was organized at the old meetinghouse on Plummer's Ridge, on September 8, 1815. People who lived in central Milton wanted a place of worship that was closer to the center of town, so a "Union" meetinghouse was built; it was dedicated on November 19, 1835. It was shared by the Congregationalists and members of other denominations. This building was later known as the "Classical Institute," and was located across the street from the Milton Hotel, which was just south of the train station. The building was later sold and the money divided between each of the denominations. The building may have also housed the Lake View Hotel. The present site of the Congregational church was bequeathed money in Lewis W. Nute's will because it was the site of the house where his mother was born.

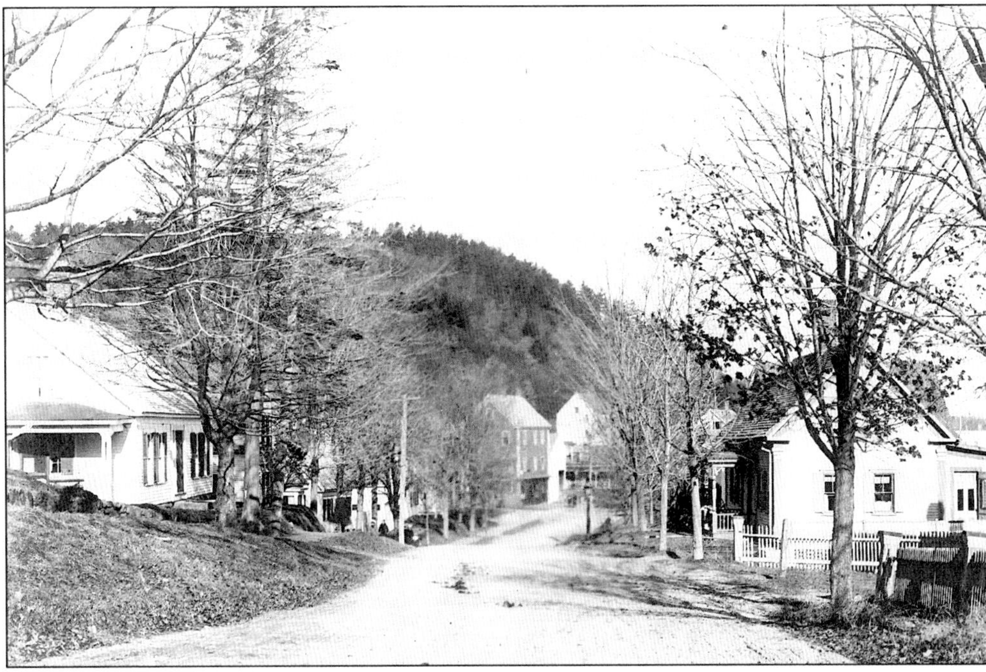

The View from the Congregational Church. This photograph is looking north toward the center of the town. The hill in the background, on which Silver Street is located, is Teneriffe Mountain. Milton was a typical New England village with its simple clapboard houses and fences. Note how close the houses are to the road. These houses were built before the fad of houses being set back from the road with large front lawns providing privacy from the neighbors. The church parsonage is on the left.

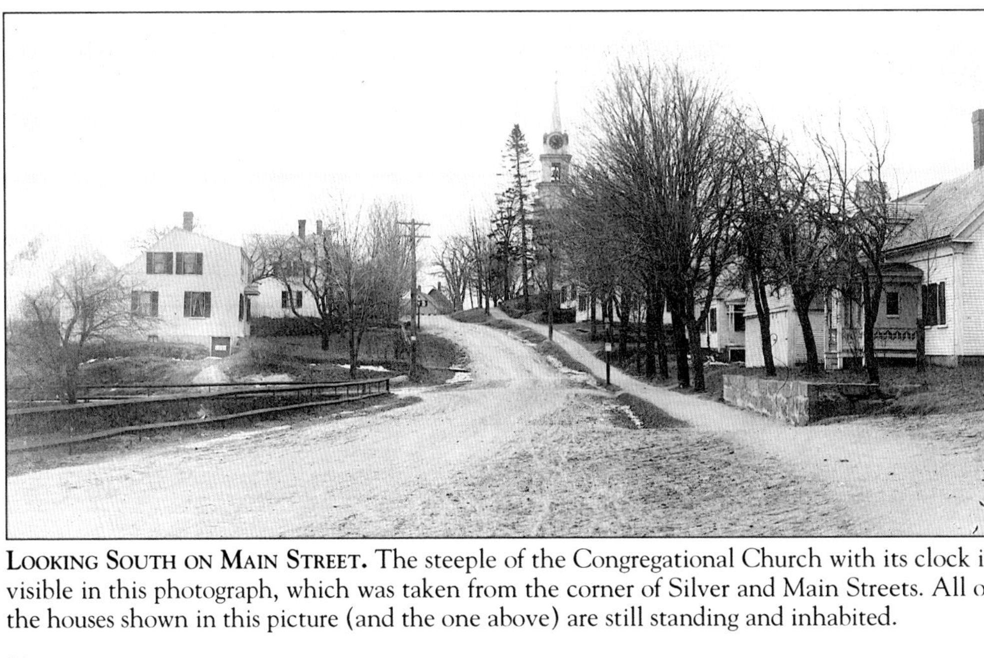

Looking South on Main Street. The steeple of the Congregational Church with its clock is visible in this photograph, which was taken from the corner of Silver and Main Streets. All of the houses shown in this picture (and the one above) are still standing and inhabited.

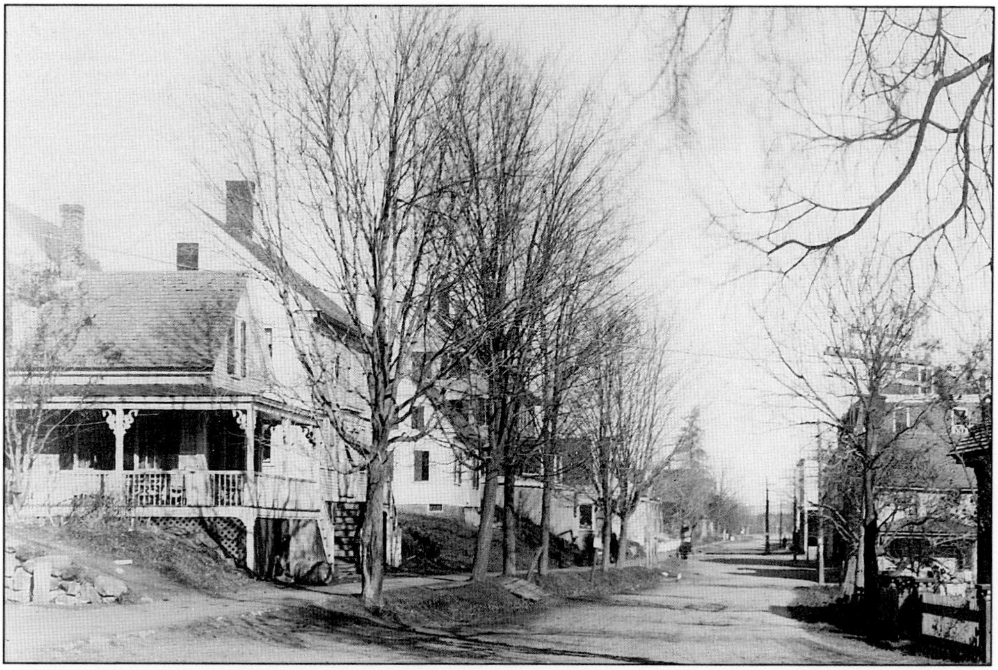

Looking North on Main Street. Main Street, or what is now more commonly referred to as Route 125, is a road that begins in Massachusetts and continues all the way to Union, New Hampshire, a small town just north of Milton. Since this photo was taken, the road has been tarred and sidewalks have been added.

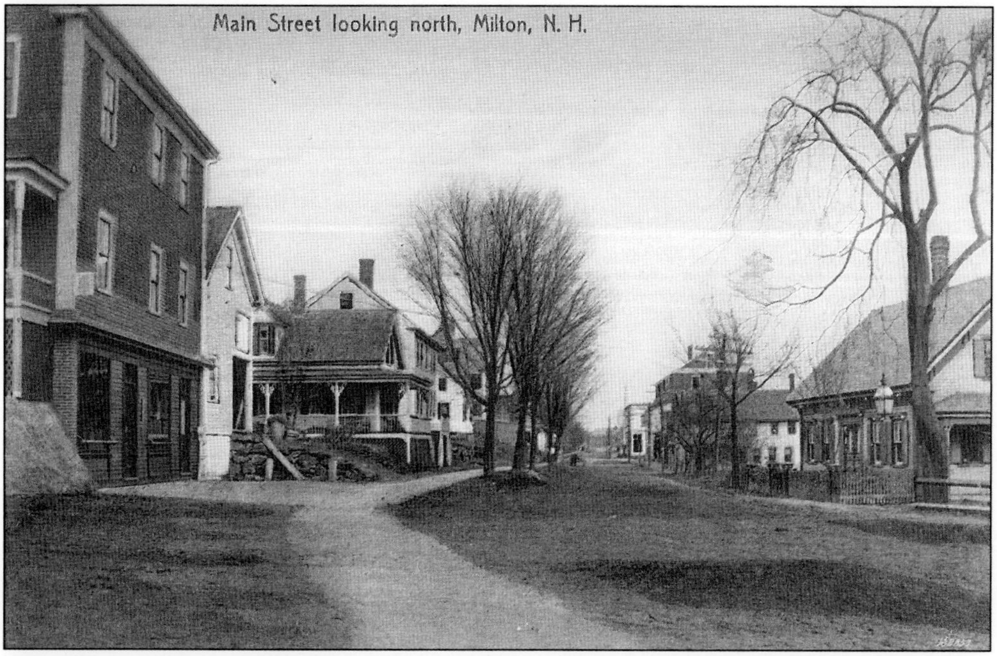

Main Street. This *c.* 1900 photograph was taken at the foot of Silver Street. The building in the left-hand corner is still there; however, the one next to it is no longer standing, and a new building has been put in its place.

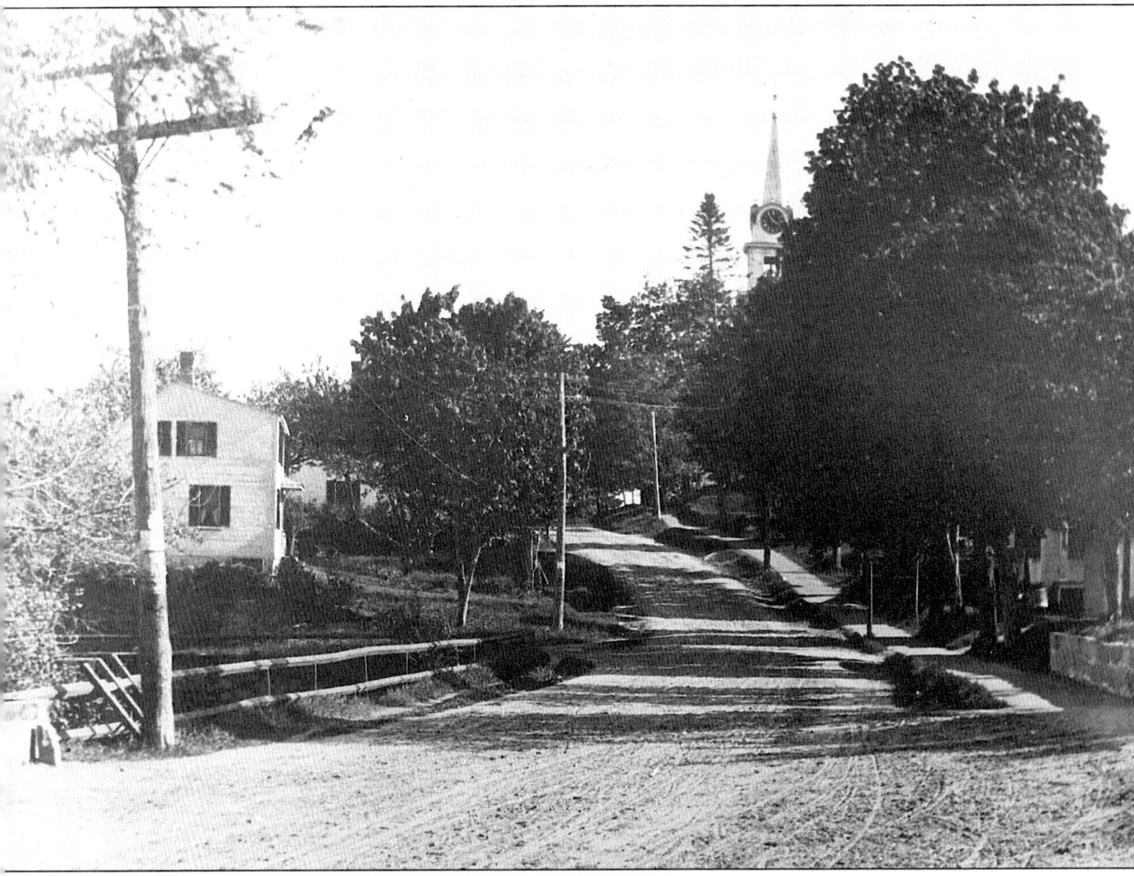

MILTON BECOMES ELECTRIFIED. Milton first used electric streetlights in 1893. This is Main Street, looking south; the large, white house on the left is still inhabited, and the grassy area just below it is used every year for the nativity scene. Though the poles appear to be just telephone poles with no streetlights, it has been documented that Milton did use electric lights at this time. Charles Appleby of Milton Mills was the last man to hold the job of lighting the kerosene lights. With the advent of electricity, Charles agreed to turn on the electric lights every night, even though his wife thought it was dangerous. The horse watering trough is on the left. Spring water from the hill fed it, keeping the water clean and fresh. In the distance is the steeple of the Congregational church.

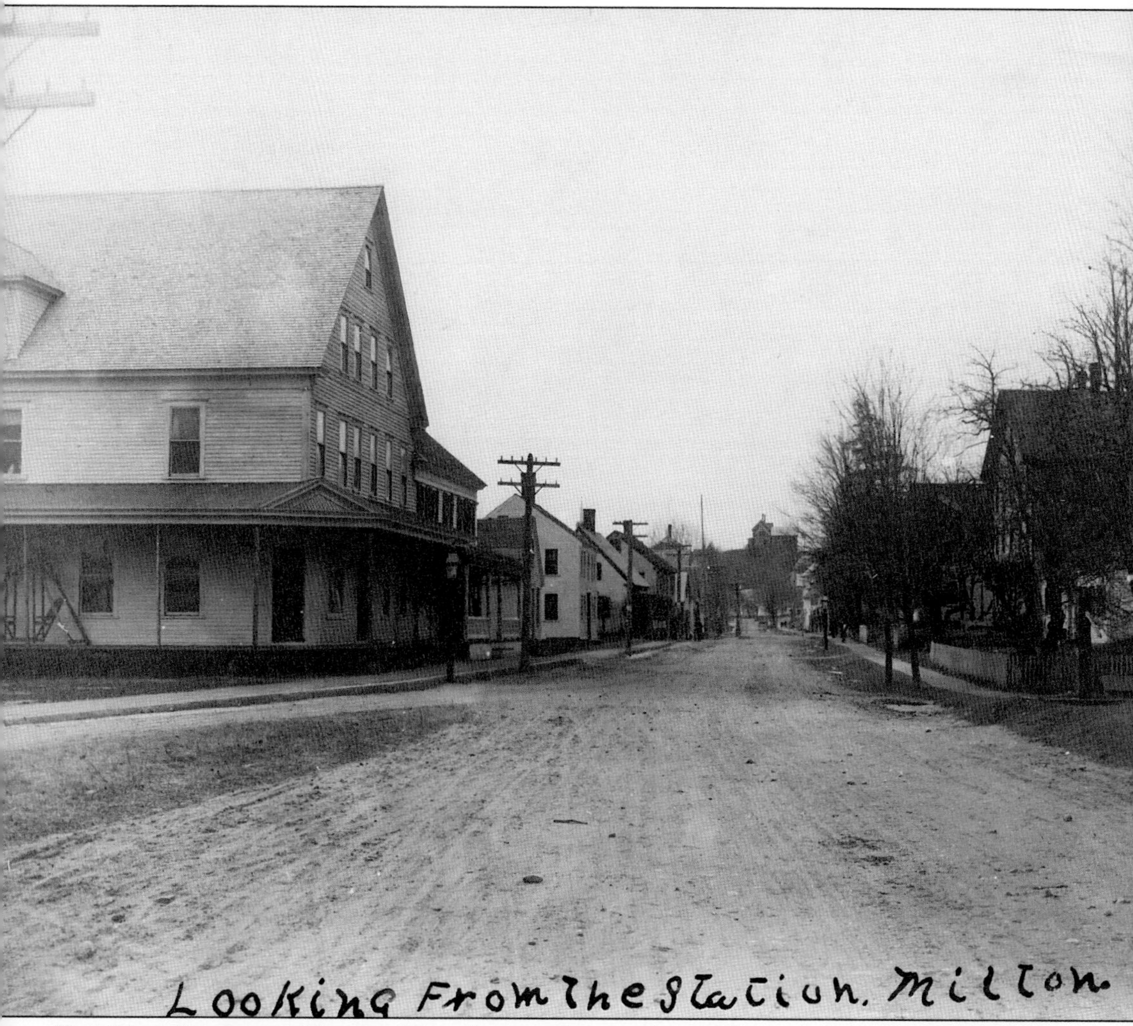

The Wide Streets of Milton. This photograph was taken in front of the train station. The large building on the left is the Lake View Hotel. This building, once the Congregational church, was dedicated on November 19, 1835. Later it became a school, and finally was used as the hotel.

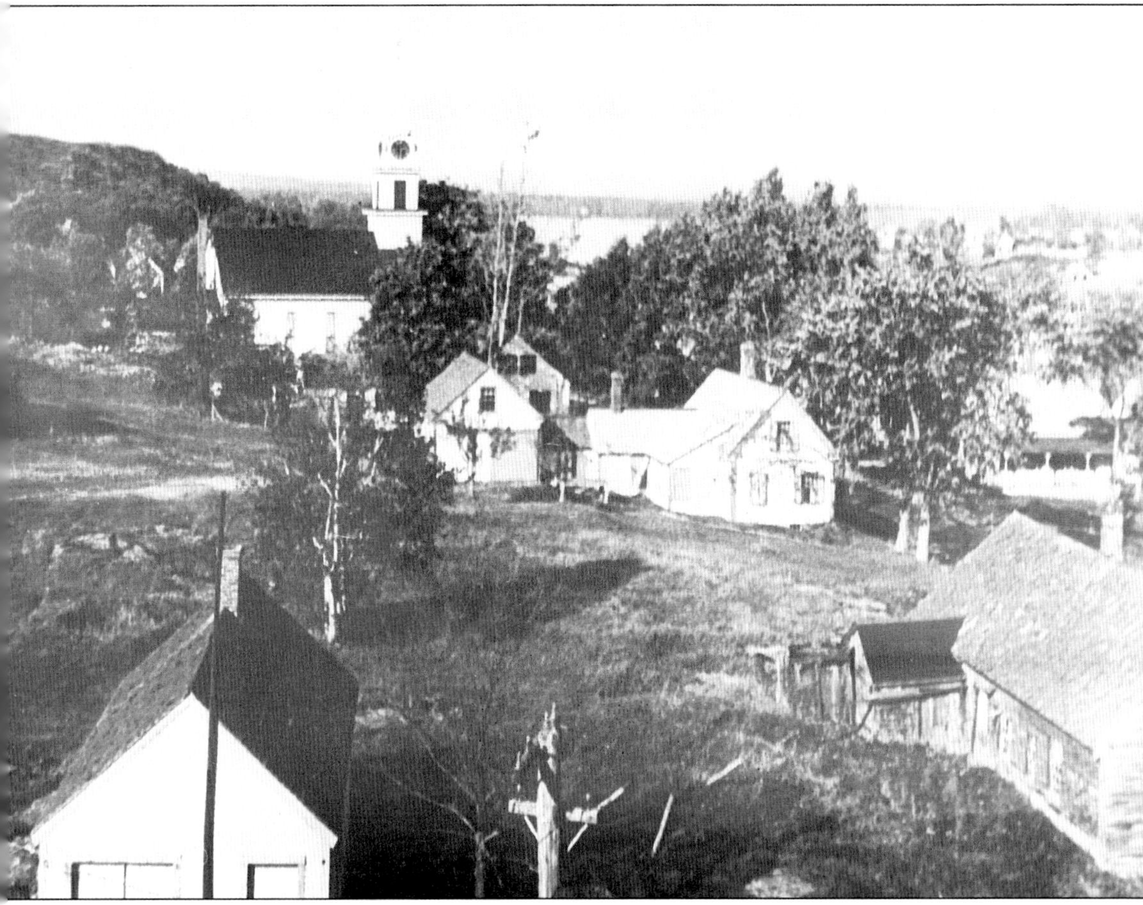

FROM JAIL TO THE CHURCH. The small building in the front is the old Milton Jail, which stood near the Baptist church. The small frame house on the right, in the front, was Mel Jones's house. It was torn down, and the Legion Hall was built on the site. The classic New England Congregational church towers over the scene.

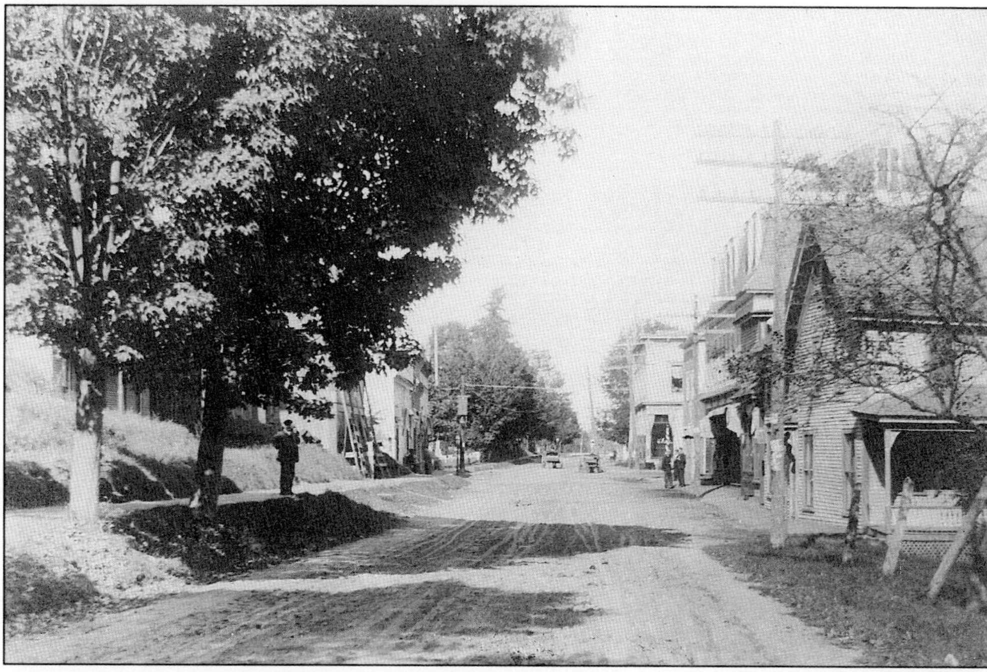

Downtown Milton. The old center of Milton was a mix of commercial and domestic buildings. The photograph was taken from in front of J.H. Willey's store. Lovely maples and evergreens lined the street and provided welcome shade for the handful of pedestrians on what appears to be a slow business day.

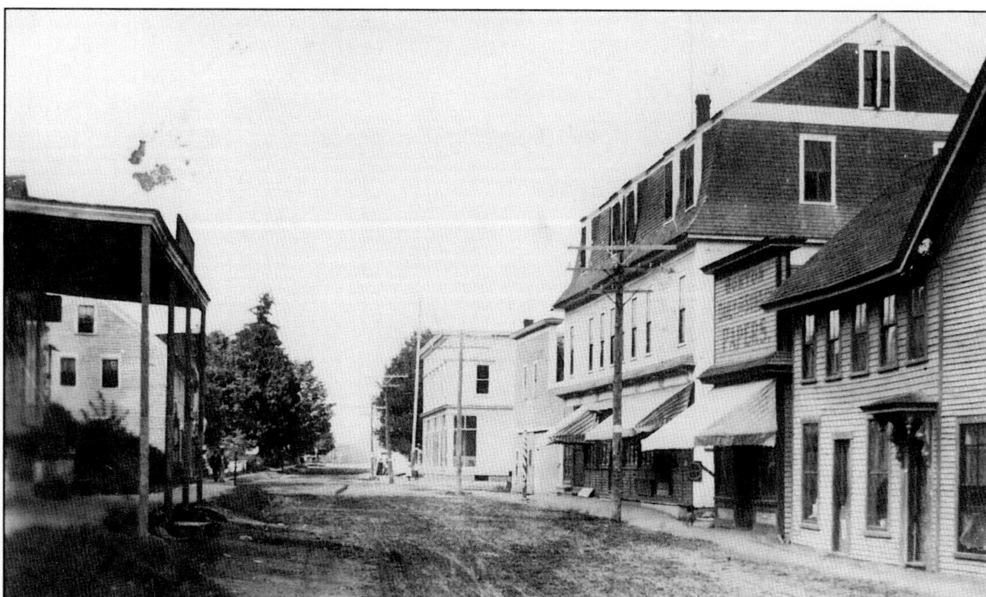

A Building from the Past. The building on the right is located in the downtown area. It was built in the Second Empire style. The mansard roof, along with a complete third floor, are indicative of a Second Empire building. At one time the building housed a ballroom, and later, for a very short time, there was a roller skating rink inside.

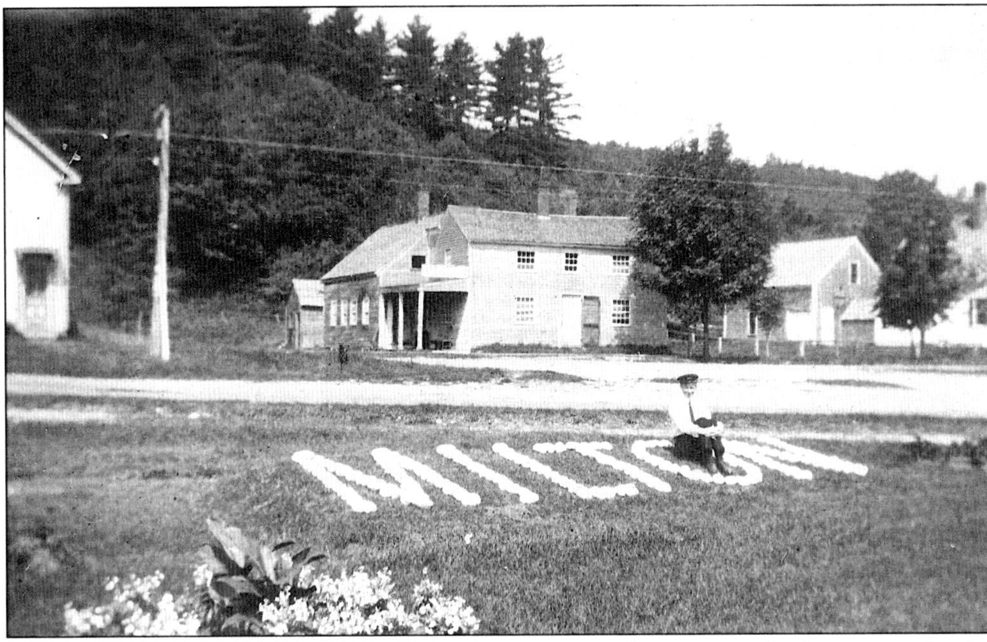

A Floral Tribute. The town's name is written out in flowers in a display set up for the Centennial Parade in 1902. Ray's Marina is presently located on this spot.

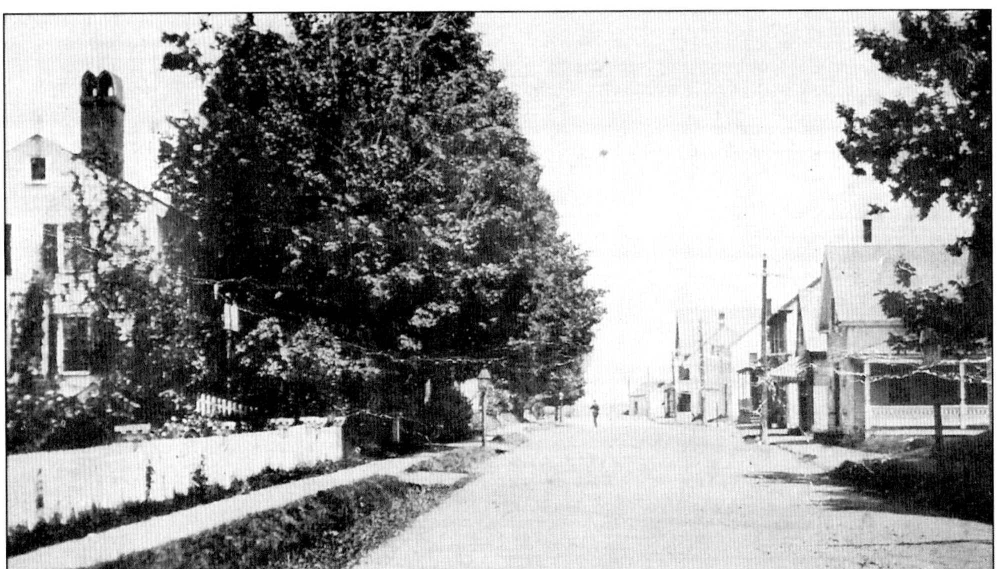

Main Street, October 11, 1921. The downtown area is little changed from its earlier appearance. The streetlights appear to still be gaslights in shape, though they were electrified. The beautiful, white house on the left is in the Georgian architectural style. Note the wonderful design of the chimney.

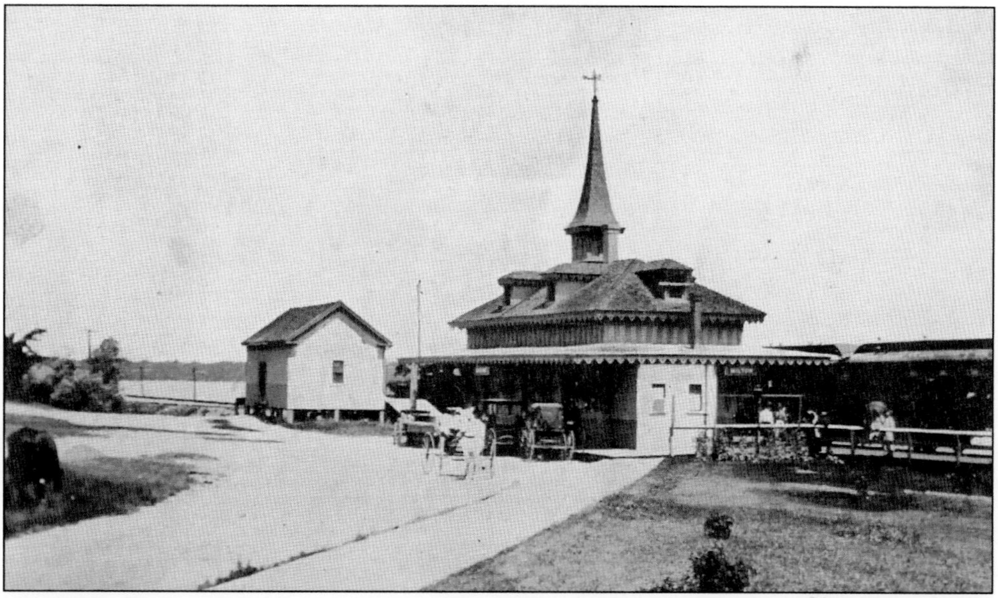

THE B&M TRAIN STATION. At one time the train traveled all the way to North Conway. In front of the station is a horse and a buckboard-type of wagon. The other may possibly be an early automobile.

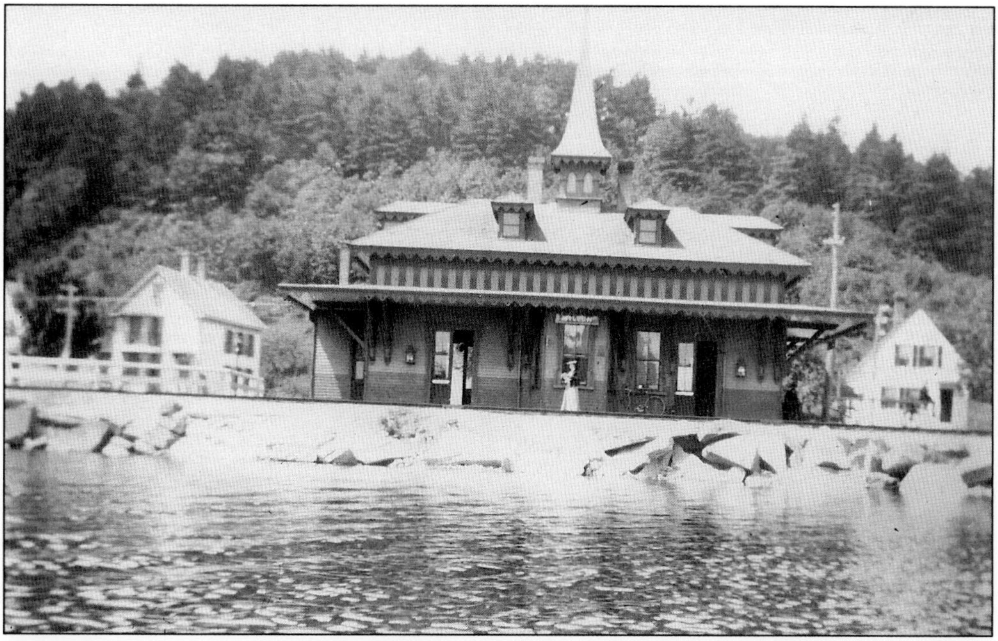

TRAIN STATION, FROM THE LAKE. Someone took this picture from a canoe in the middle of the pond. At this time, in the early half of this century, the pond was known as Depot Pond. Later it was changed to Lower Pond, though some people still refer to it by its old name. The people coming in from Boston had such a lovely view. A train station could not be more perfectly located.

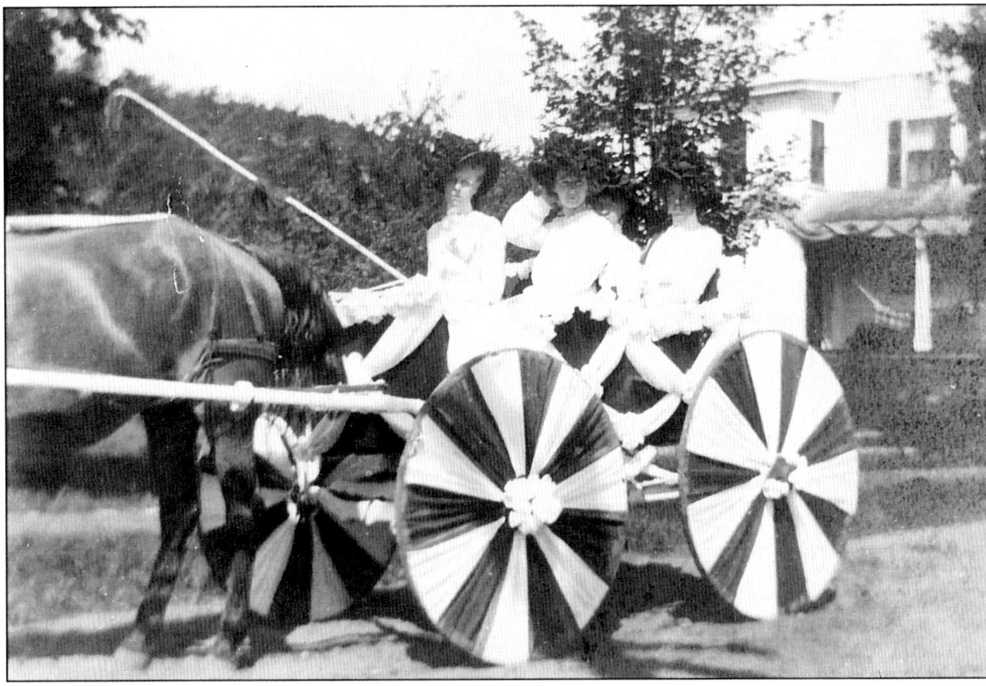

Getting Ready for the Centennial Parade. Milton celebrated the 100th anniversary of its separation from Rochester in 1902. A grand parade was held with numerous floats. The local citizenry decorated its houses with banners and flags. The people of the town were very festive; almost everyone helped build a float to display.

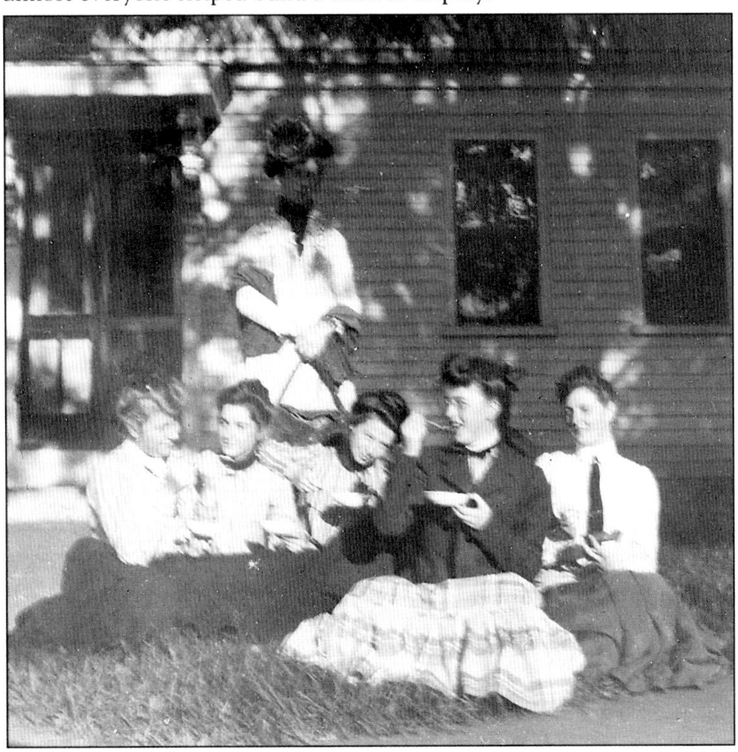

Ice Cream before the Parade. This photograph was taken before the parade happened. It came from the scrapbook a Plummer girl kept, showing what activities she participated in in 1902. Here, she wrote under the picture, "We were Robbie's guests."

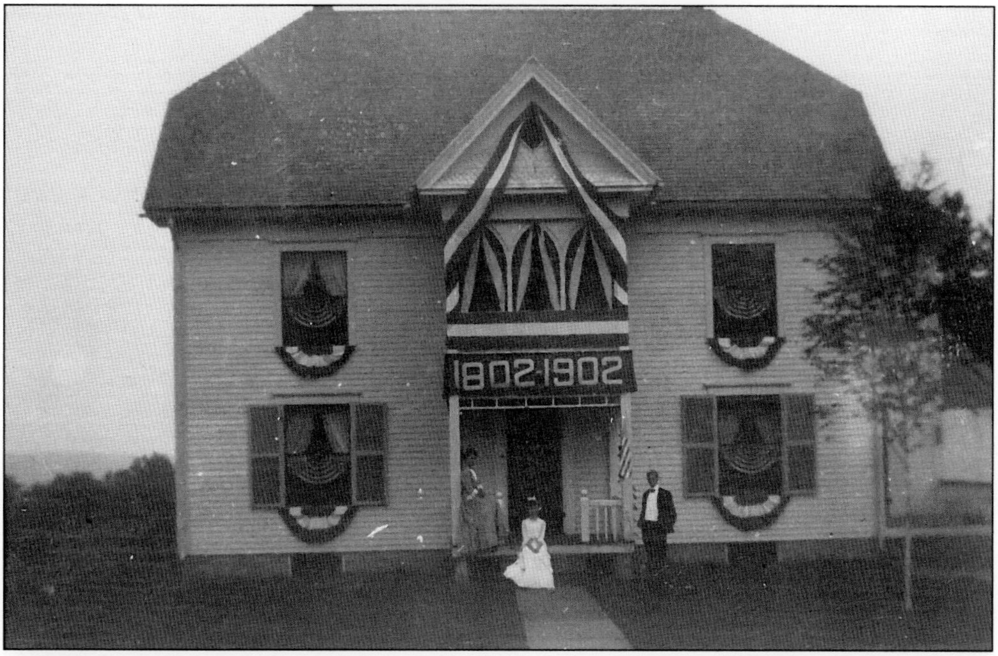

A Downtown Plummer Home. The centennial parade was an event that everyone was proud of. The people of the town worked hard to make the parade a success. The Plummer family was no exception. The banner hanging in front of the house reads: "1802–1902." Red, white, and blue were most likely the colors used in this banner.

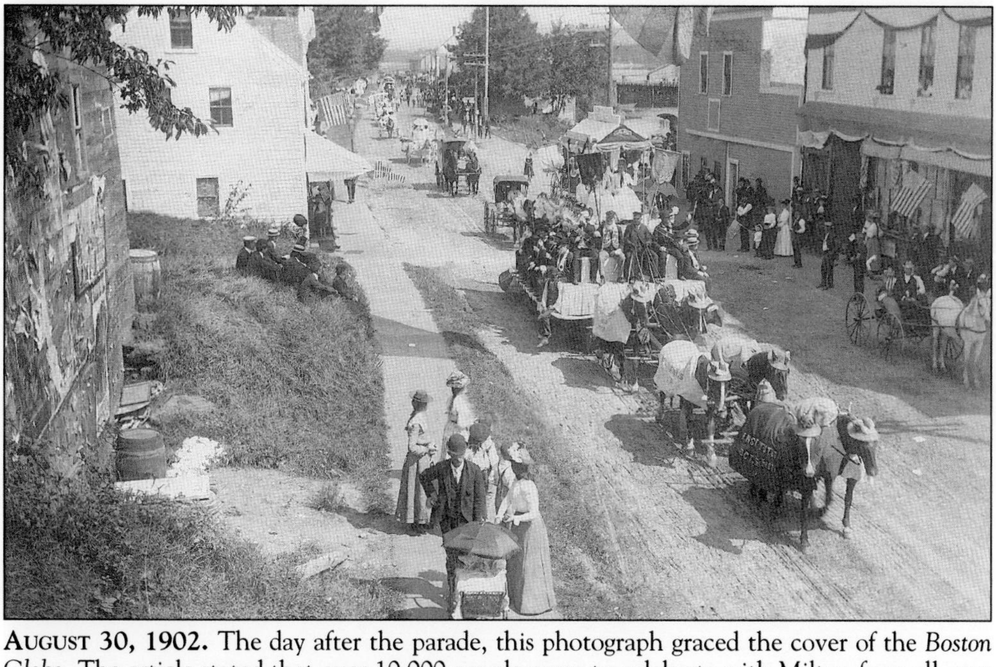

August 30, 1902. The day after the parade, this photograph graced the cover of the *Boston Globe*. The article stated that over 10,000 people came to celebrate with Milton from all over New England. The trains started pulling up to the station early in the morning and didn't stop until the celebrations were almost over. Notice the straw hats on the horses and the beautiful wicker baby carriage on the sidewalk.

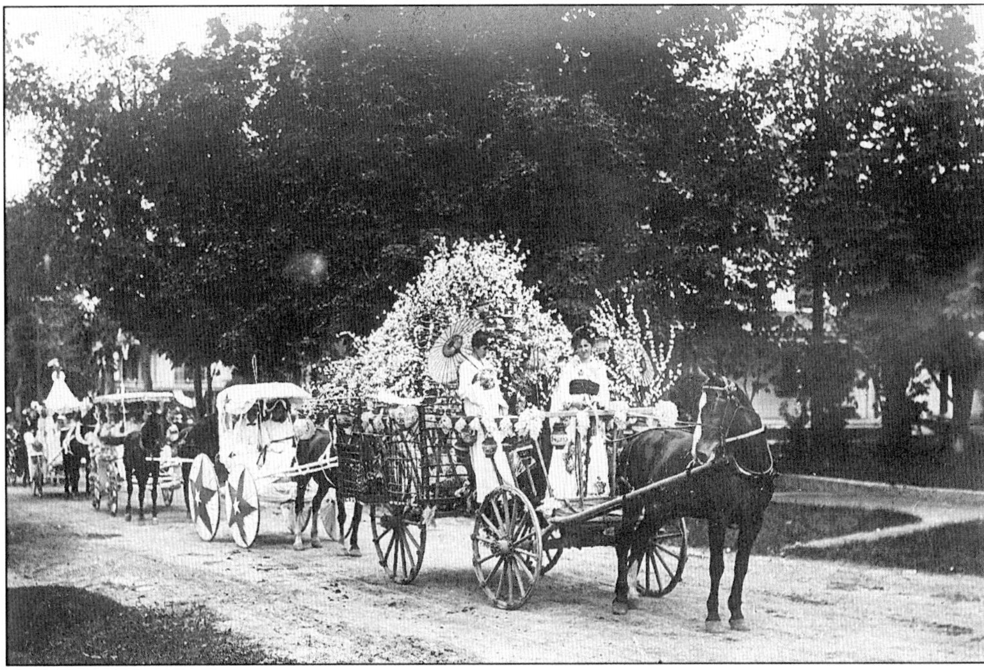

The Line Up. Everyone in town put their all into this great event. Here, at the start of the parade, we see the first horse and float. The parade line-up seems to continue far into the distance. It was said in the *Boston Globe* that people stayed up until four in the morning dancing and having a great time.

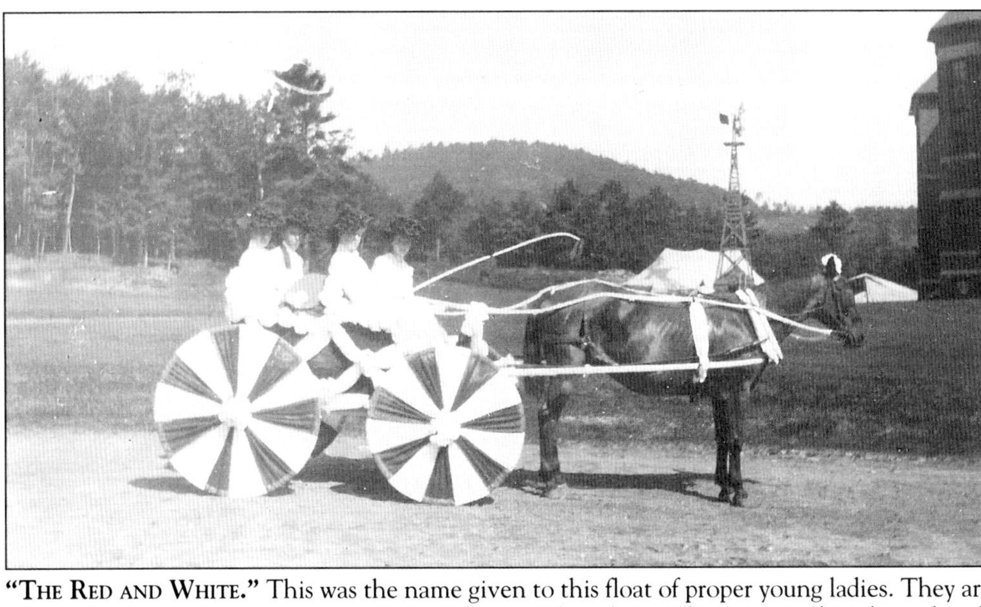

"The Red and White." This was the name given to this float of proper young ladies. They are all dressed in their best clothes, sitting in the float they designed. Imagine what the red-and-white wheels must have looked like when the float was in motion.

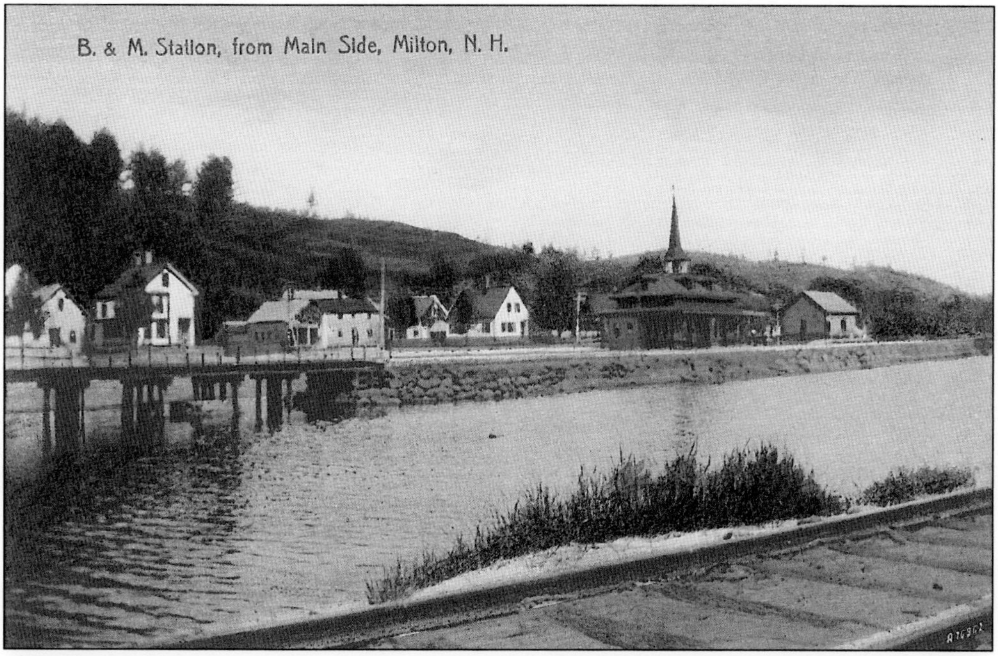

The Train Station as Seen from the Other Side of the Pond. This photograph was taken in the early part of the 20th century. The photographer was standing opposite the railroad station.

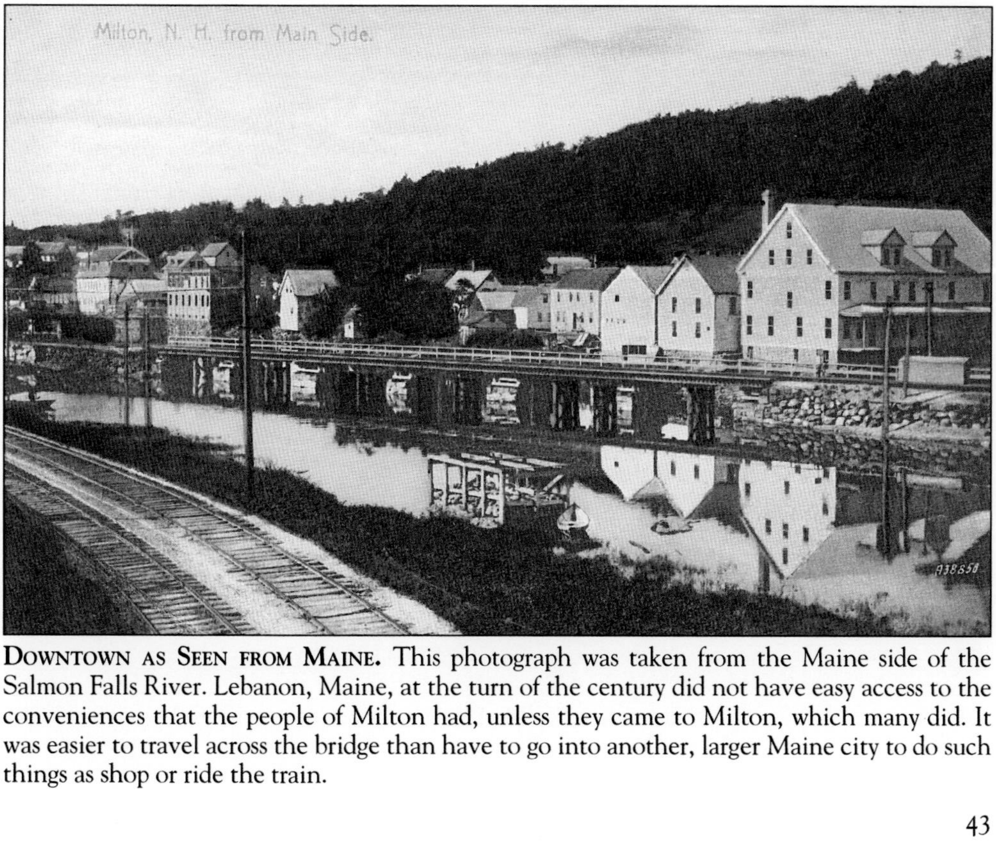

Downtown as Seen from Maine. This photograph was taken from the Maine side of the Salmon Falls River. Lebanon, Maine, at the turn of the century did not have easy access to the conveniences that the people of Milton had, unless they came to Milton, which many did. It was easier to travel across the bridge than have to go into another, larger Maine city to do such things as shop or ride the train.

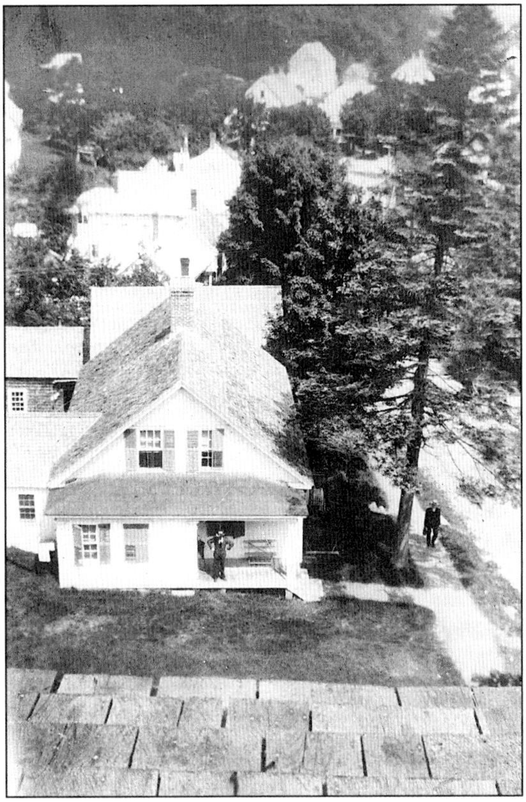

CONGREGATIONAL CHURCH PARSONAGE. This photograph was taken from one of the upstairs windows of the Congregational church. It is looking down upon the Cape Cod-style parsonage. The parsonage is on the right-hand side of the church, if you were standing in front of it. In the distance, the corner of Silver and Main Streets is visible.

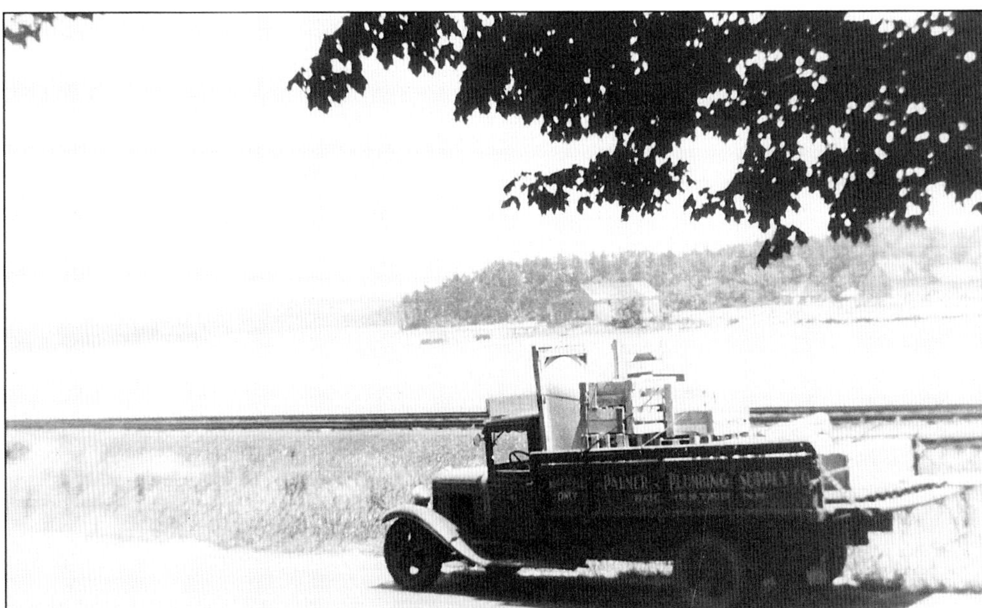

THE ISLAND. When people drive through Milton, by the pond, they can't help but notice the small island with the camp nestled between the pine trees in the middle of the pond. In the forefront of the photo is the Plumbing Supply Co. truck, probably doing some business in town.

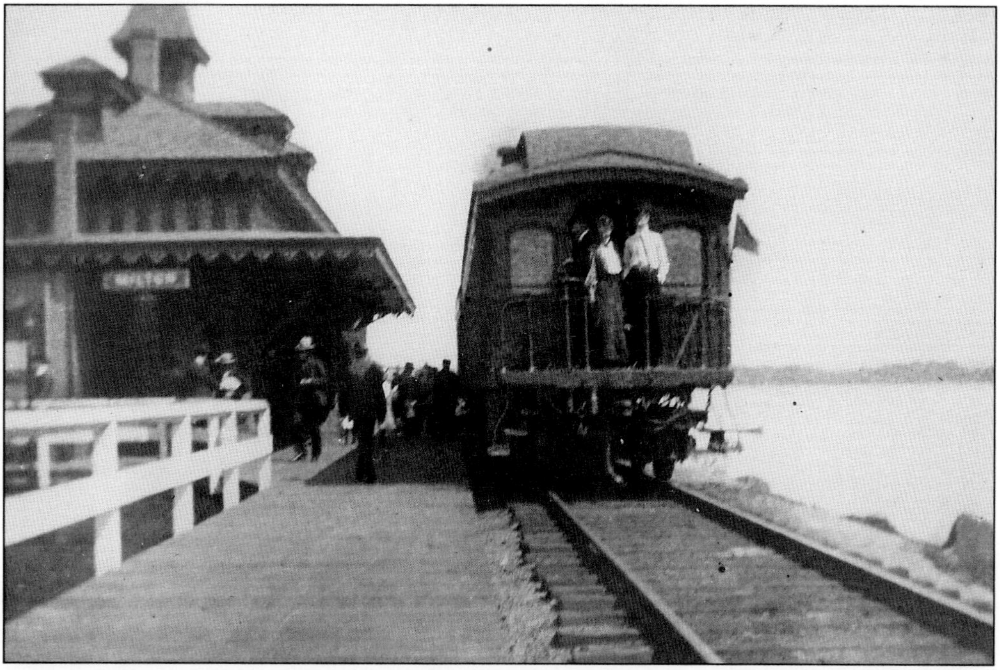

Leaving Milton. These two young people are leaving on the train; their destination is either north toward Ossipee or south toward Boston. This photograph was taken in 1902; it is part of the chronicles of the Plummer girl's scrapbook.

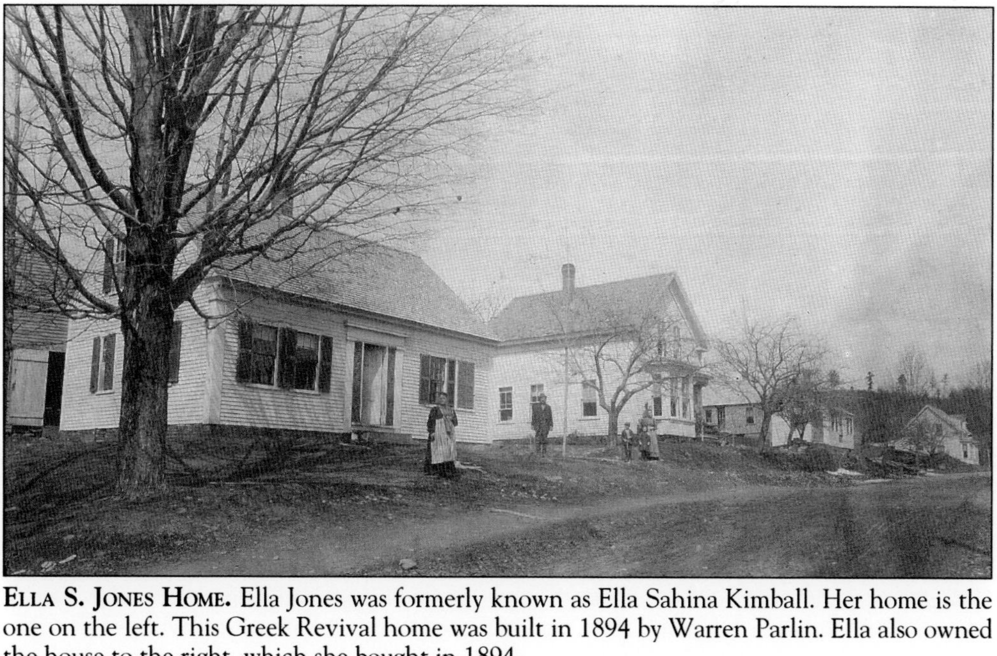

Ella S. Jones Home. Ella Jones was formerly known as Ella Sahina Kimball. Her home is the one on the left. This Greek Revival home was built in 1894 by Warren Parlin. Ella also owned the house to the right, which she bought in 1894.

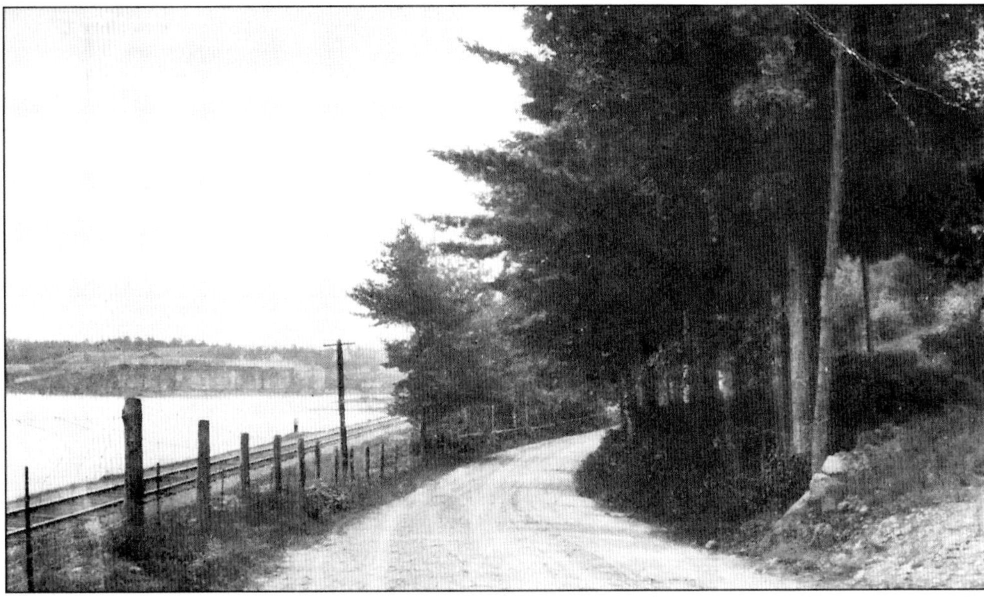

WAKEFIELD ROAD. This photograph is looking south toward the center of town. Lower (or Depot) Pond is on the left. This road is now more commonly referred to as Route 125. This picture was a postcard from J.H. Willey's General Store. It is titled, "Wakefield Road, looking South, Milton, NH."

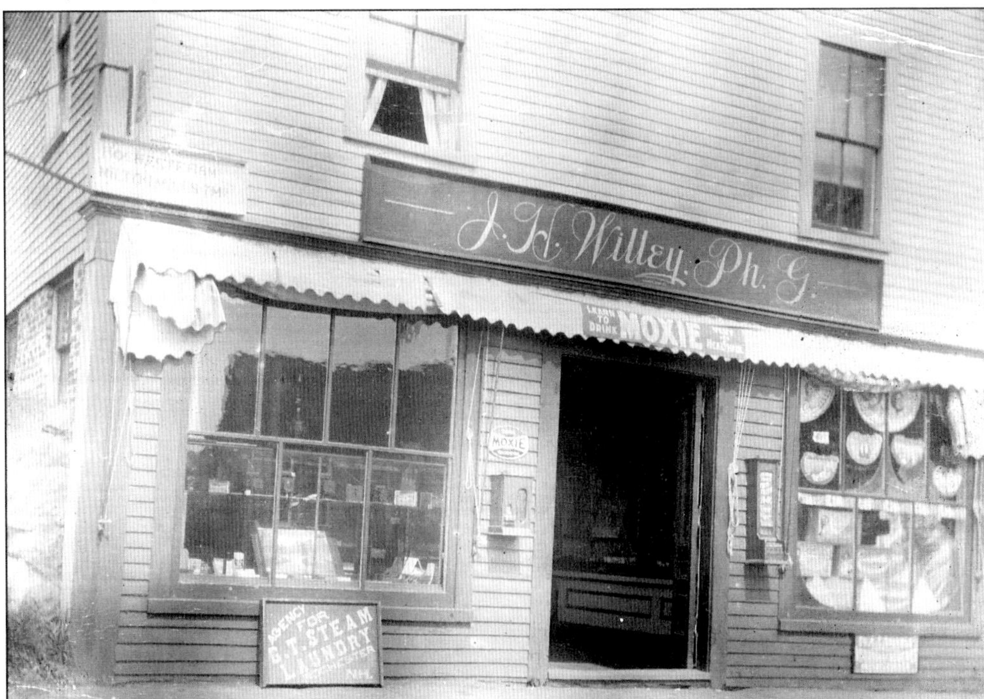

WILLEY'S STORE. You could buy anything from soda pop to medication at this general store, located at the corner of Silver and Main Streets. The building is still being used today. Notice the wonderful signs hung in front of the store, such as "Rochester 8M Milton Mills 7M," or the "Learn to drink Moxie, very healthful."

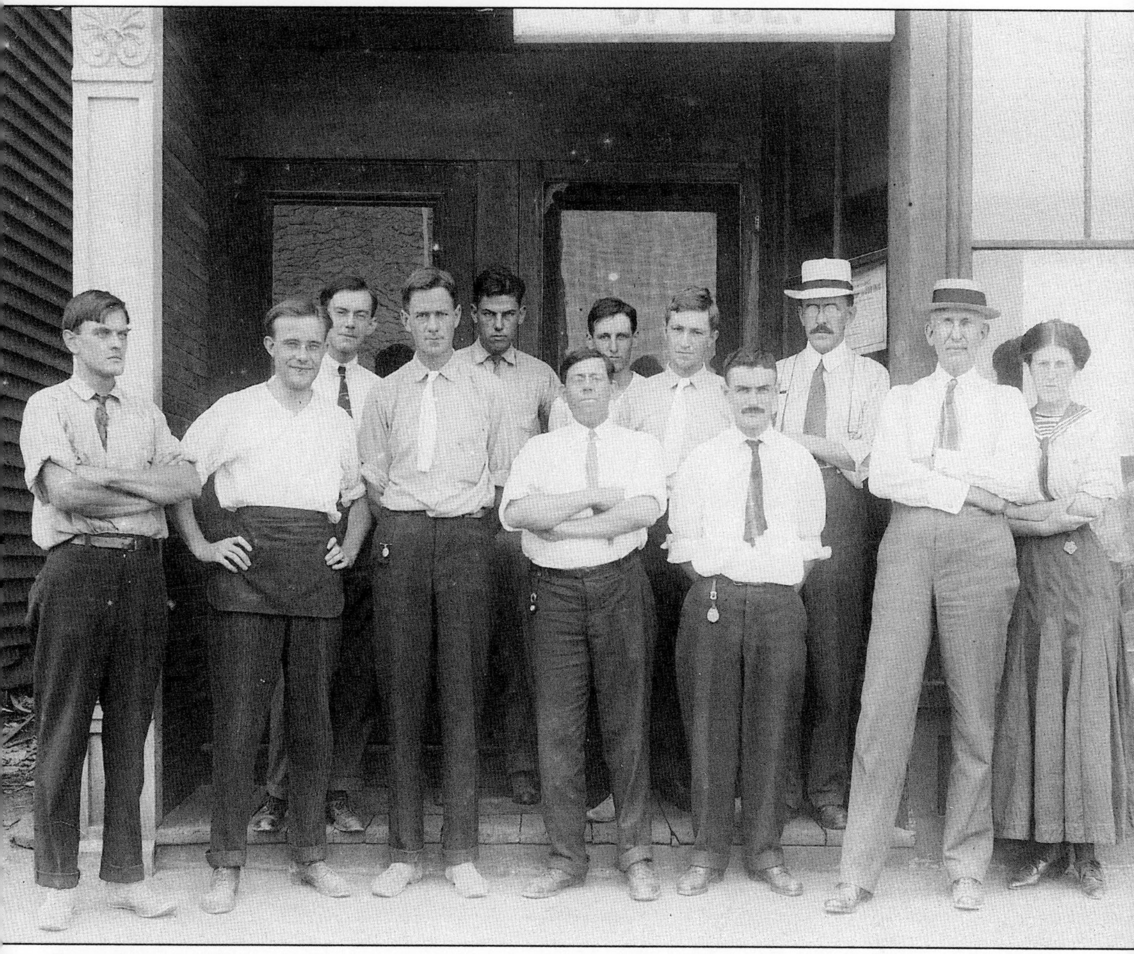

Post Office. These are the employees of the Milton Post Office. The photograph was taken in the early 1900s. At this time the post office was located in the large Second Empire-style building, which was located right before the bridge. The building was recently torn down.

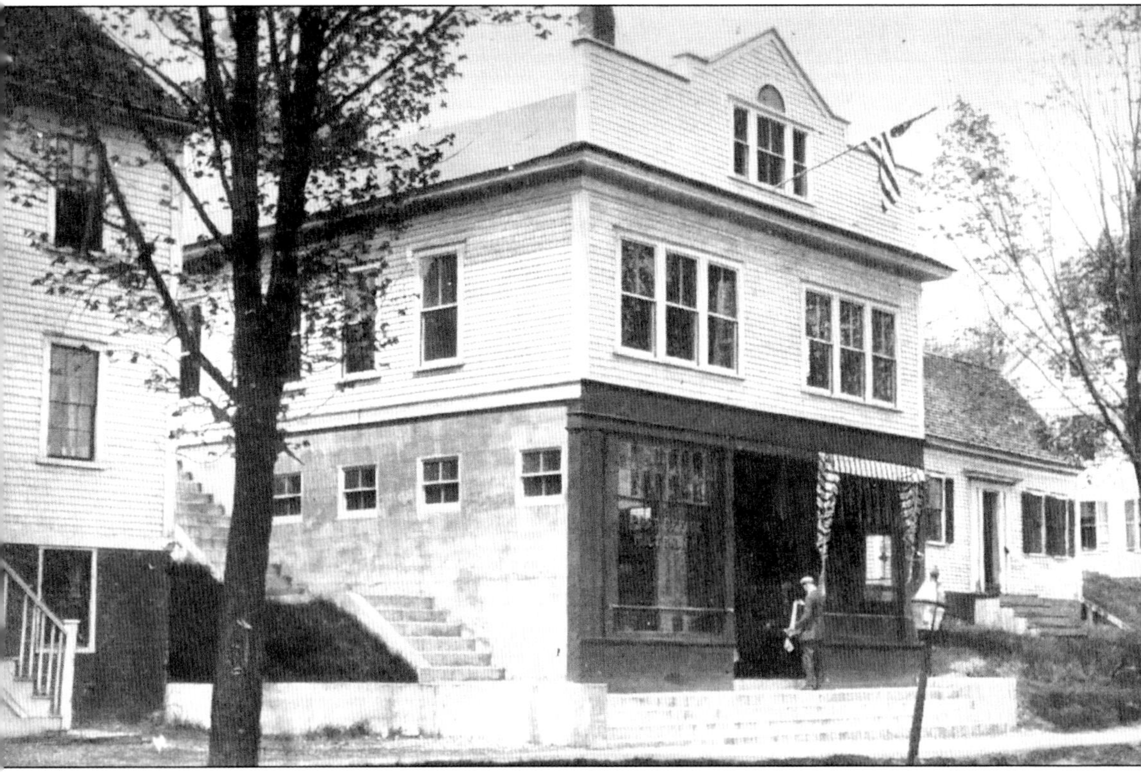

The Newer Post Office. This postcard was labeled "Milton Post Office." This building is still in use, near the corner of Silver and Main Streets. Notice the street lamp in front of the building.

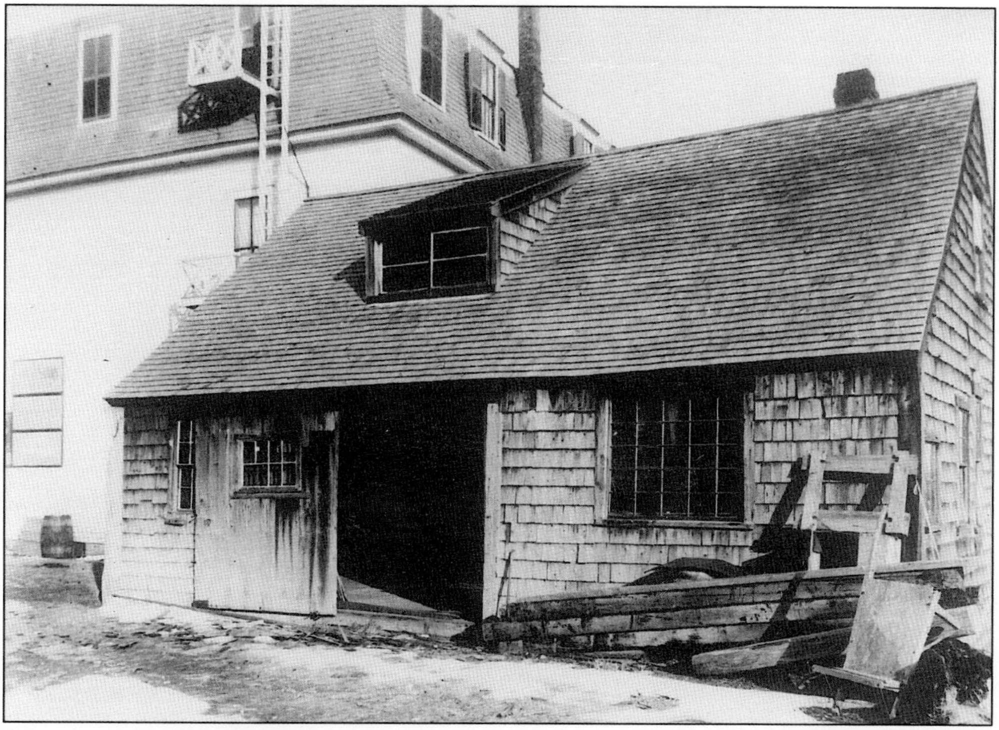

Blacksmith's Shop, Side View. At the time of this photograph, the local blacksmith's shop had already been abandoned for years. It was located in the center of town, near where the police station used to be housed.

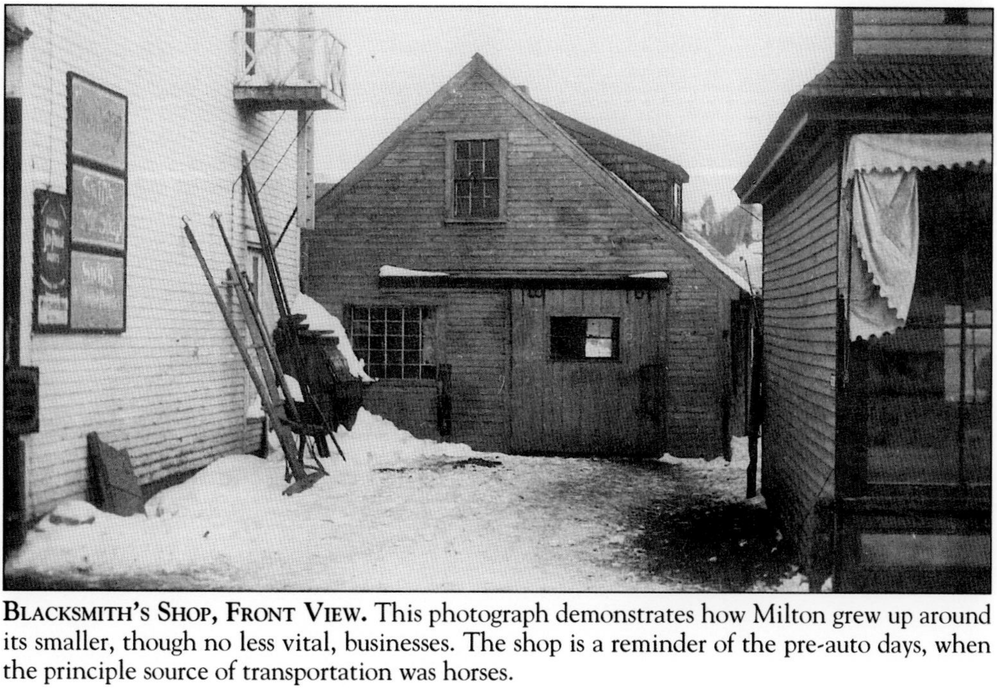

Blacksmith's Shop, Front View. This photograph demonstrates how Milton grew up around its smaller, though no less vital, businesses. The shop is a reminder of the pre-auto days, when the principle source of transportation was horses.

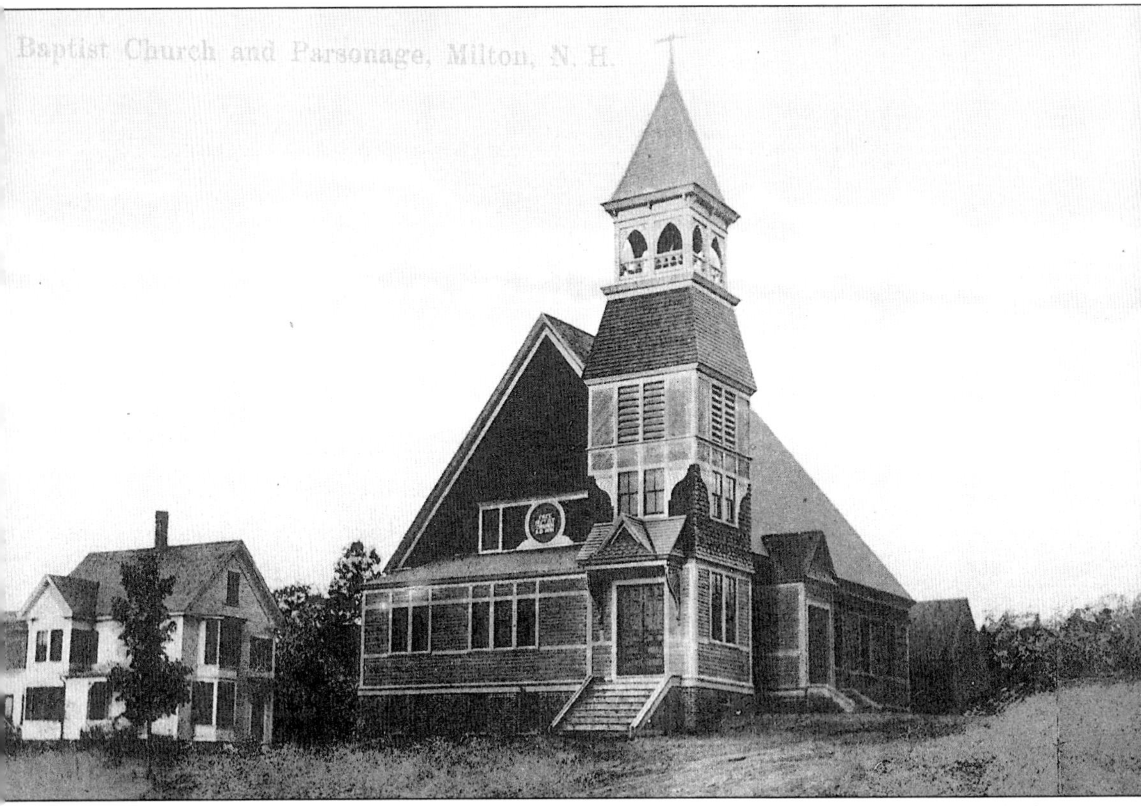

THE FIRST BAPTIST CHURCH. The First Baptist Church of Milton was first organized in the home of Theodore Lyman in 1843, but the church was not actually built until 1860. On December 12, 1890, at 11:30 p.m., the church burned. Only the parsonage was saved, protected by the heavy snow and ice on the roof. Until the new church was built, which is shown in this photograph, services were held at the Burley and Usher Shoe Company.

Baptist Church Interior with Pulpit. This unknown pastor was one of many men to serve the congregation. Here, he stands at the pulpit, proud and tall.

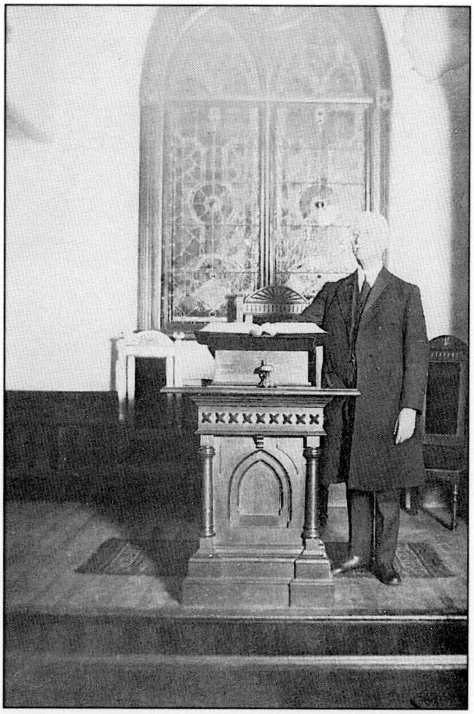

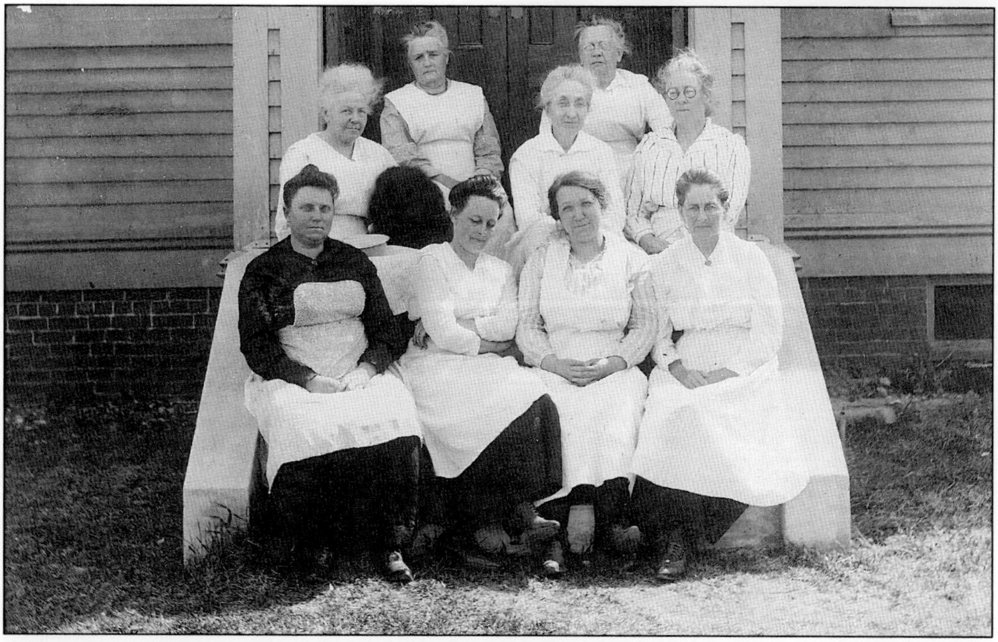

Preparing a Church Dinner. Though the actual reason these women are posing for this photograph is unknown, it seems a likely guess, by their aprons, they were preparing a church dinner. The women are, from left to right, as follows: (front row) Blanch Downs, Georgie Dixon, Emma Bruce, and Annie Hayes; (middle row) Emma Avery, Ester Cate, and Salley Avery; (back row) Clara Ramsdalle and Hattie M. Butley. Note that Emma Avery is holding her cocker spaniel.

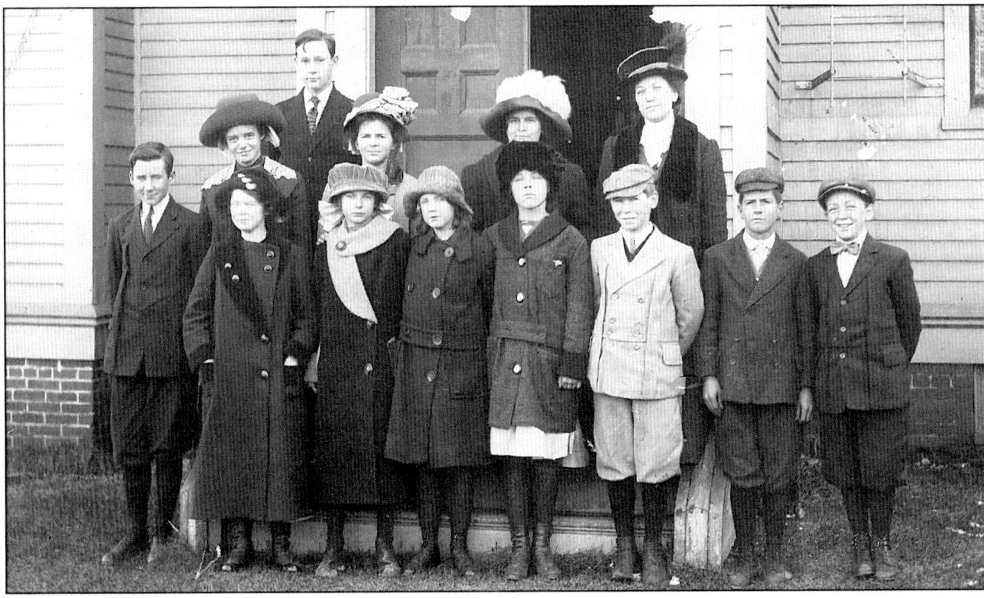

SUNDAY SCHOOL CLASS, 1914. This was one of the Baptist Church Sunday School classes. Members from left to right are (front row) Josephine Downing, Helen Hayes, Marta Parker, Francena Nutter, Charles Twombly, Leo Corson, and Arthur Bruce; (middle row) Harold Roberts, Marion Webster, Mary Corson, Alice Hodges, and Emma Bruce (the teacher); (back row) Willard Cleveland.

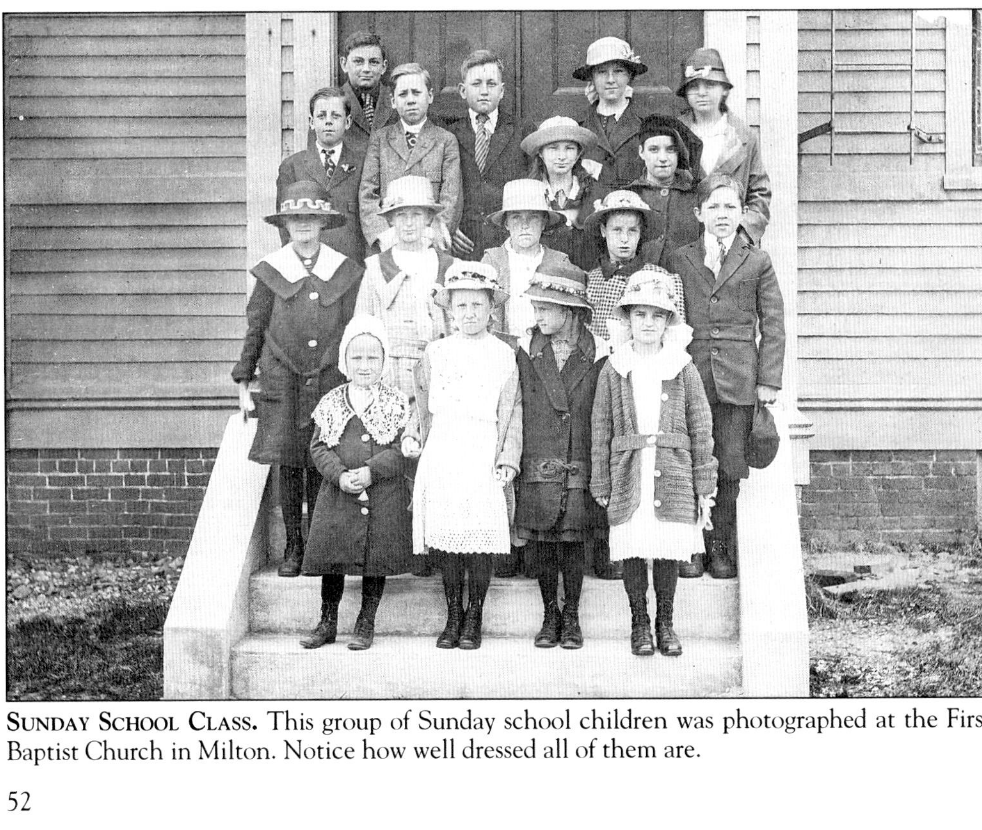

SUNDAY SCHOOL CLASS. This group of Sunday school children was photographed at the First Baptist Church in Milton. Notice how well dressed all of them are.

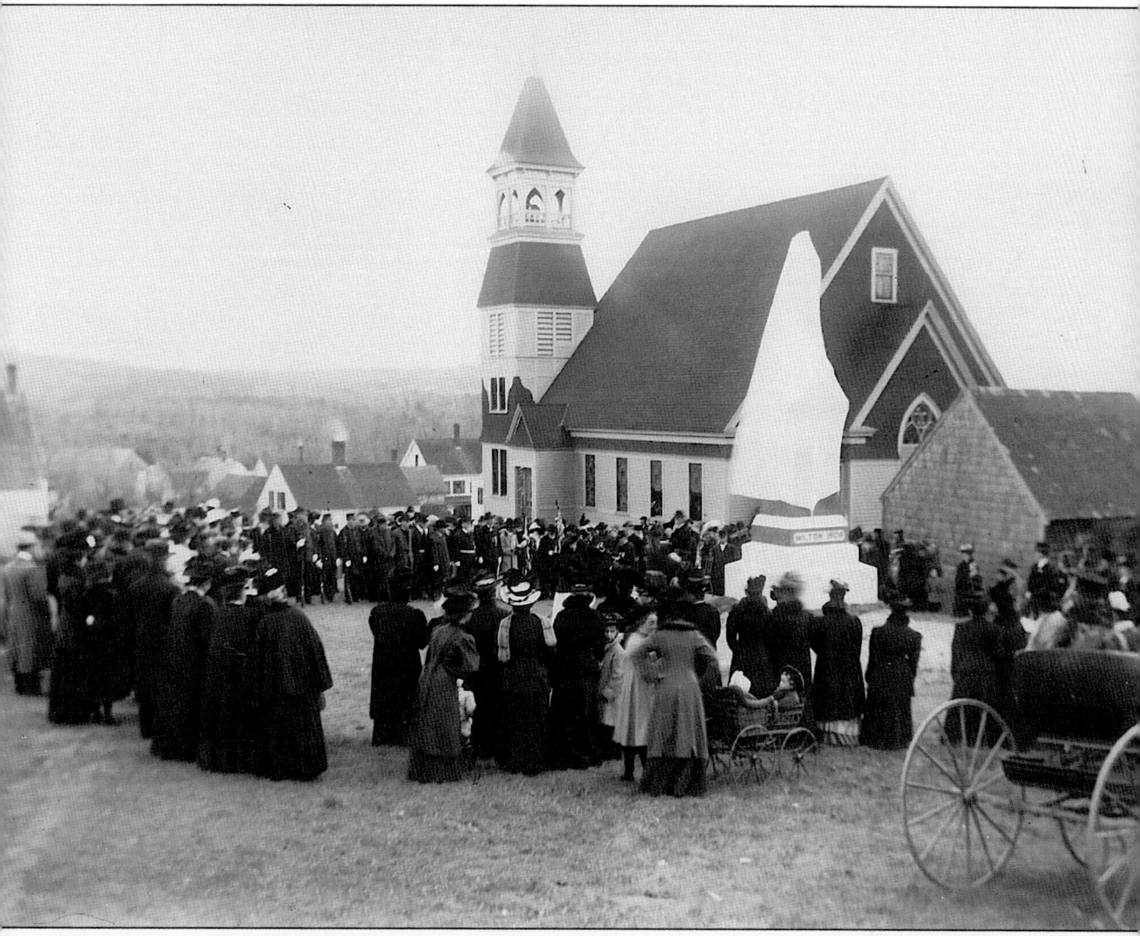

WAITING FOR THE UNVEILING. Townspeople eagerly await the unveiling of the statue to commemorate the Civil War Veterans. Notice the large, horse-drawn carriage on the right.

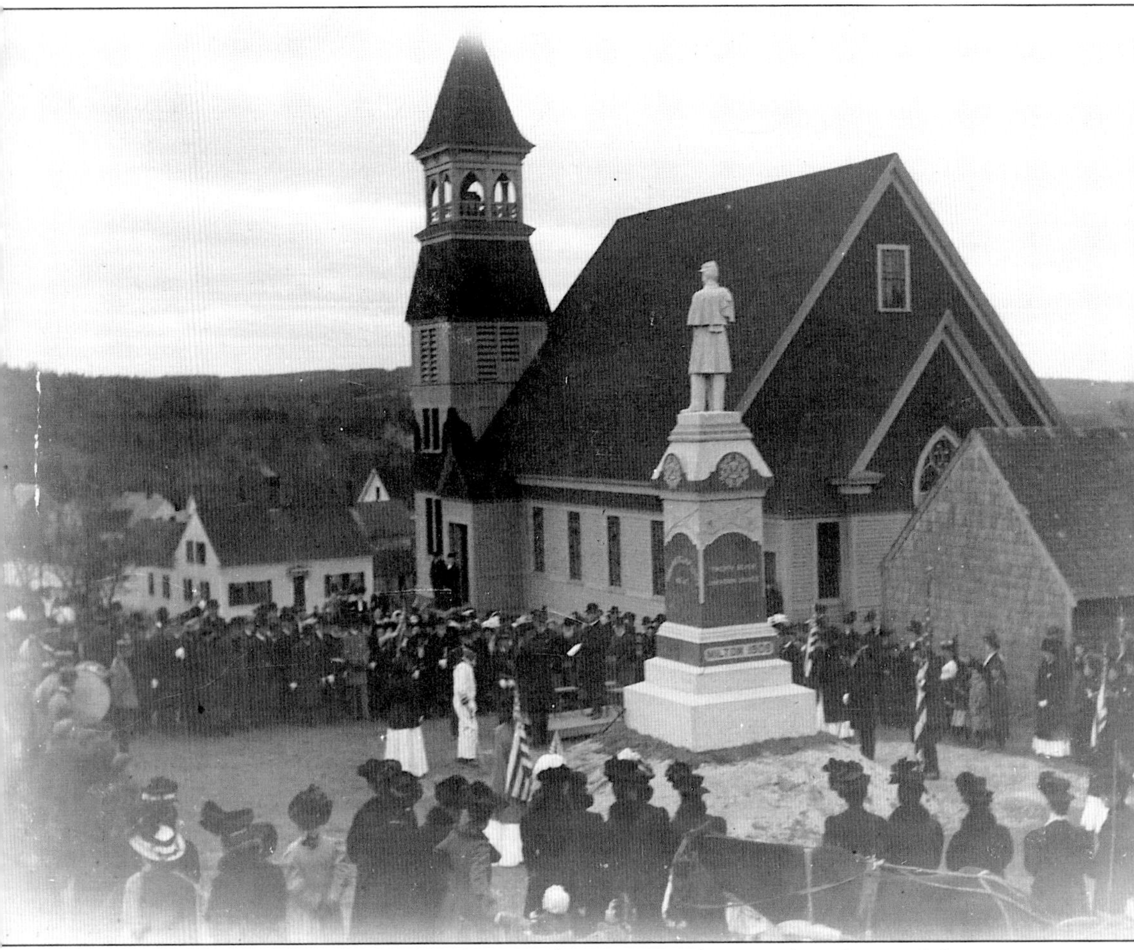

The Unveiling. The statue is dated 1909. The townspeople are gathered around the new statue, excited about the addition to the town. The statue is right next to the First Baptist Church, and in clear view of the elementary school.

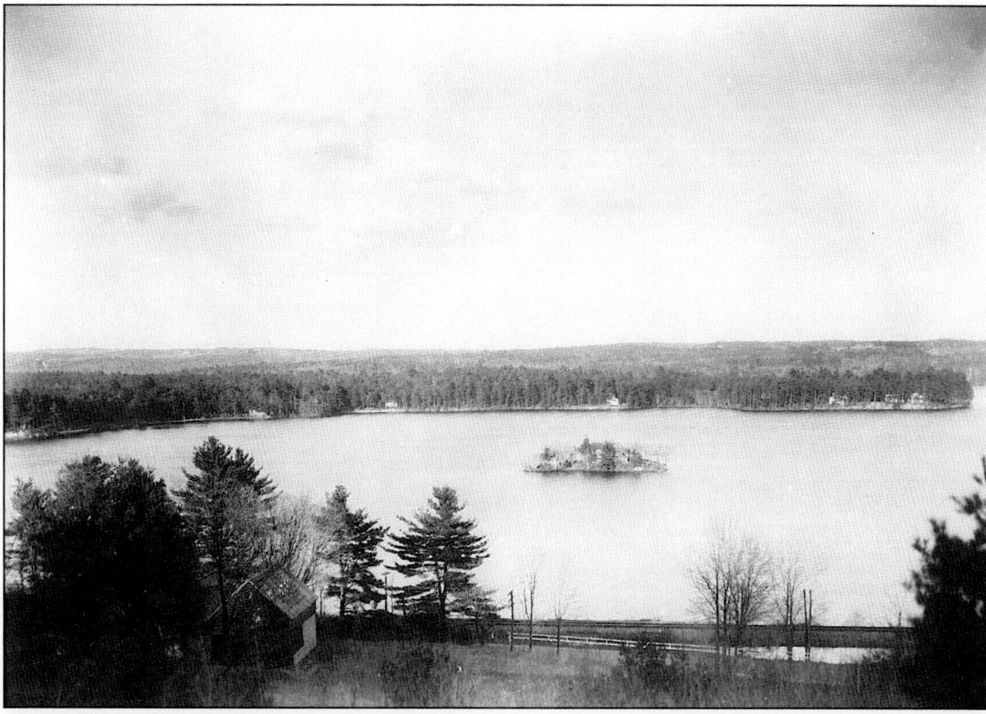

The Island. The island in the middle of Lower Pond has a lovely house settled in the center. It is picturesquely situated very close to the railroad station, and everyone traveling through Milton had a chance to see the sight.

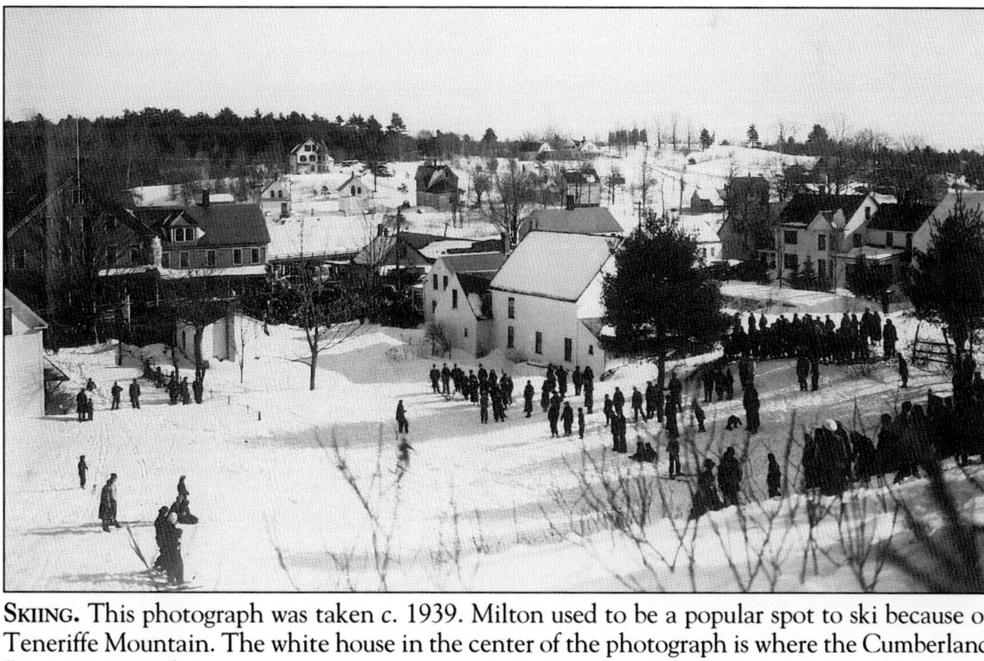

Skiing. This photograph was taken c. 1939. Milton used to be a popular spot to ski because of Teneriffe Mountain. The white house in the center of the photograph is where the Cumberland Farms now stands.

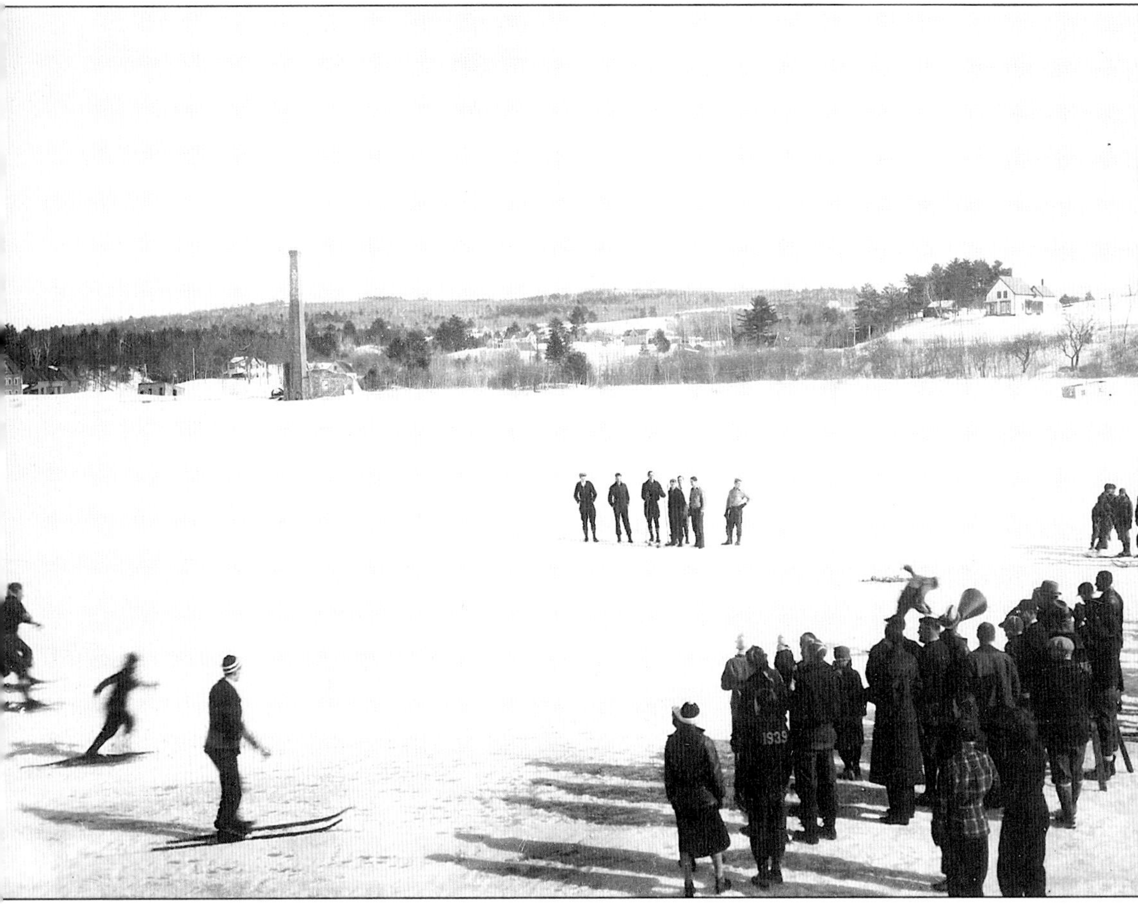

Winter Carnival. This photograph was taken in 1939, according to the man's sweater. This is out on Lower Pond, and it appears that a skating competition is in the works. The people on the left seem to be moving quite fast.

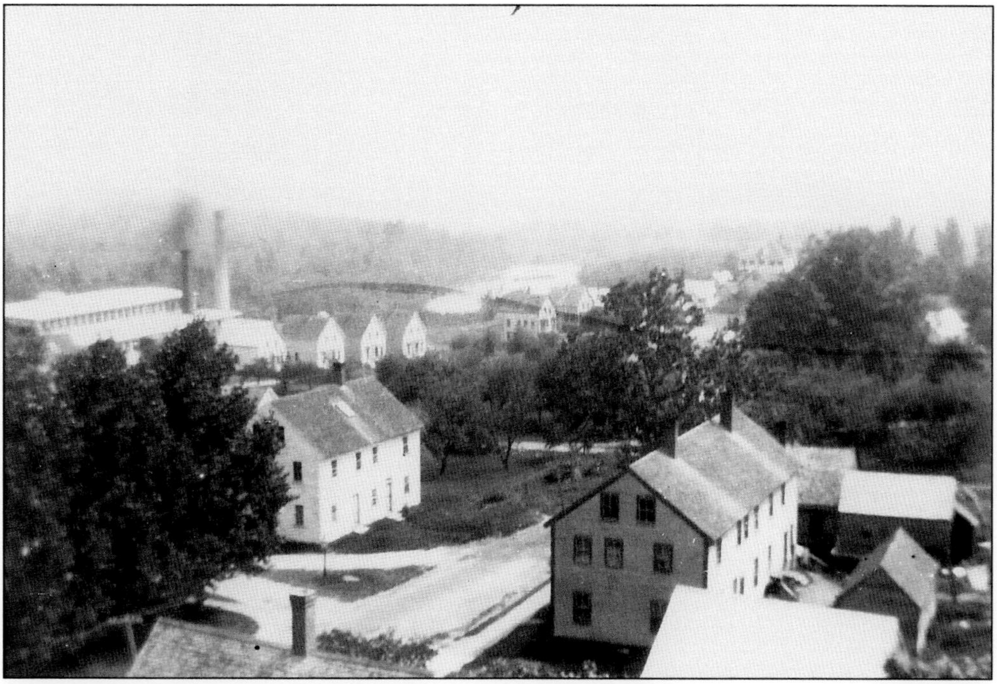

View from the Baptist Church. In the foreground is the Teneriffe Sports Club. The houses in the front are all double houses. A row of similar houses in the back could very well be factory housing. In the distance is the Milton Leathboard Factory.

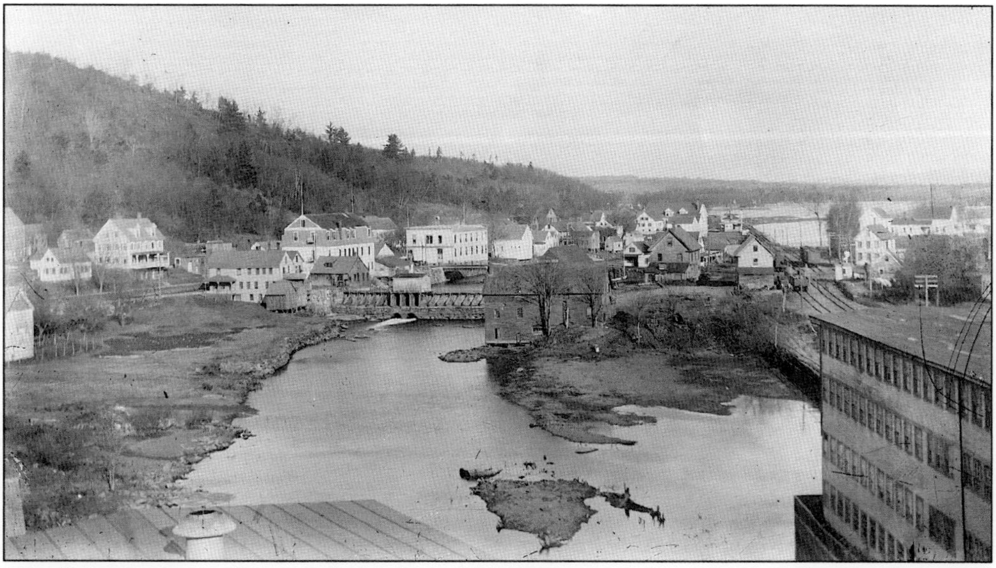

The Salmon Falls River. The Salmon Falls River was a very powerful river that could have easily supplied power to dozens of factories. Here we see a view of the river from a factory window.

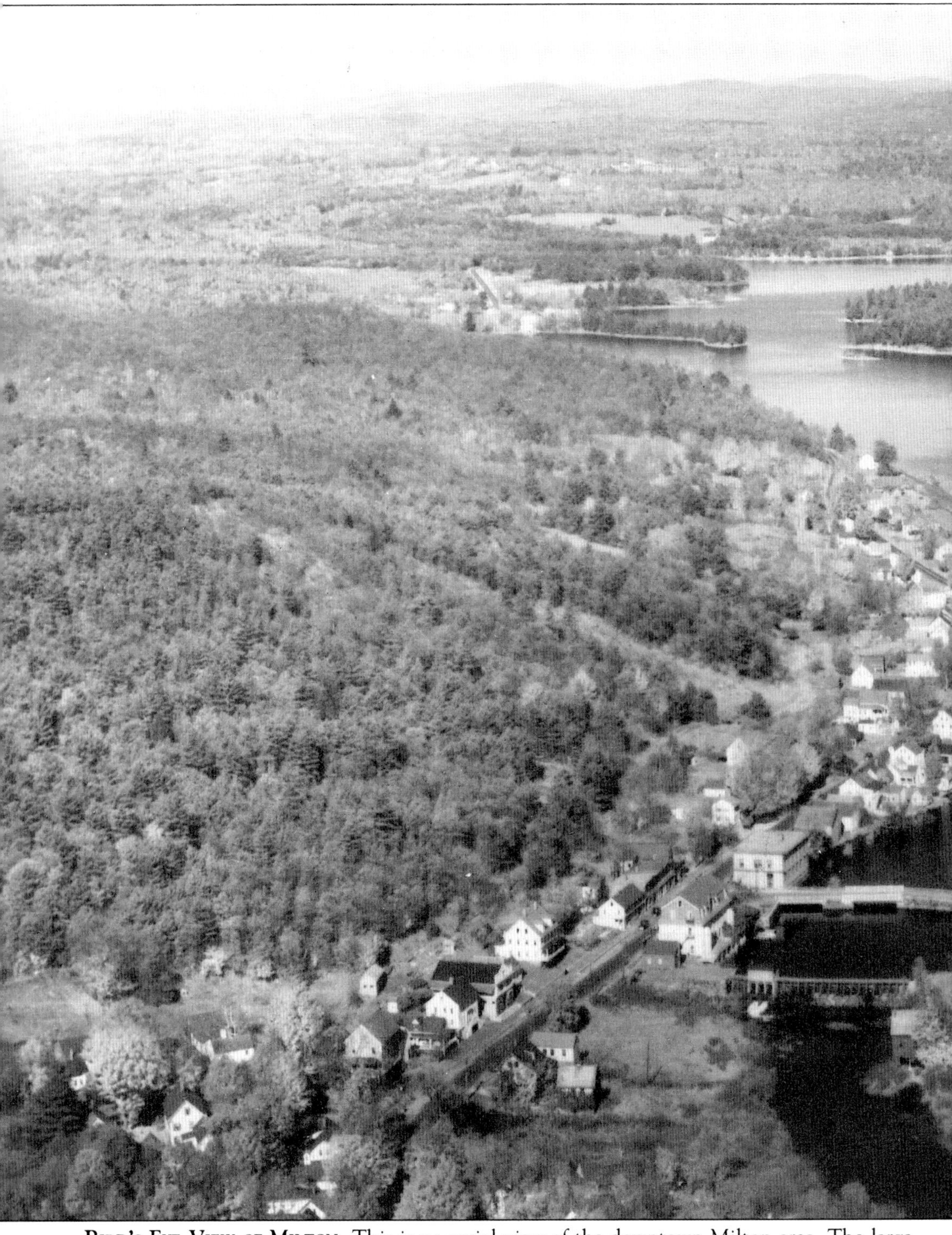

BIRD'S-EYE VIEW OF MILTON. This is an aerial view of the downtown Milton area. The large body of water in the center of the picture is Lower (or Depot) Pond, and the small island is also visible. The railroad tracks run across the Salmon Falls River, from Maine to Milton.

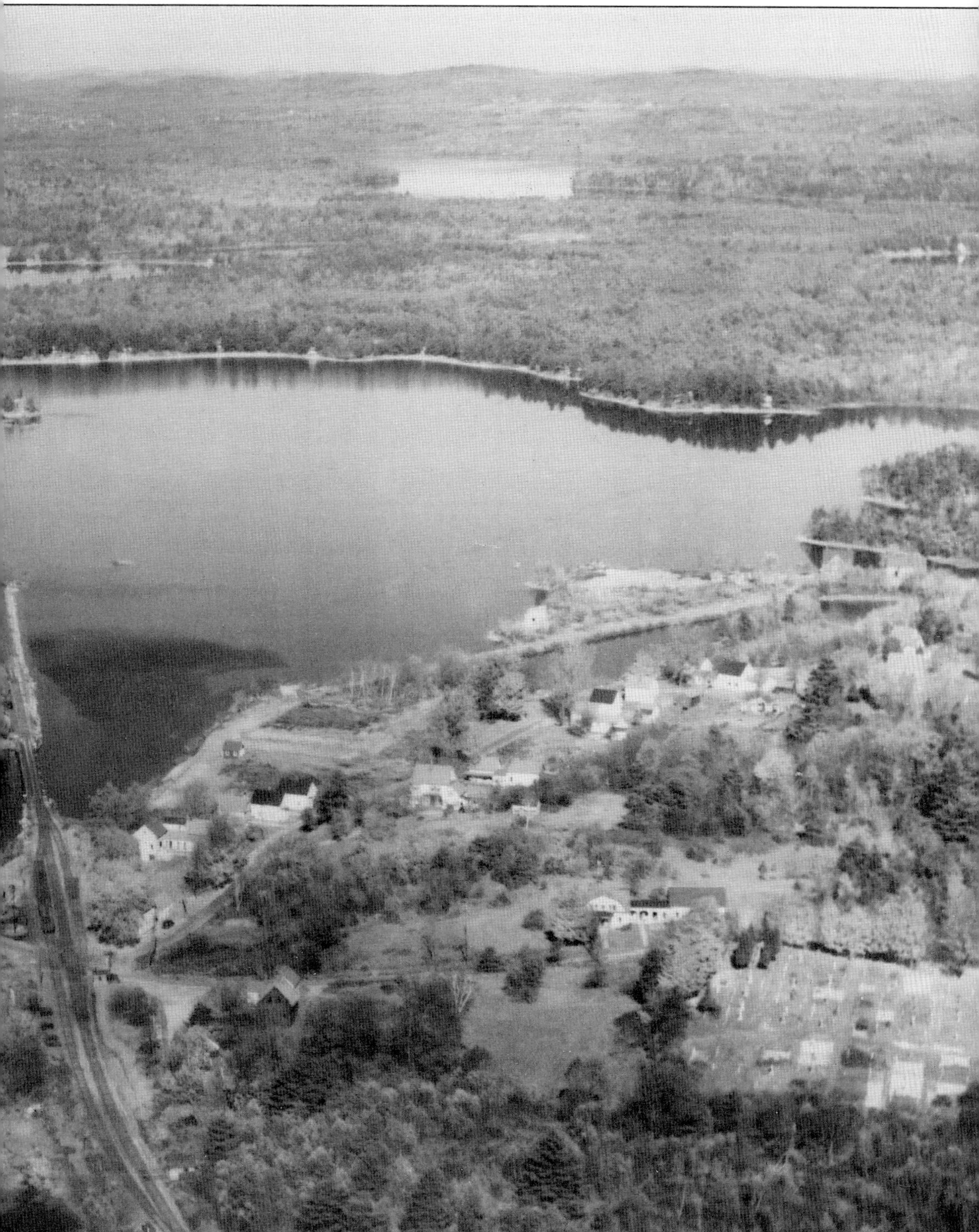

The bridge that connects Milton and Maine is just above the dam. A Maine cemetery is on the right.

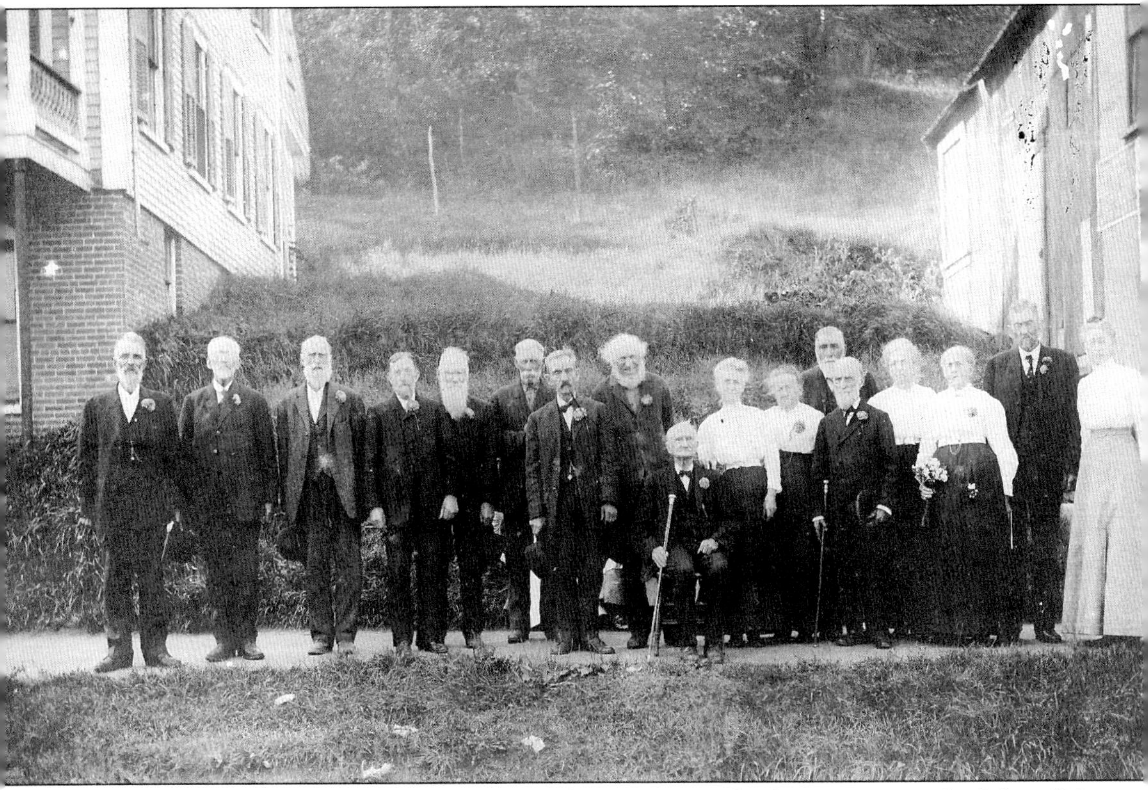

OLD-TIMERS CLUB. This photograph was taken in 1911. The first person on the left is G.I. Jordon, and the eight, ninth, and tenth people, respectively, are as follows: Leander Clements, Eli Foss, and Abby Foss (later Cole). The women are all in shirt waists and plain skirts, the style of the time. Many of the men have facial hair, even though it had gone out of style. It seems that the healthy air of Milton produced long-lived people.

Four

Milton's Ponds and the Flume

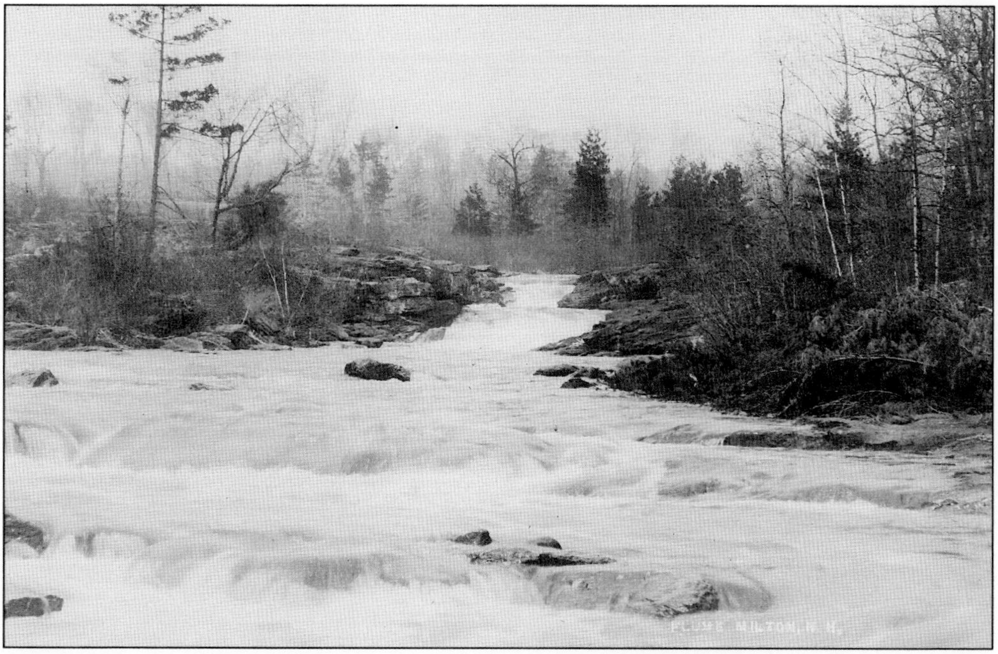

The Flume. New Hampshire has always been known as the Granite State. The Flume is a gorge with a stream running through it. It is part of the Salmon Falls River and is a natural wonder of Milton that many don't know about today. The evergreens that forest the area around the Flume also supply a natural beauty.

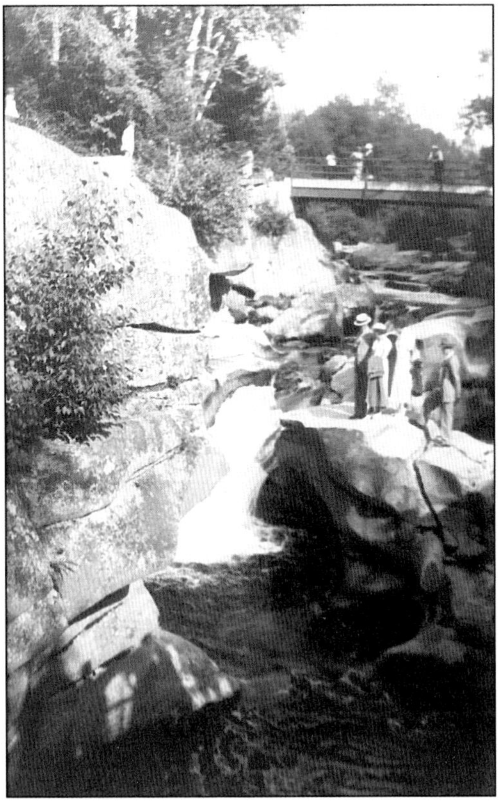

Sightseers at the Flume. This photograph was taken in the early 20th century. The Flume was a natural attraction that many flocked to during the summer months. It was a wonderful place to bring a picnic lunch and gaze at the beautiful water while sitting under the birch trees. In the back, people are seen strolling across the bridge. There are also two young, unsupervised children on the bear rock on the left. In the foreground, the Flume opened up, enough to probably entice younger people to swim.

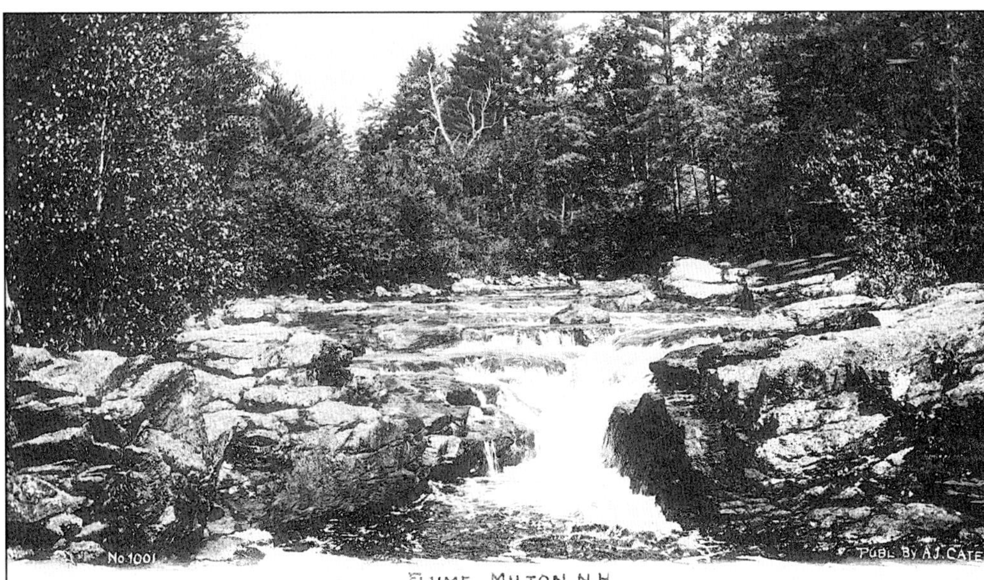

The End of the Flume. This picture was probably taken in the summer, since the trees have leaves on them. Here the granite Flume opens up, and the Salmon Falls River is able to travel faster, hence the white water.

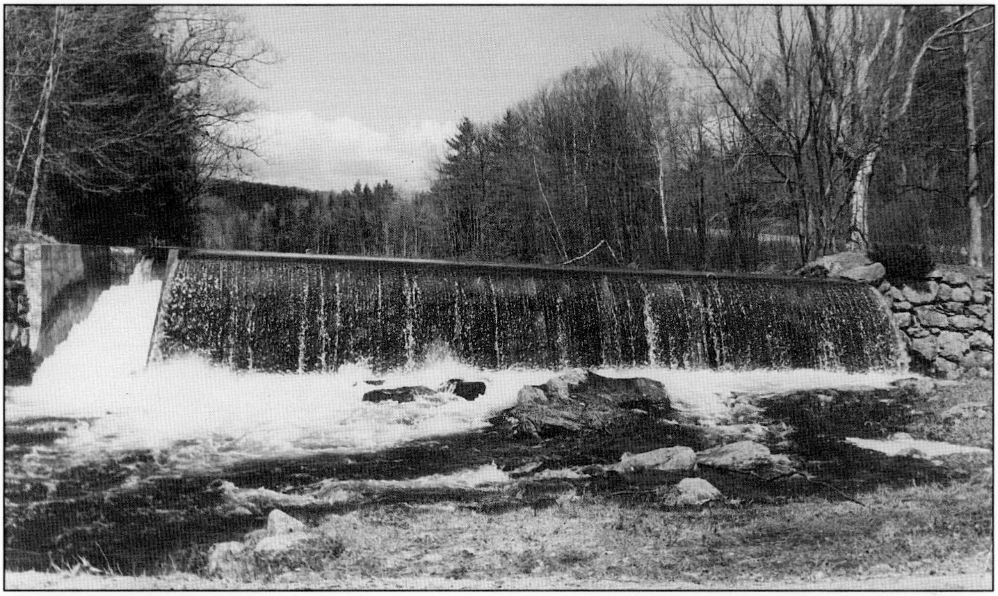

The Rowe Dam. This dam is located beside Hopper Road in Milton Mills. The dam was named for a family that lived in the area over a century ago. It is used to control the water level from Great East Lake and several small ponds as they feed into the Northeast pond in Milton, combining with the Branch River to form the Salmon Falls River.

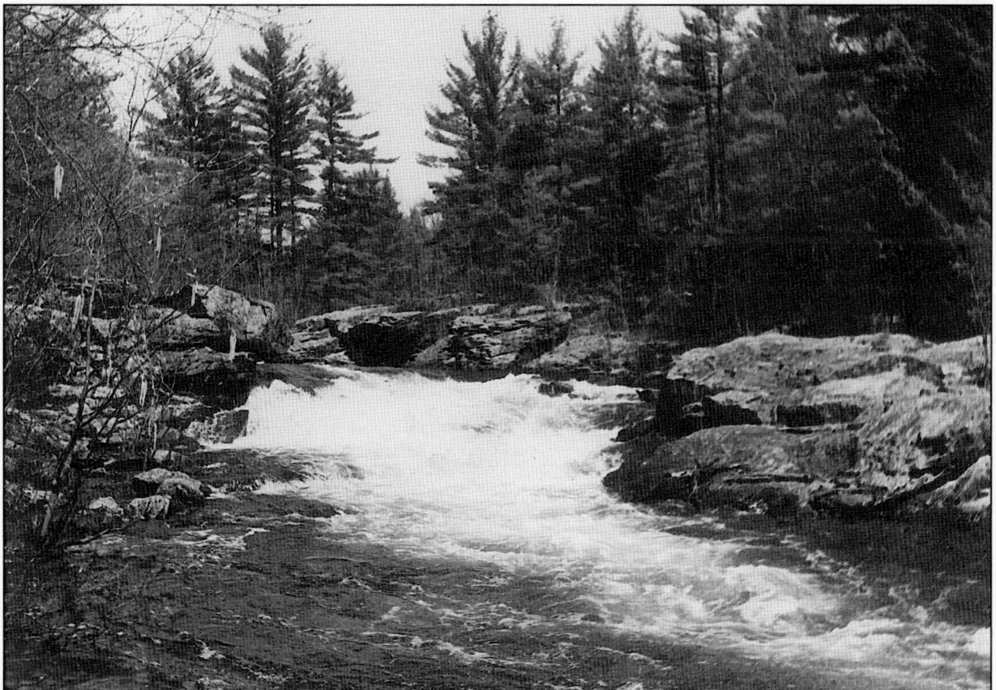

Rapid Water below the Flume. From the dam on the Salmon Falls River that controls the water level for use by Spaulding Fibre Company, the river becomes very rapid white water as it spills over a continuous ledge until it reaches the dam located opposite Spaulding Fibre Mill.

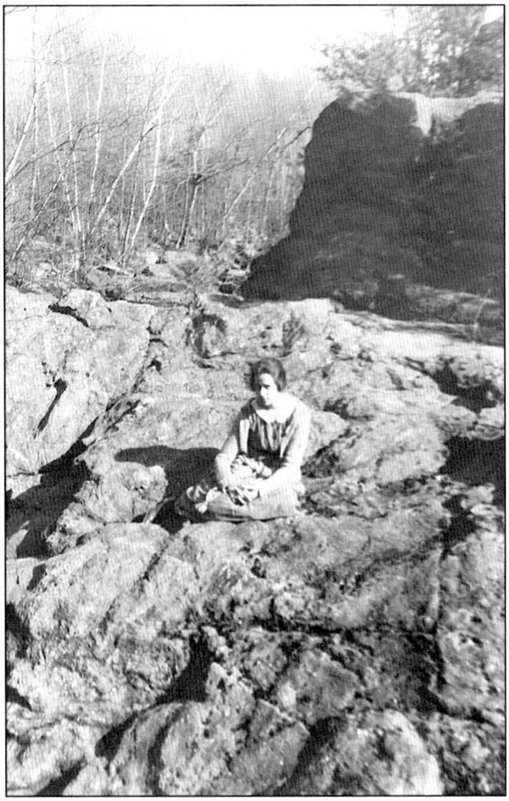

Remnants of the Ice Age. Hundreds of thousands of years ago, during the great Ice Age, glaciers moved over Earth's surface. The soil was rubbed away until only bare rock was left behind. The ice scraped along, leaving marks on the rock.

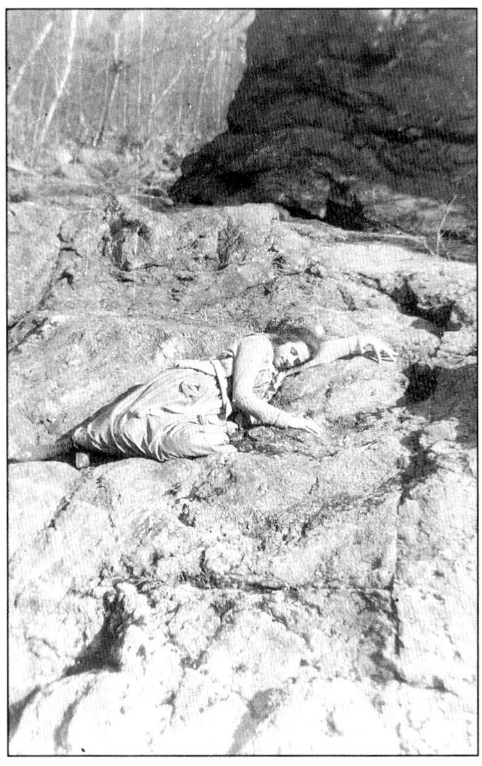

Art. This picture was marked only with the date "1920." During this part of our century, the flappers wanted to break free from the art of their elders. To do this they tried many different art forms, one being photography. This picture demonstrates this perfectly, as the woman is sprawled out on the rocks.

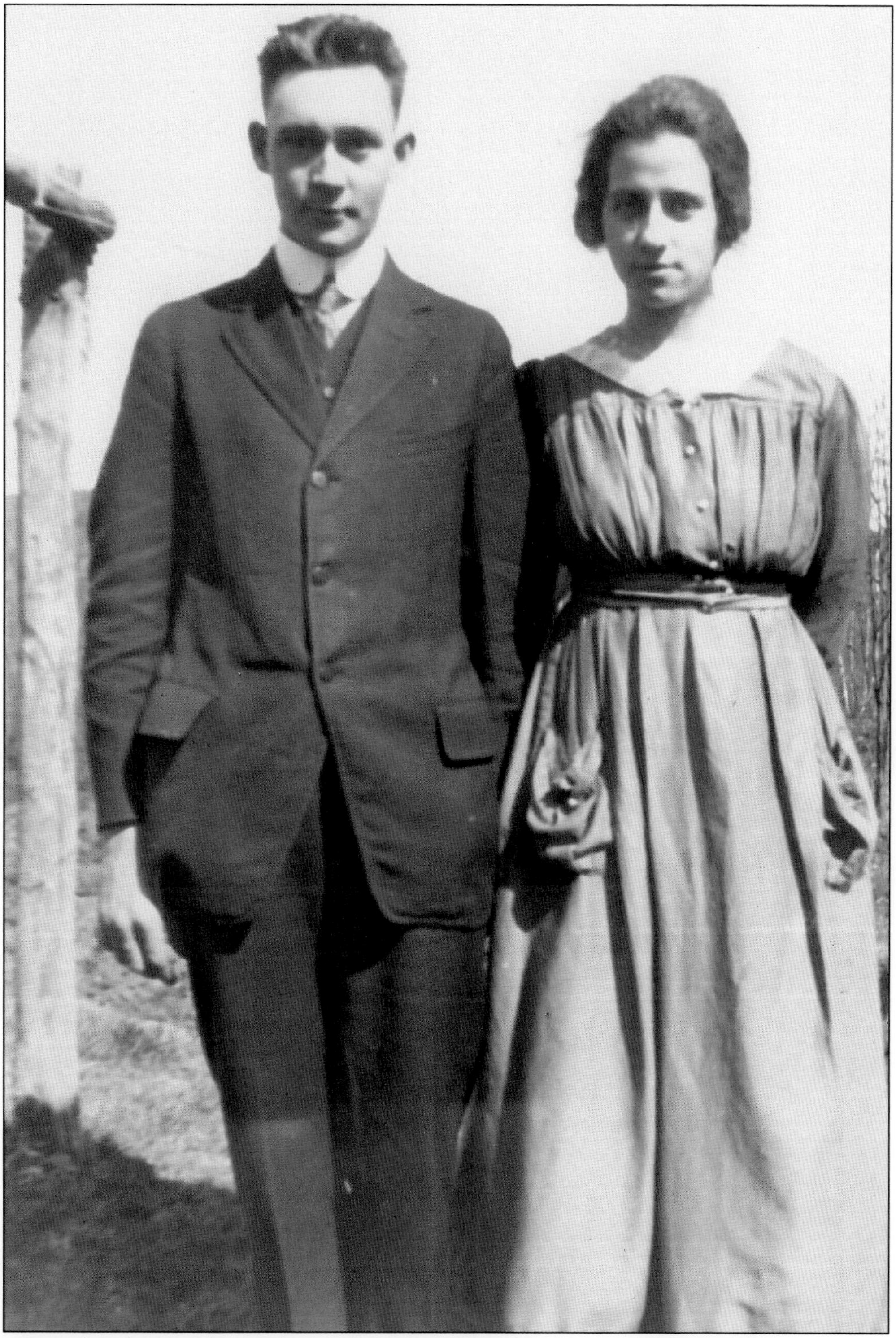

1920. This photograph was also marked with only the date of 1920. It is the same woman who is in the two previous pictures; her young escort may have been the photographer.

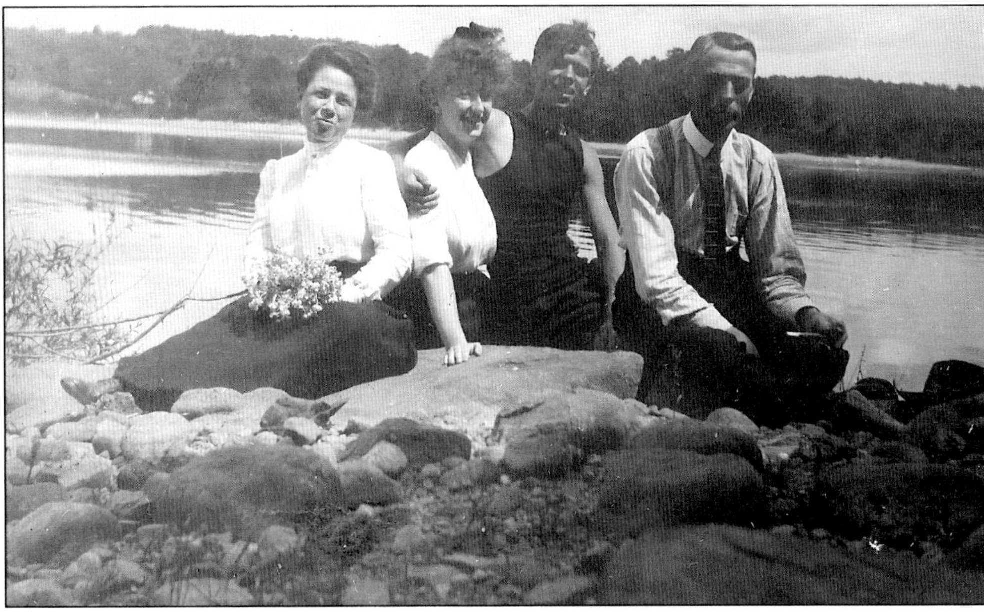

Visiting the Pond. These young adults are pictured near where Ray's Marina is now located. This photograph at Depot Pond is from a scrapbook kept by a Plummer girl. The scrapbook was dated 1902, so the picture was probably taken around that time. One of the men appears to be wearing a bathing suit.

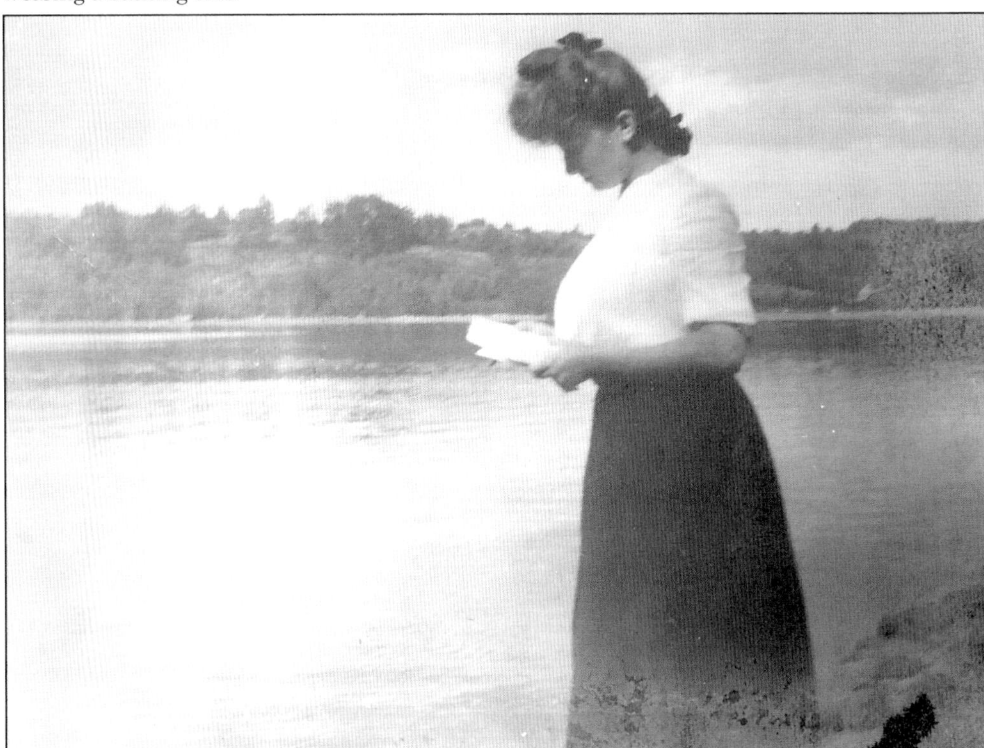

Posing in front of the Pond. This girl has been identified as a Plummer, but her first name is unknown. This picture is also from the above mentioned scrapbook.

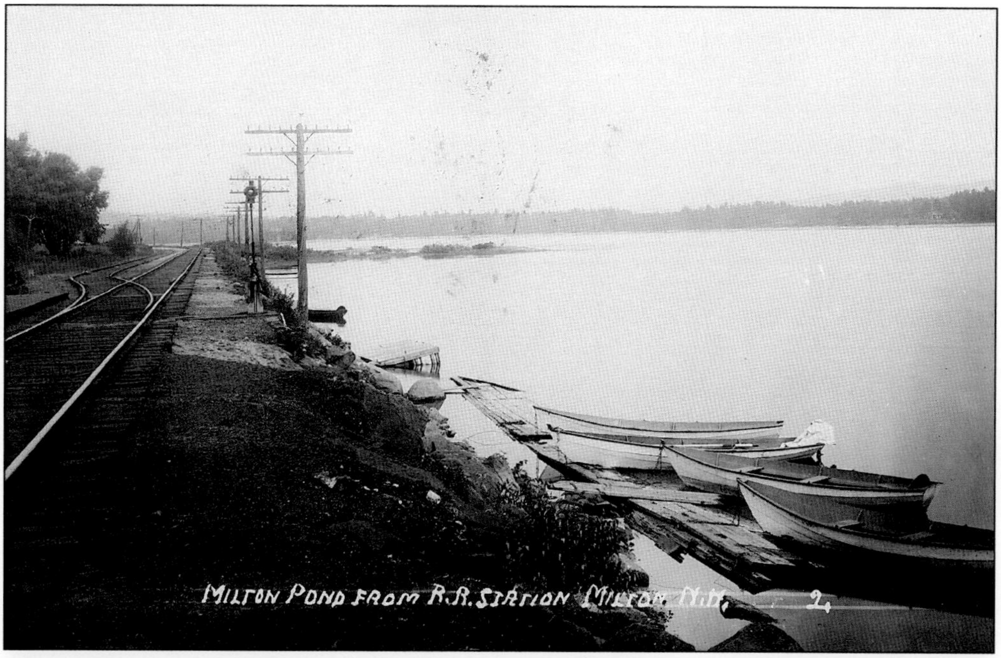

MILTON POND FROM THE RAILROAD STATION. This postcard shows the view facing north, toward Milton Mills. The railroad station was near the center of town, and the tracks follow the pond for quite a ways, making a beautiful scenic route for those traveling north. Notice the row of canoes along the shore.

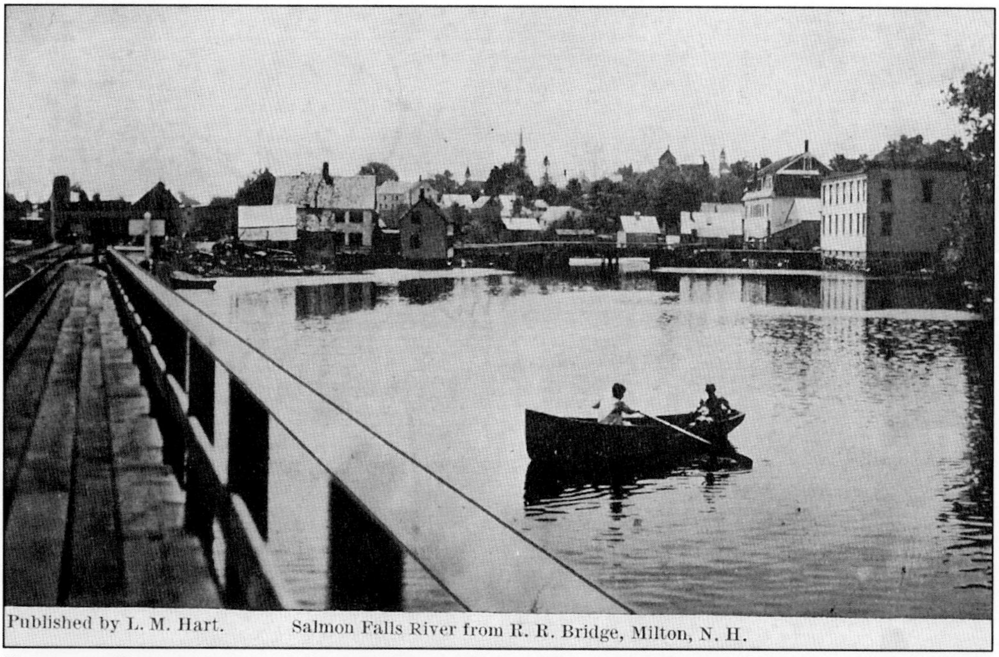

RAILROAD BRIDGE OVER THE SALMON FALLS RIVER. The railroad bridge, which connects Maine and New Hampshire, is located in the downtown area of Milton, near the dam. Today the train runs from the Ossipee Aggregate Corporation (which is north of Milton), carrying crushed rock to Boston on a regular basis.

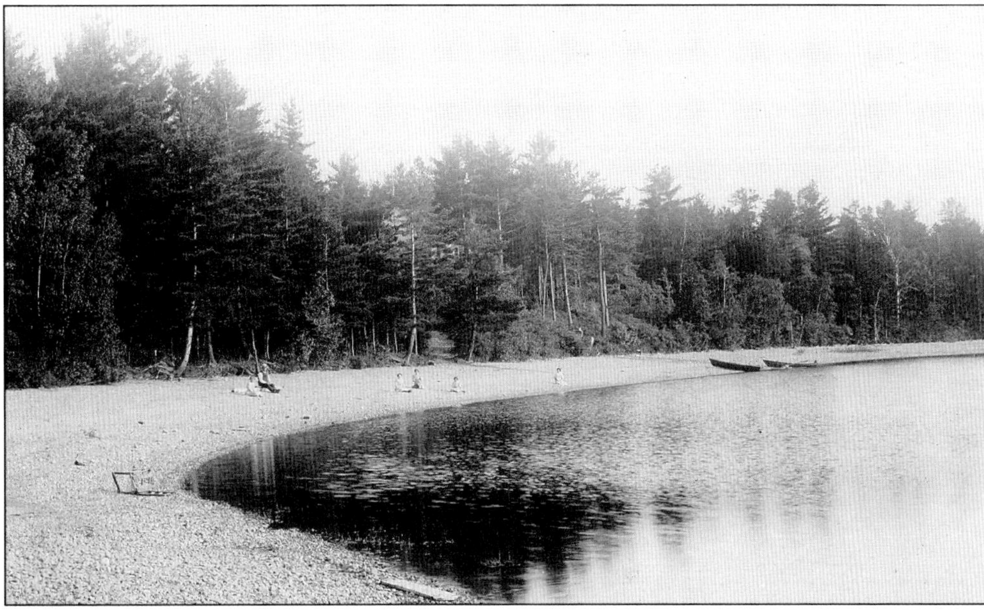

Meeting House Pond. This is a shore scene at the Meeting House Pond. The Meeting House Pond is one of the three ponds in Milton, the other two being Northeast Pond and Depot Pond. This stretch of pebbly beach is on the way to Pine Land Park, on Town House Road. From the look of the clothing the people are wearing in the distance, the picture was taken in the early 20th century.

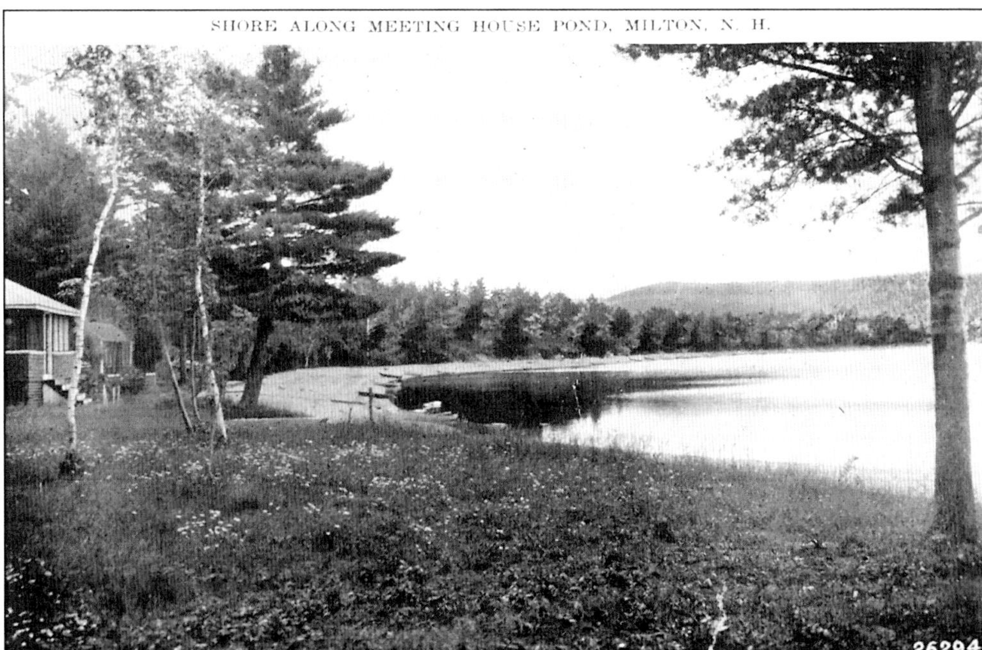

The Shore. This is also part of the shoreline of Meeting House Pond. This section of the beach, however, is a more sandy place, where children and adults alike can frolic in the sun and build sand castles.

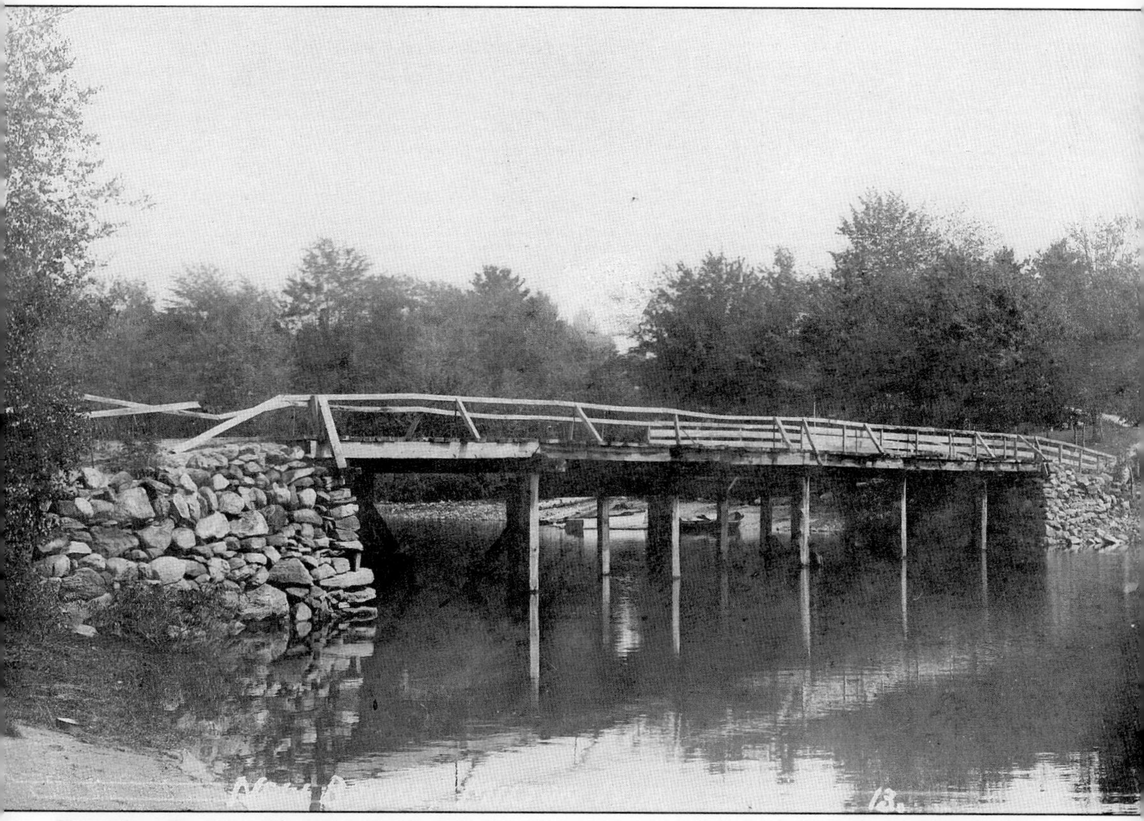

THE NEW BRIDGE. The New Bridge allows travel between Milton and Lebanon, Maine. The bridge is located near where the Mi-Ti-Jo Campground is located today. This rustic bridge is virtually unchanged. The rough stone still lines the shore, and the wood pilings are still in the water.

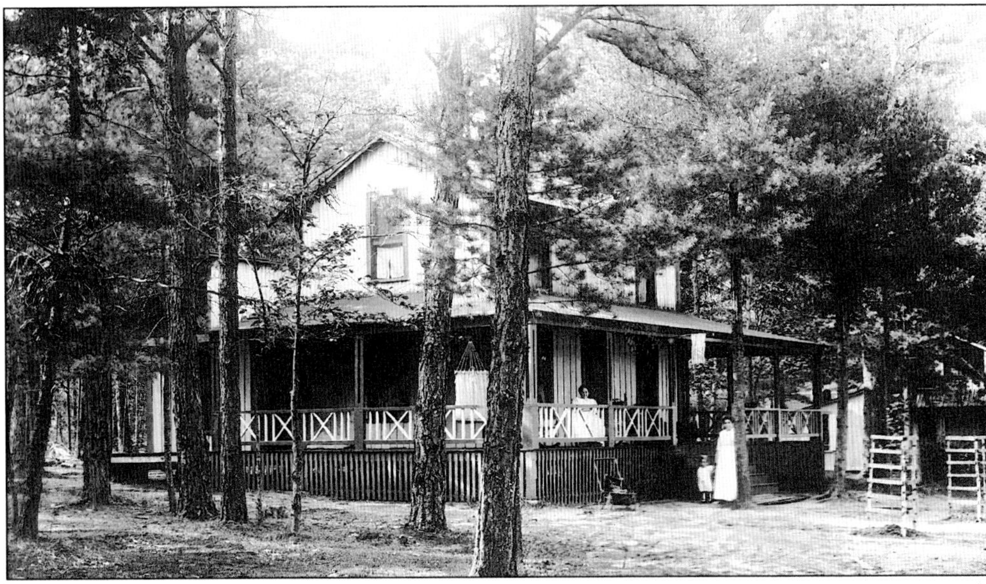

Camp Roberts. During the summer months, Milton was a very popular tourist site. People would come from as far as Boston to spend their summer at the ponds in Milton. This camp was probably built and owned by the Roberts family, who spent their summer months here. The large, wide porch must have provided a cool pleasant spot for the family and friends to relax. This camp is located near the New Bridge. Notice the woman sitting in a chair on the porch and the woman and child standing in front of it.

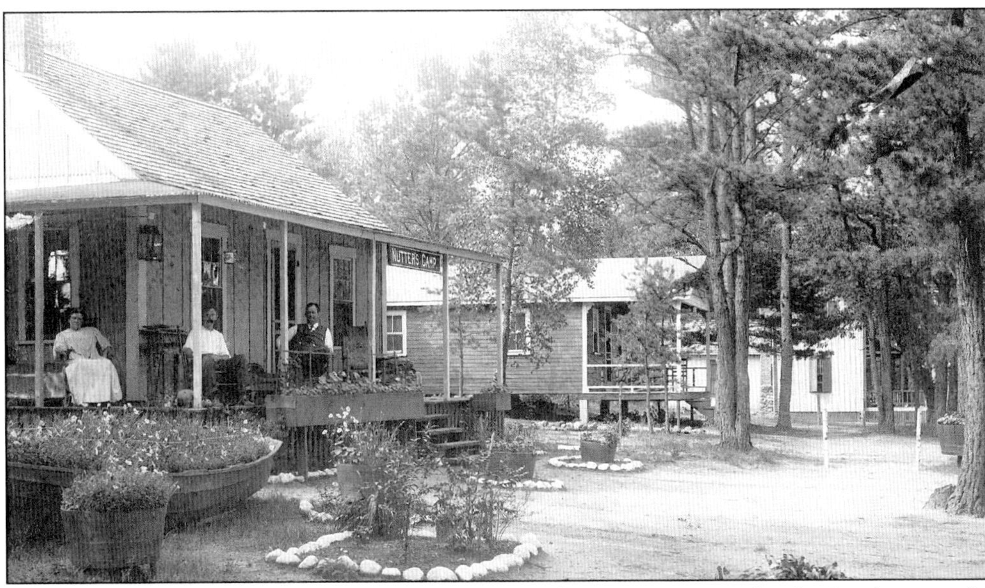

Summer Vacation. At the turn of the century, it became very popular for families to take summer vacations. These camps are much smaller and simpler than the above camp. This type of campground was the predecessor of the auto court or motel. This was also the time when the resorts at beaches like Hampton began to flourish. People were attracted to this spot because of the close location of the pond. People may have also preferred the fresh water of the pond to the salt water of the ocean.

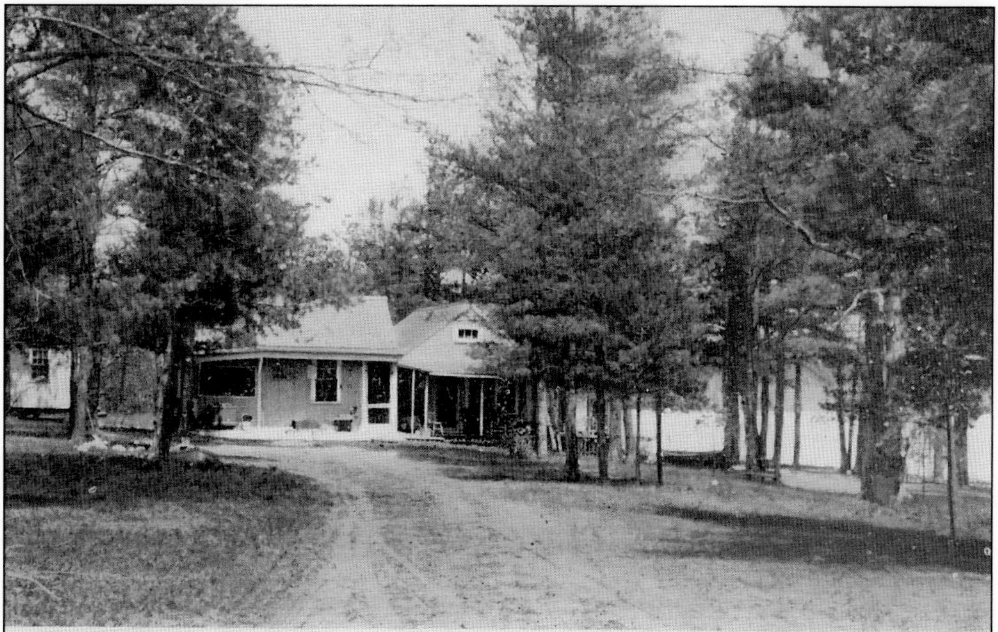
Published by J. H. Willey The Camps, Milton, N. H.

CAMPS. Because of the growing popularity of summer vacations, people would look for a place to go that would have many different activities to offer. At the camps alone, many water activities, such as swimming, canoeing, and fishing were available. Also, because of the availability of the train, tourists could easily go up to the White Mountains, which was only 60 miles away, to spend the day.

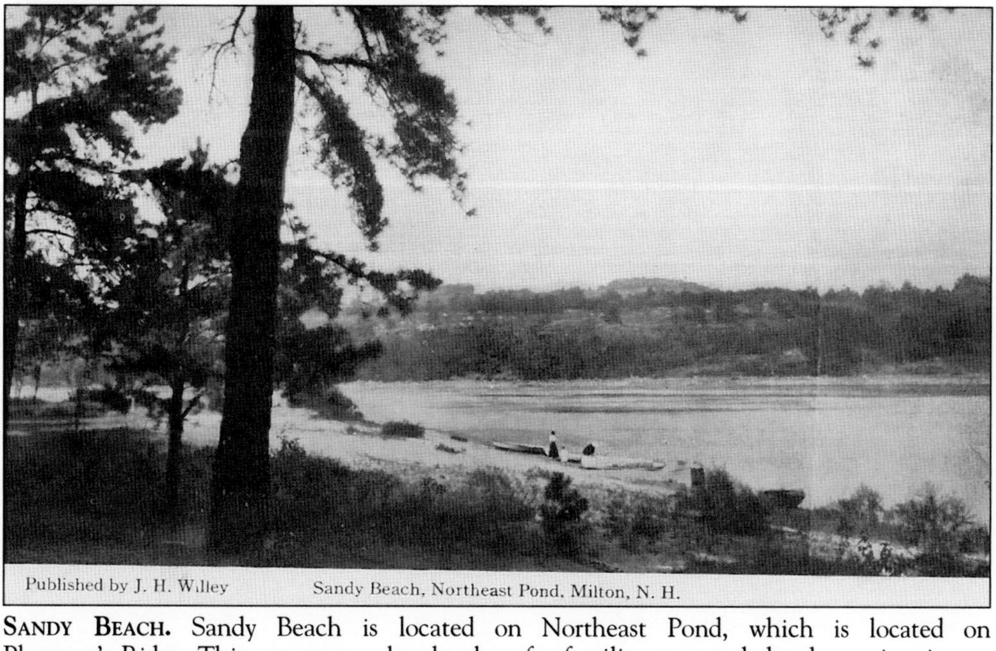
Published by J. H. Willey Sandy Beach, Northeast Pond, Milton, N. H.

SANDY BEACH. Sandy Beach is located on Northeast Pond, which is located on Plummer's Ridge. This was once a lovely place for families to spend the day, swimming or building sandcastles.

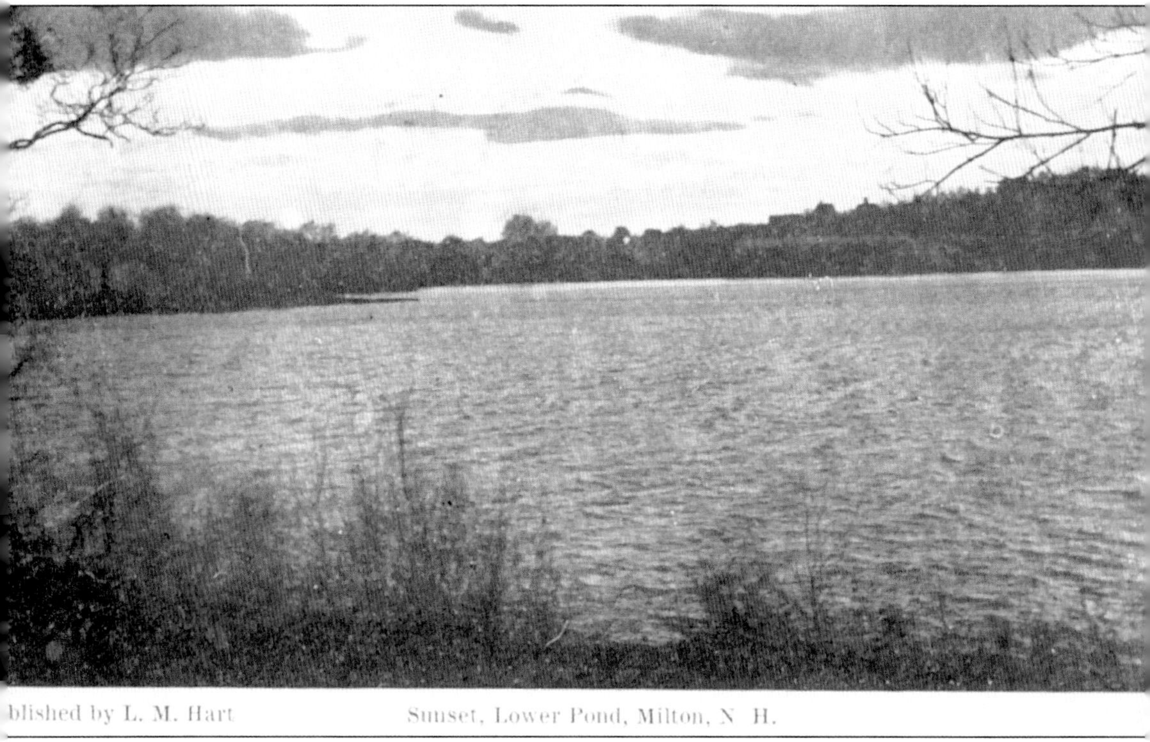

LOWER POND. This photograph was taken at sunset, at Lower Pond in Milton. In the distance, the silhouettes of rooftops are visible.

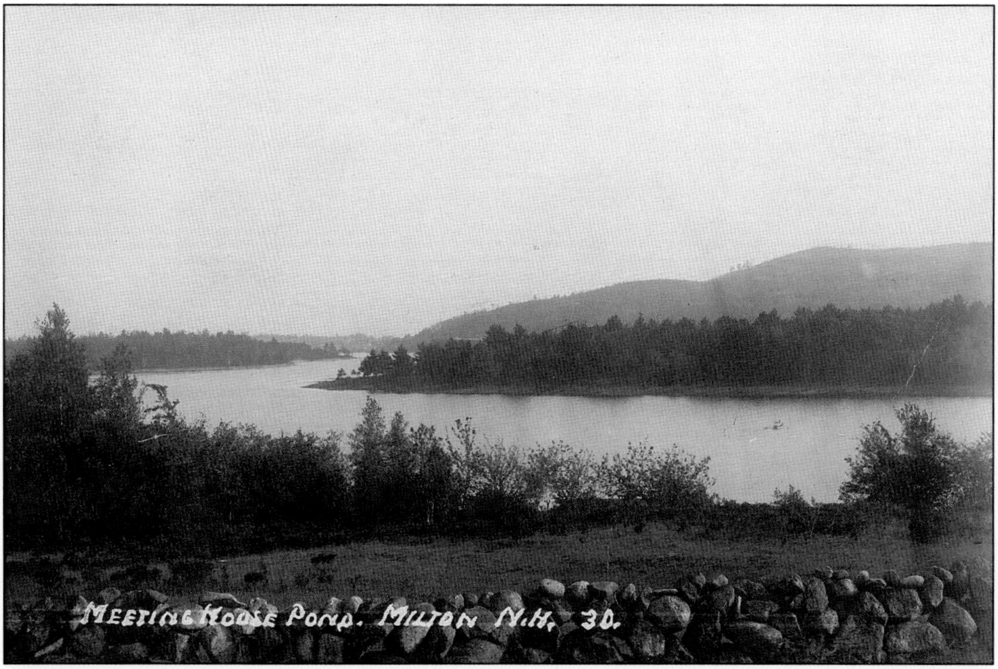

Meeting House Pond. This photograph was taken *c.* 1930. It clearly shows the beauty the pond offered the town. Not only did the pond supply jobs in the winter with the ice industry, it also supplied endless means of fun in the summer.

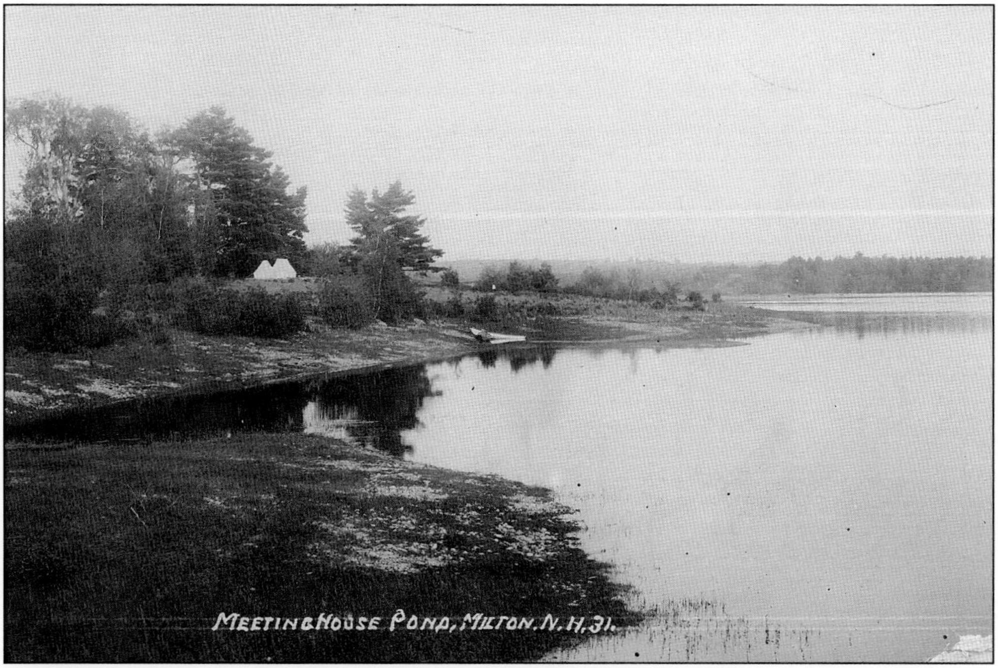

Shoreline of Meeting House Pond. Though this part of the shore did not supply a sandy place for children to play, they never ran out of new and exciting ways to play around the pond.

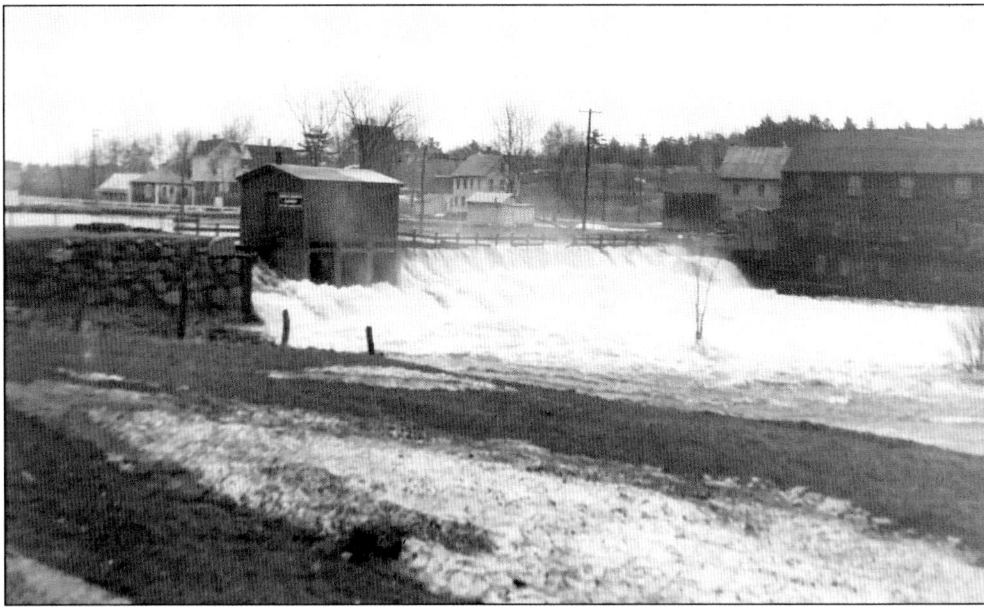

The Dam. The dam has been the center point of the town for many years. This is where the water level for the Salmon Falls River is controlled. The first dam in Milton was built by Samuel Palmer *c.* 1784. Sawmills and gristmills were built on either side. For a time, Milton was known as Palmer Mills.

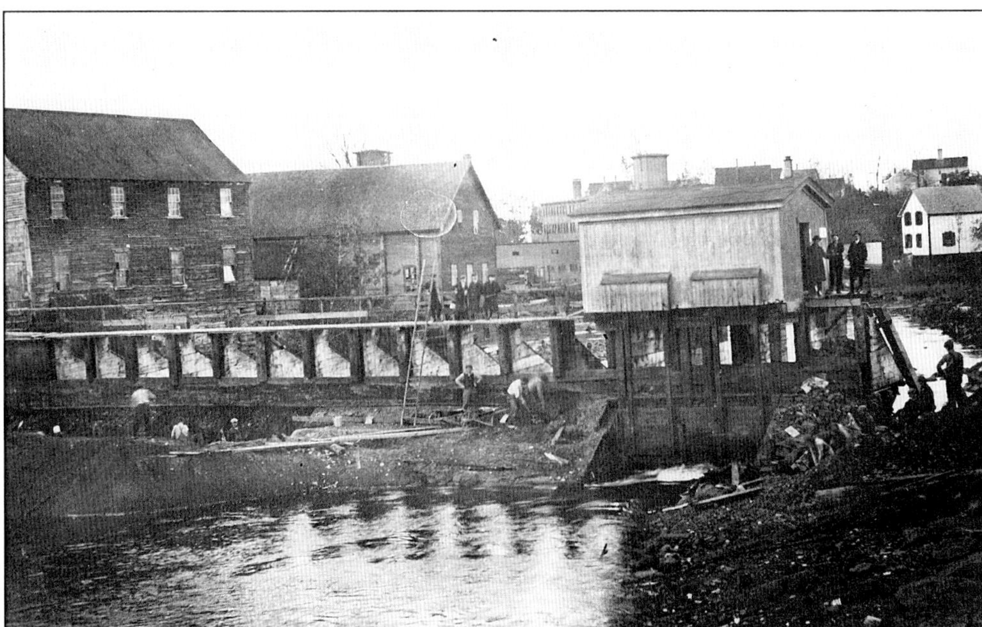

Working on the Dam. The annual spring freshets (the high water) has always been a regular concern for the people who maintain the dam. When the snow melts off, the water would bring debris down river and it would pile up at the dam. These men are cleaning up the debris.

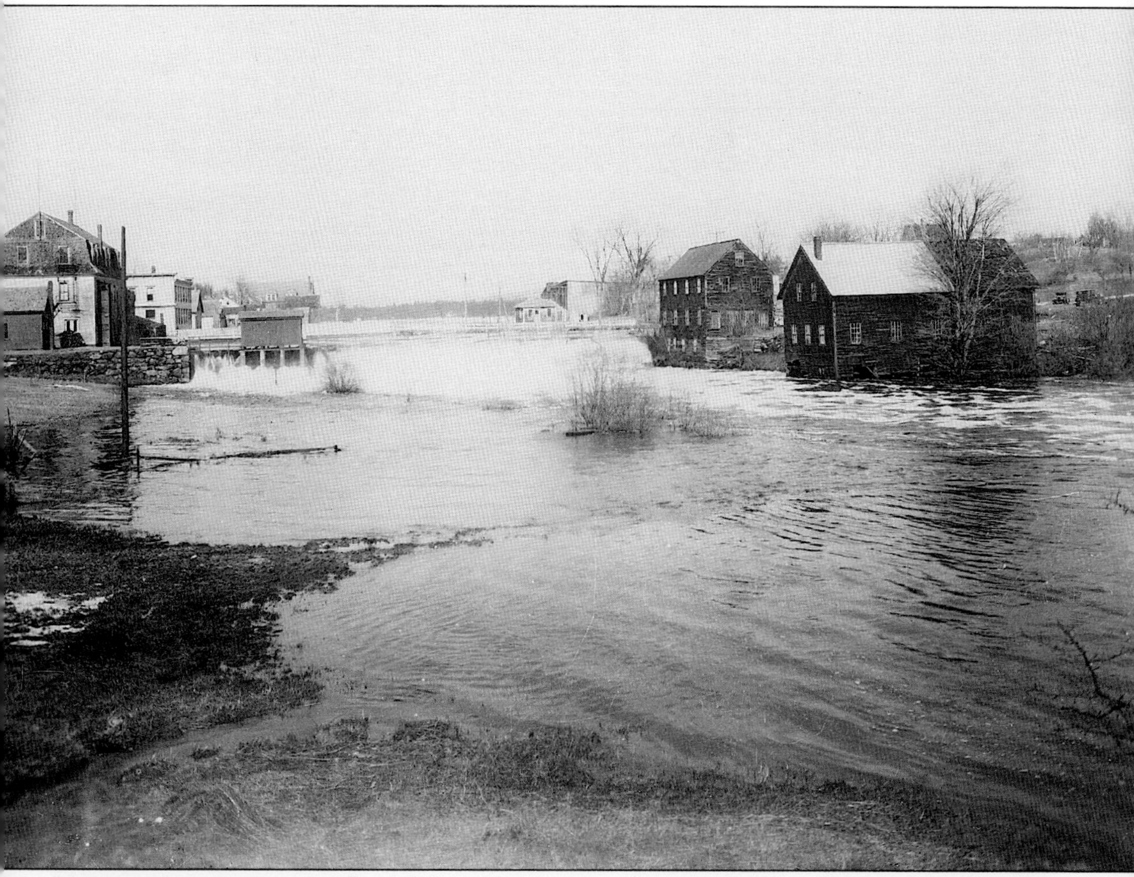

THE FLOOD OF 1932. The flood did not destroy any of the buildings on Main Street, but the water did cause damage to the Maine side of the river. Note how high the water is in comparison to the building foundations along the river.

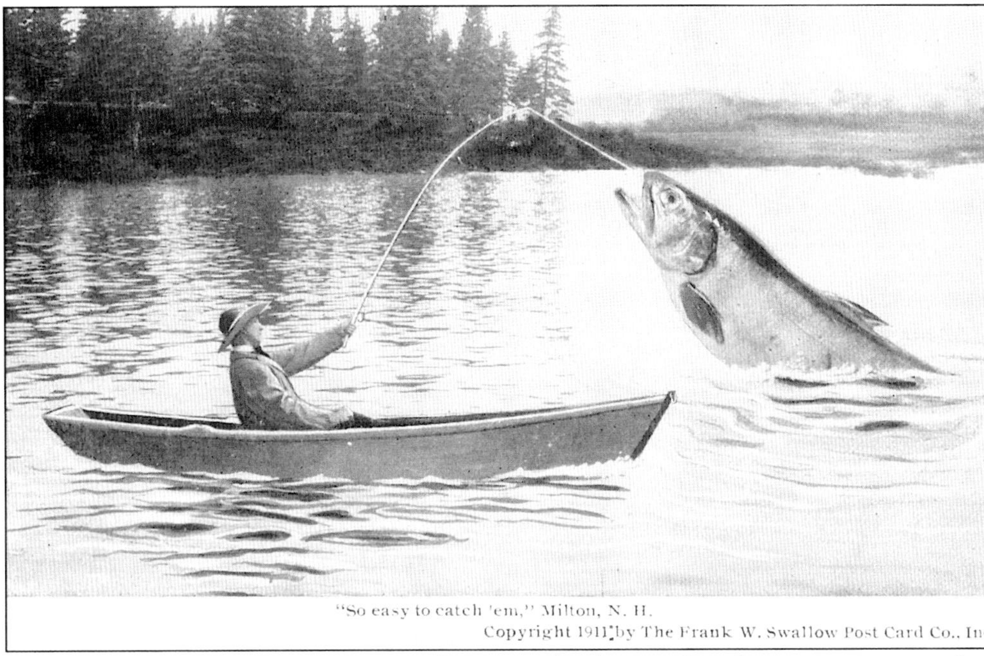

"So Easy to Catch 'Em." This postcard is copyrighted 1911, though it was not postmarked until 1913. This outlandish postcard was an easy way for Milton to advertise to tourists who enjoyed fishing.

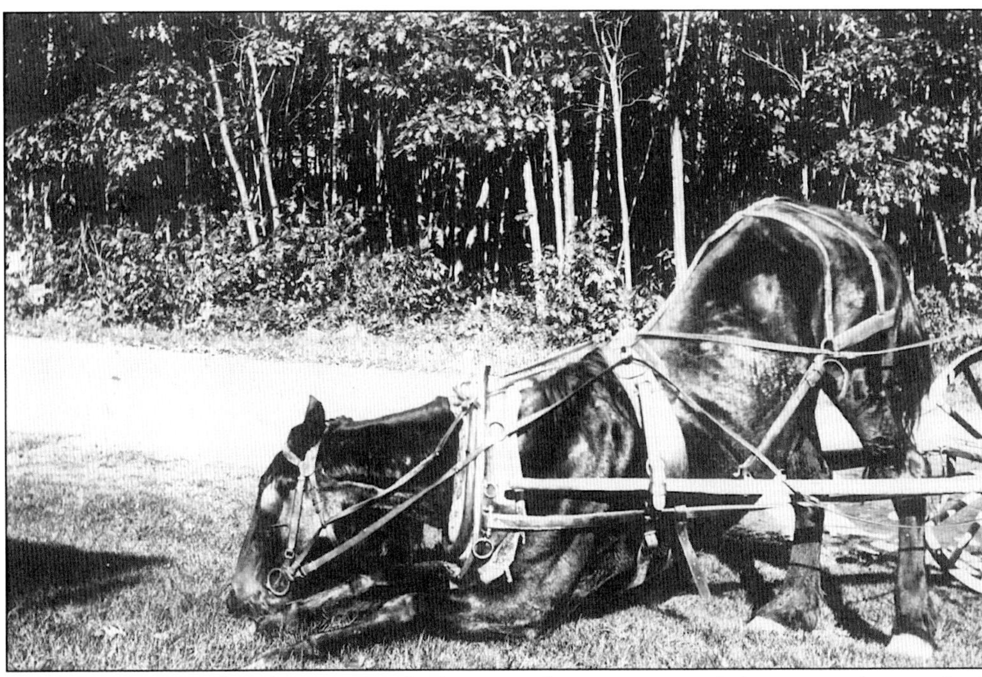

A Milton Horse. This photograph, which was made into a postcard, does not make one think that the horses in Milton have a very promising future. But it is a fun postcard; on the back, the sender asked: "Have you seen this horse?" Postcards were a very easy way to advertise. They were for sale at all the general stores as well as at the train station.

Five

INDUSTRIES

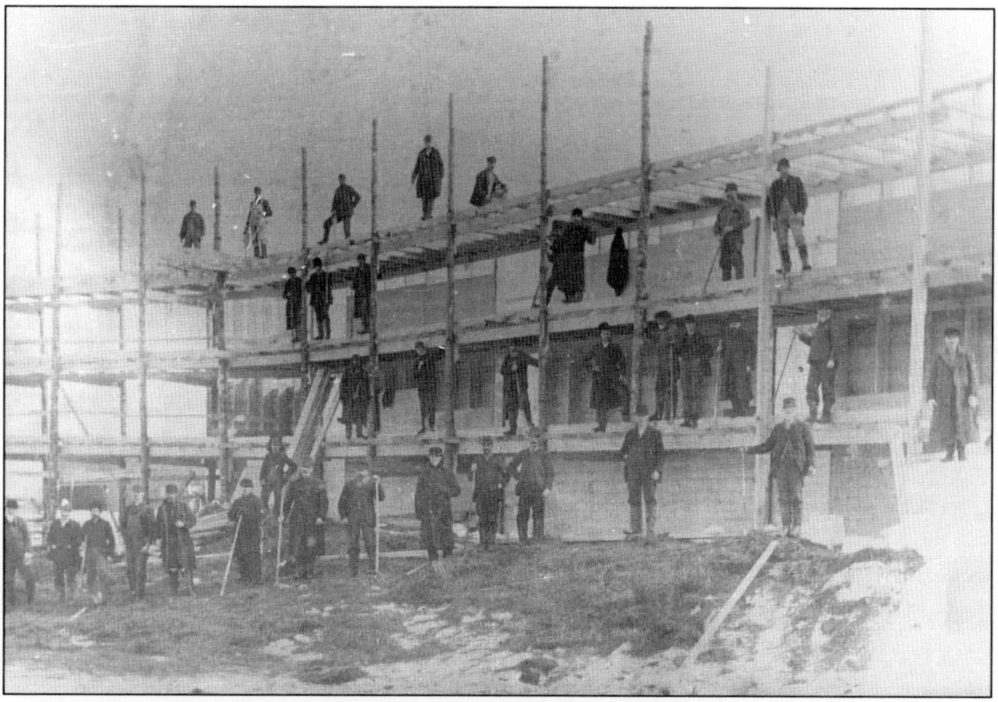

ICE LOADING CREW. This ice loading crew took time out of their busy schedule to have this photo taken, *c.* 1915. Every day (during the winter of course!) over 100 railroad cars carried ice to Boston. The man in the center of the photo seems to be dressed in a suit; he is probably the boss or owner. The other men are warmly dressed, and most have ice hooks in their hands.

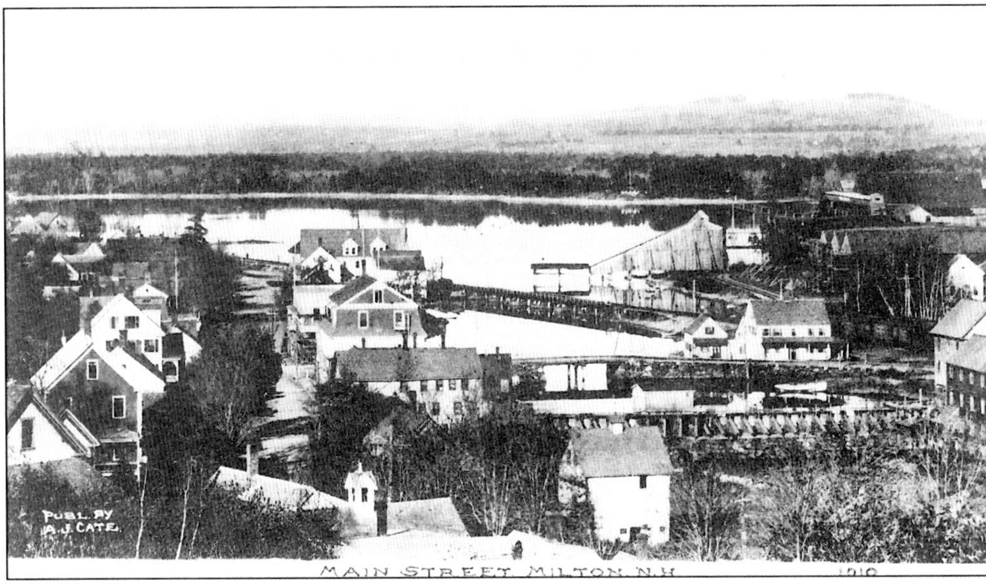

BIRD'S-EYE VIEW OF MILTON. This photograph was taken from Main Street. Even though the ice industry was not the center of town, it was never far from the thoughts of the townspeople. In the distance, the ice slope is visible. This postcard was published by A.J. Cate, possibly Aaron Juddy Cate, of South Milton.

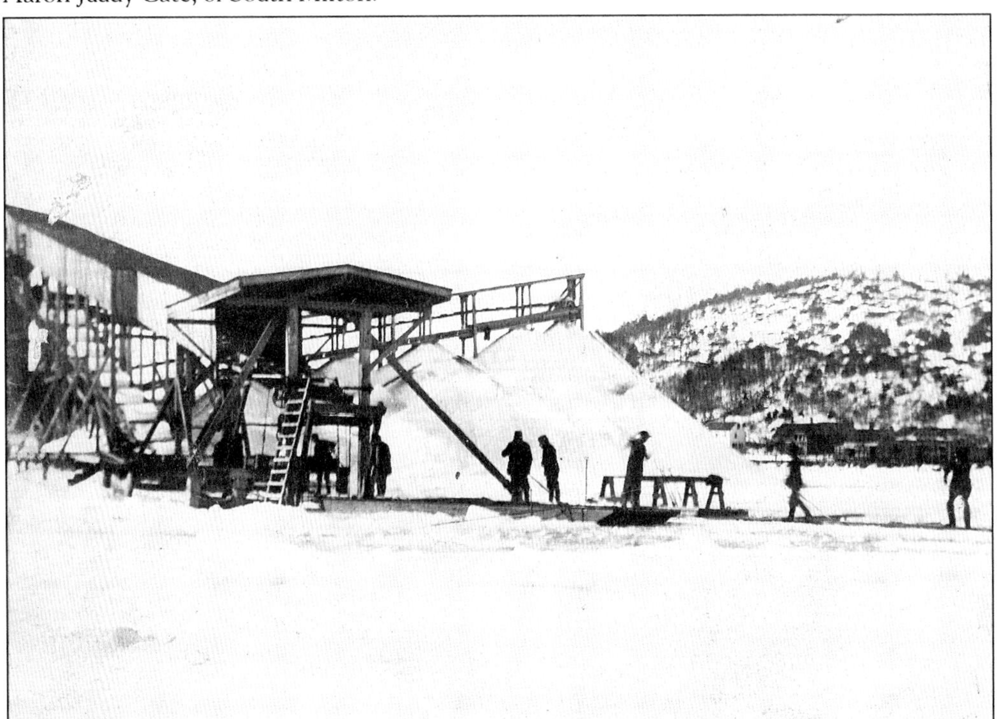

LOWER POND IN THE WINTER. The ice industry was very important to other industries in Milton. People came from all over to cut ice in Milton and stayed in the many different hotels, and had to buy supplies from the general store. Here, there are at least nine men hard at work, probably trying to meet their daily quota.

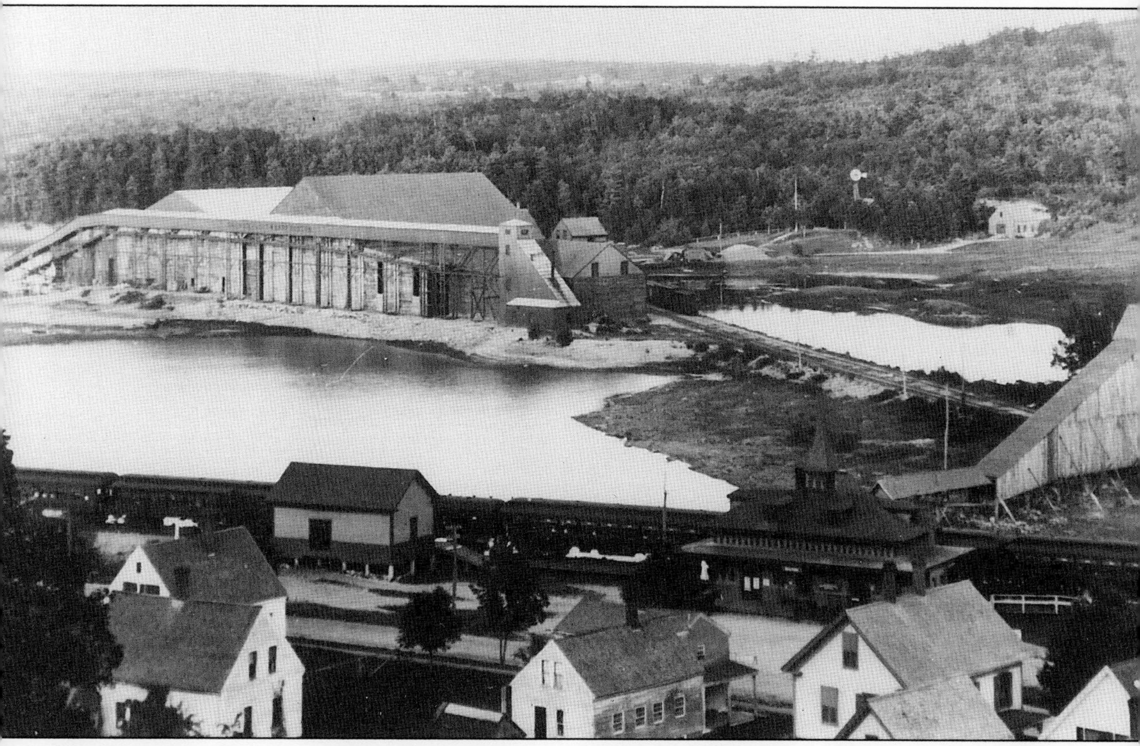

THE FIRST ICE SHIPPED, 1858. The first ice was shipped by railroad to Boston in 1858. The Milton Town Beach was opened in 1938, but before that, it was the home of the Downing Ice Company. This photograph seems to have been taken before the ice was actually frozen, but it shows how ice cutting must have been thought of all year.

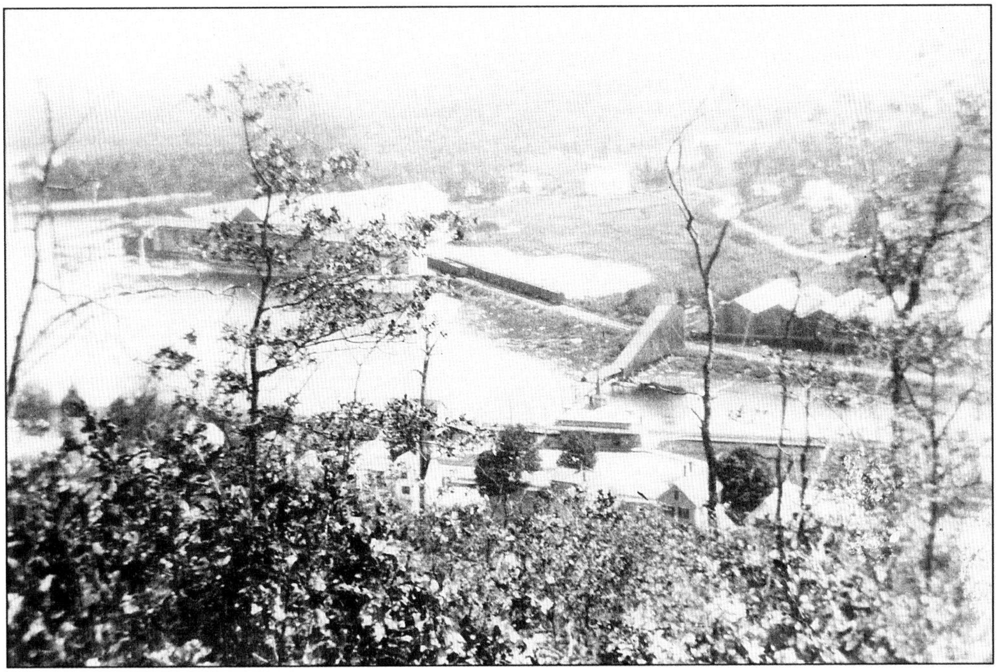

The Refrigerator! With the advent of the refrigerator, the ice industry slowly began to fade. This affected not only the ice cutters and their families; it also affected the businesses around the town, such as the hotels and the stores, which soon began to shut down.

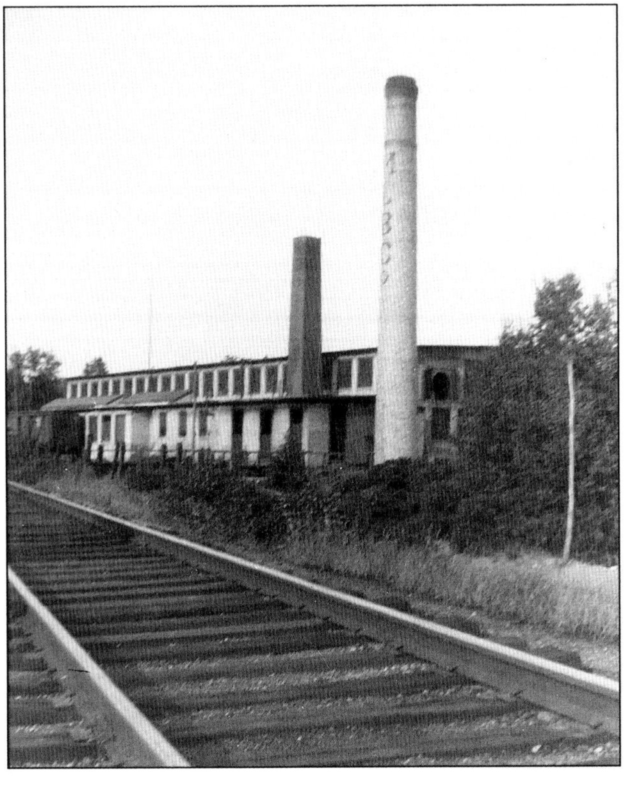

Milton Leather Board. The smoke stack reads: "MLBCo.," which stands for the Milton Leather Board Company. This factory is located behind Charles Street. It was recorded that in 1912, the Leatherboard was still in operation.

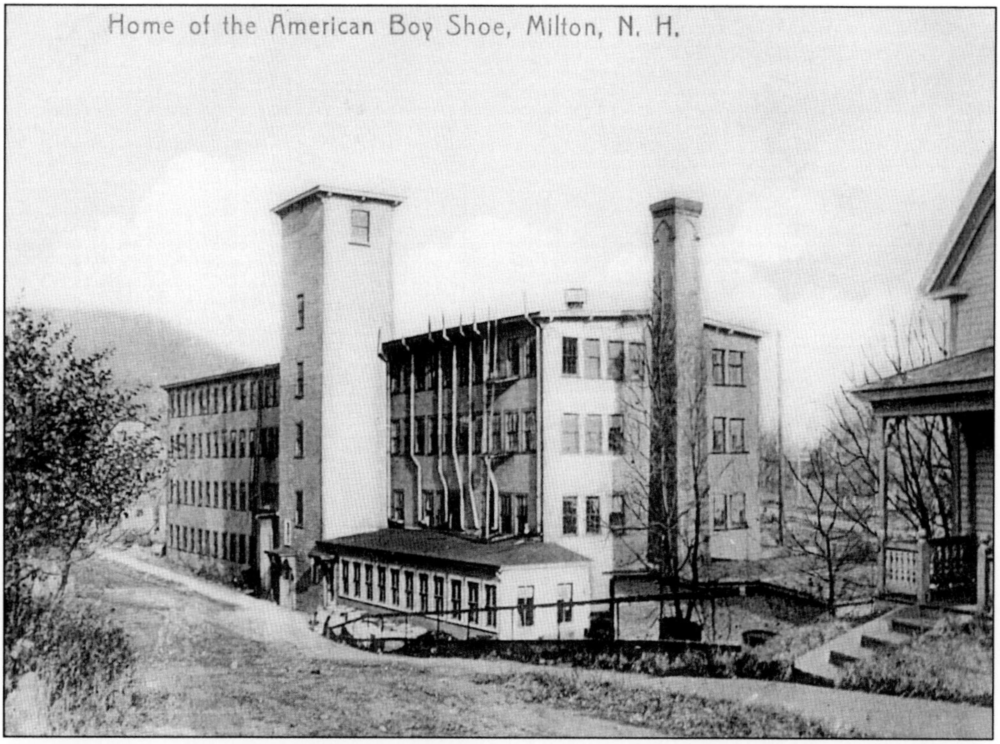

The American Boy Shoe Factory. This shoe factory is located in Milton, on the Salmon Falls River. This postcard was distributed from J.H. Willey's general store on Main Street. This factory was also known as the Kennebunk Mills. It was converted into a shoe factory *c.* 1936 and operated for about ten years before going out of business. It burned in 1959.

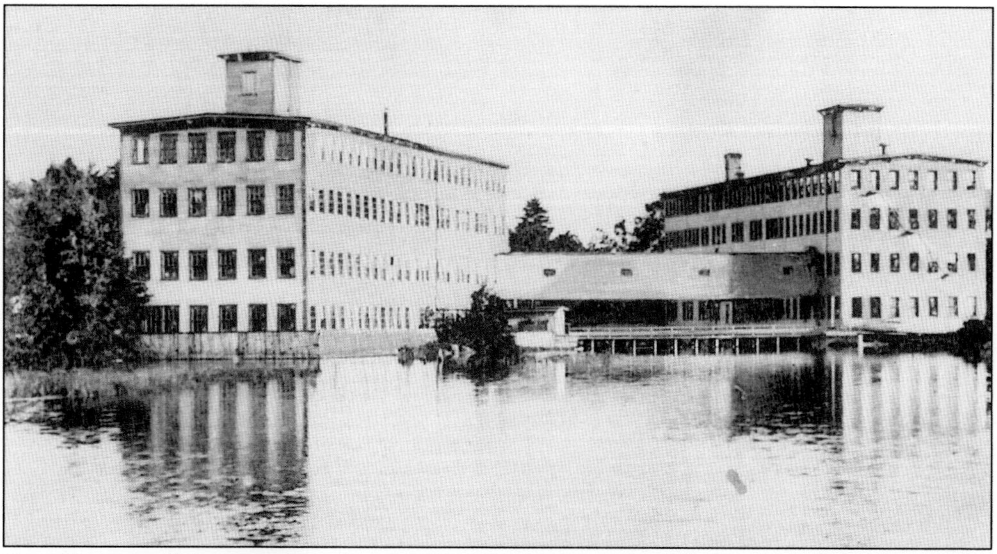

Shoe Factory. This is another photograph of the American Boy Shoe Factory. This photograph, which shows the entire factory, was taken from the Maine side of the Salmon Falls River. After it closed down in 1936, it was converted to a place to raise chickens.

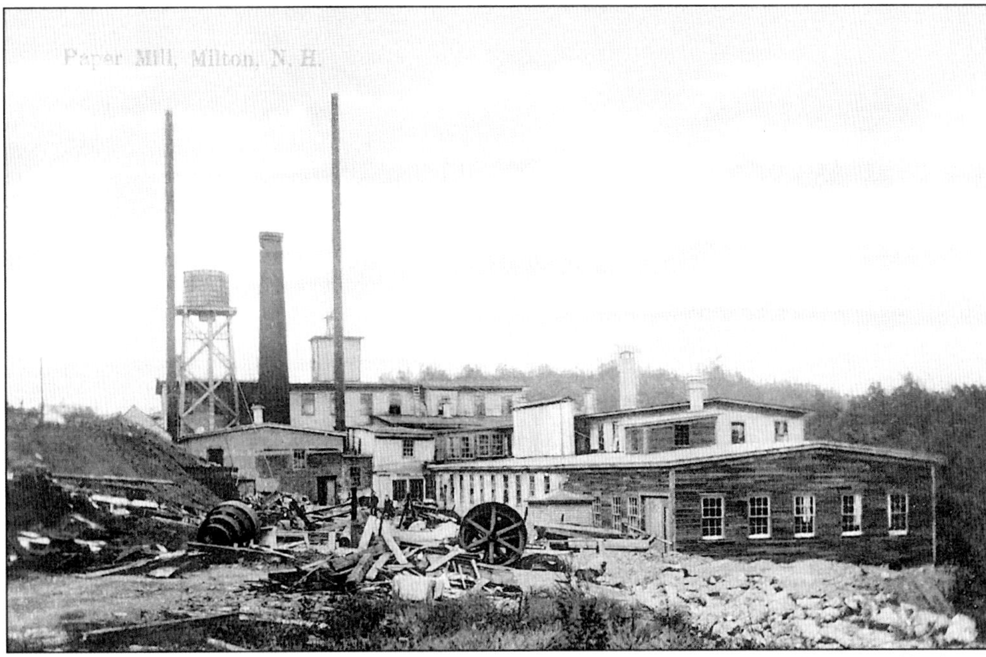

Paper Mill. This paper mill does not show the cleaner side of the factory, but actually shows the waste on the back side of the factory. This mill was located just south of Milton Village, and it supplied the paper for Milton's Centennial programs.

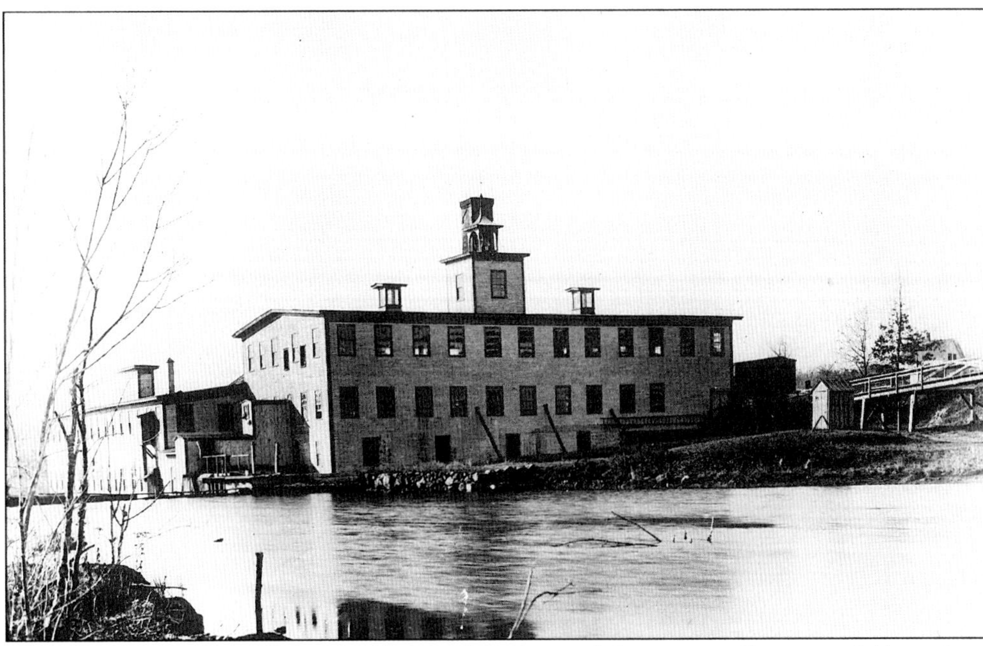

Front View of the Paper Mill. This is a front view of the paper mill as it would have been seen from across the Salmon Falls River. Notice the bell tower (or steam whistle) on the top of the building. It was probably used to summon people back from their lunch break.

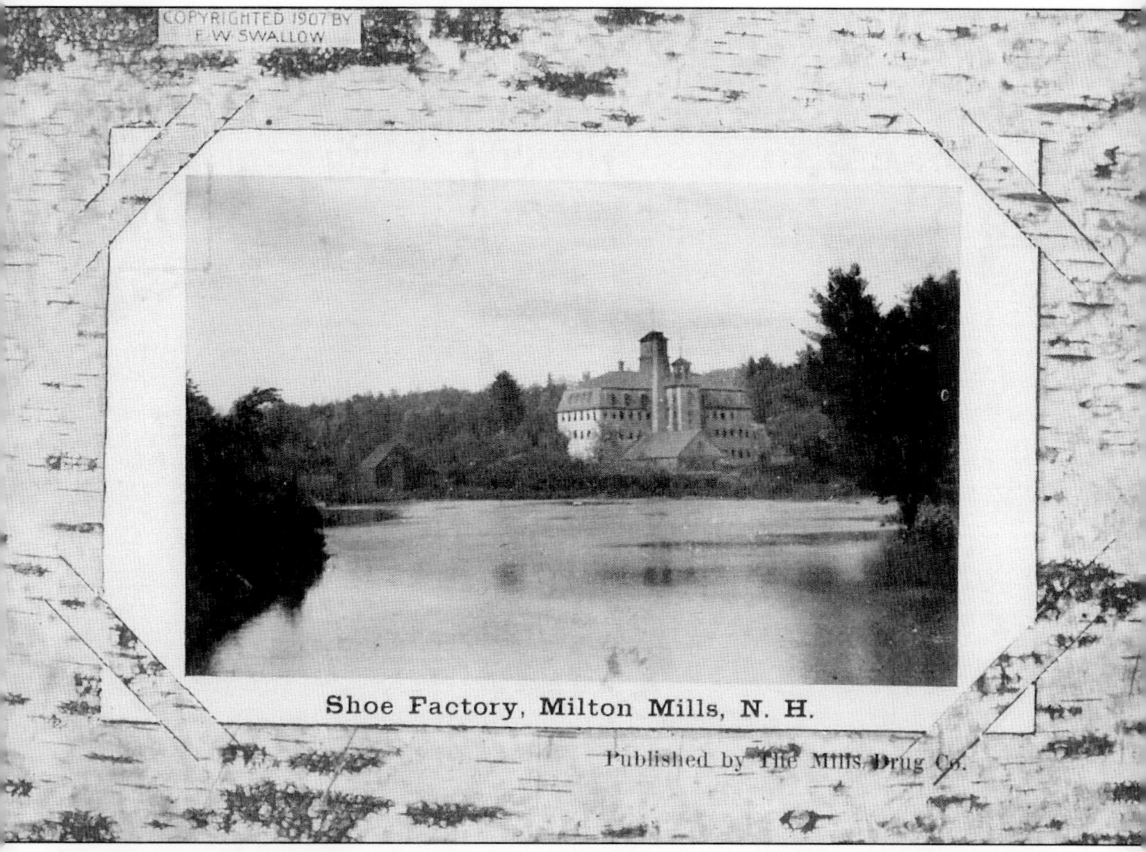

SHOE FACTORY, MILTON MILLS. This shoe factory lot was once owned by Edward Brierly, who had a felt mill here in 1860. His business was large, employing many people until it burned in 1873. He rebuilt the mill, and it later became the property of David H. Buffam, from Somersworth, New Hampshire. After his death, his son, Harry Buffam, sold it to Varney & Lane, who began to manufacture shoes. The next owners were from Haverhill, Massachusetts, and the business became the Gale Shoe Co. After several years of success, they leased the factory to Andrews & Co., who under the name of Boynton Shoe Co. were also very successful.

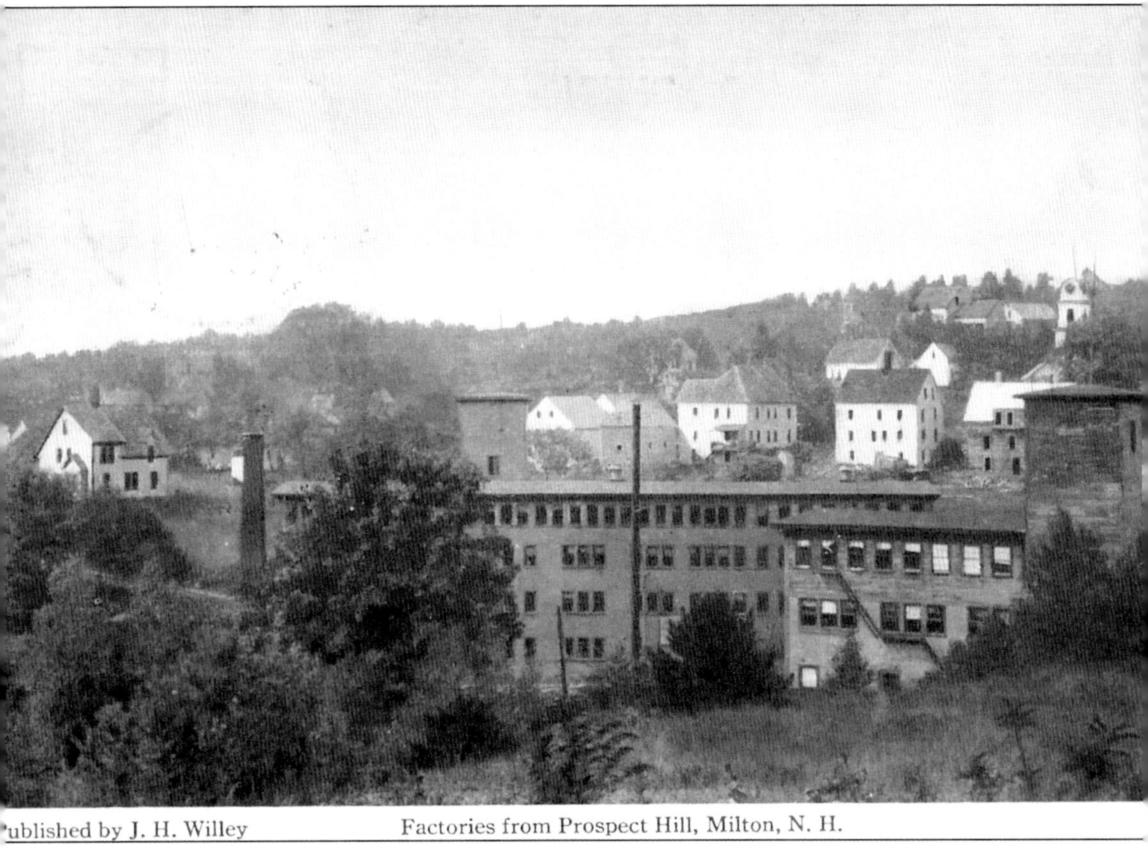

FACTORIES FROM PROSPECT HILL. This photograph was taken in 1910. In the upper right-hand corner, the steeple of the congregational church is visible. The steeple must have been a religiously inspiring sight, but also the clock on the tower must have been looked at often as the day came to a close.

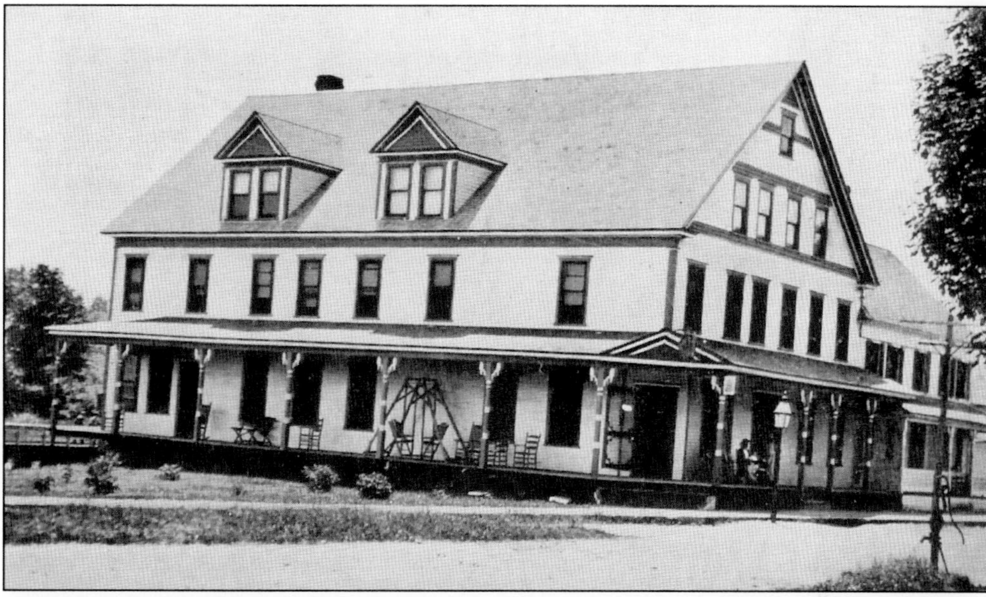

THE CHAMBERLAIN HOTEL. This hotel, along with the others, served as a place for the ice cutters and their families to live during the winter months while working in Milton. The hotel was built in the Greek Revival style, which was a very popular style in the United States during this time period. The Greek Civil War was just ending, and archaeological digs were starting all over Greece, making Americans more aware of the Greek architectural styles. This building was torn down in 1975.

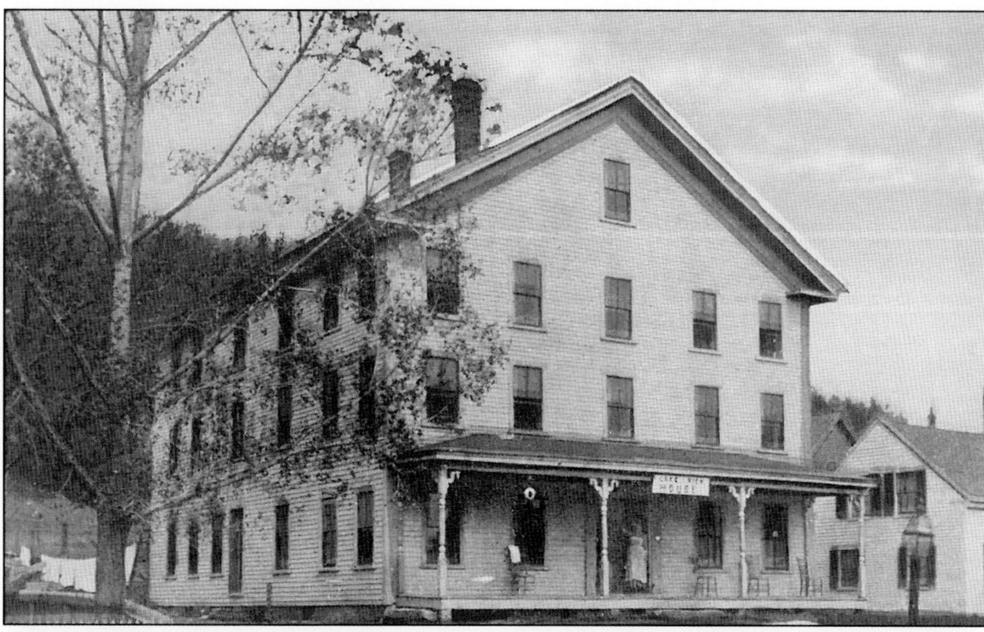

THE LAKE VIEW HOUSE. This hotel, also built in the Greek Revival style, was constructed in 1835. It was located across from the railroad station. Before it finally became a hotel, it housed the Classical Institute, and before that, the Congregational Church community, along with other denominations who used the building for their weekly meetings.

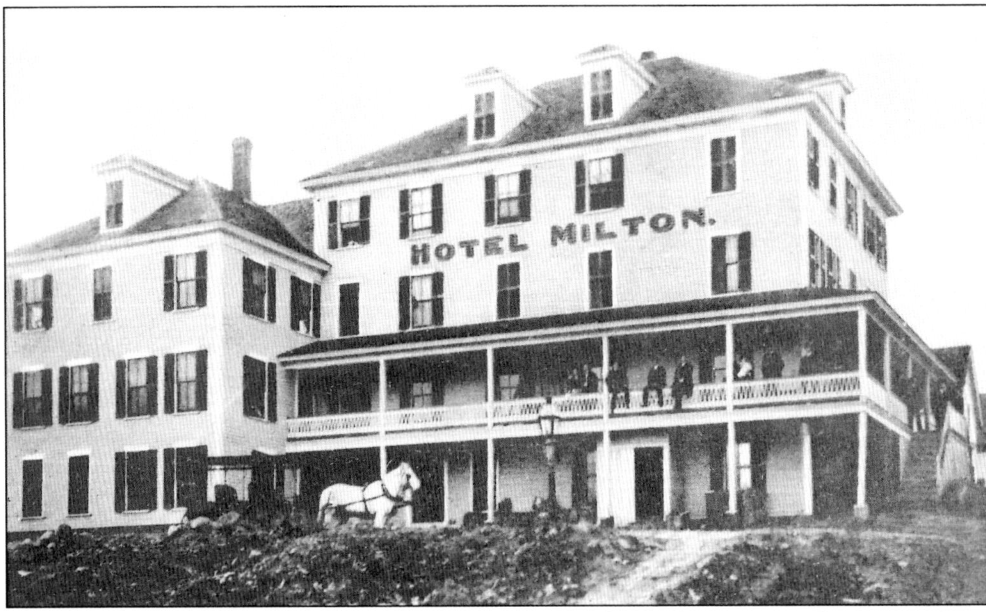

The Hotel Milton. The Hotel Milton was located on the corner of Tappan Court and Charles Street. It burned to the ground in the early 1900s. It was a hotel used mainly by the ice cutters.

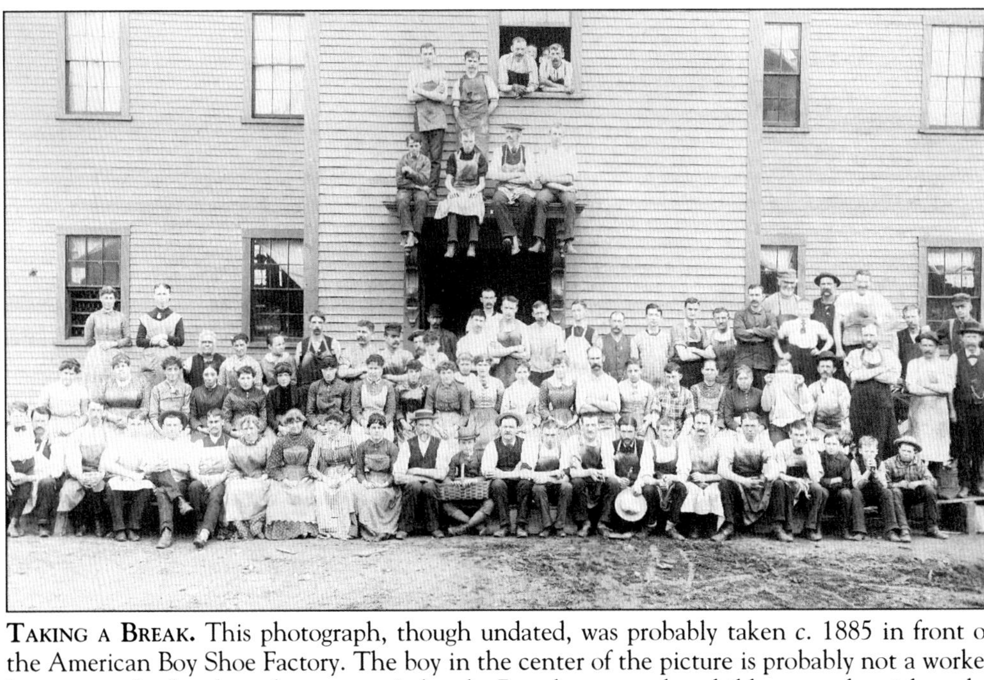

Taking a Break. This photograph, though undated, was probably taken *c.* 1885 in front of the American Boy Shoe Factory. The boy in the center of the picture is probably not a worker but a son who has brought a parent's lunch. But there are also children on the right, who are probably workers. The man in the second row (right) is camera shy and has pulled his apron up over his face!

Six

Plummer's Ridge

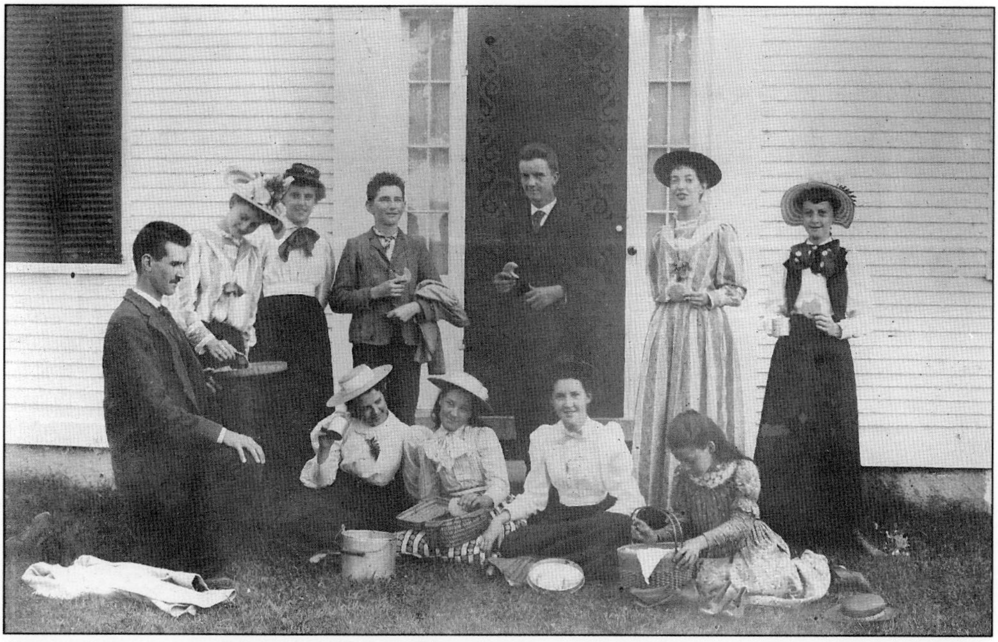

South Side of the Plummer Home. This photograph was taken *c.* 1900, by the look of the straw "boater" hats and the style of dresses. This may have been a reunion or just an afternoon spent relaxing with family and friends. The house was built in the Greek Revival style; the frame around the front door and the lights (windows) along the door confirm this.

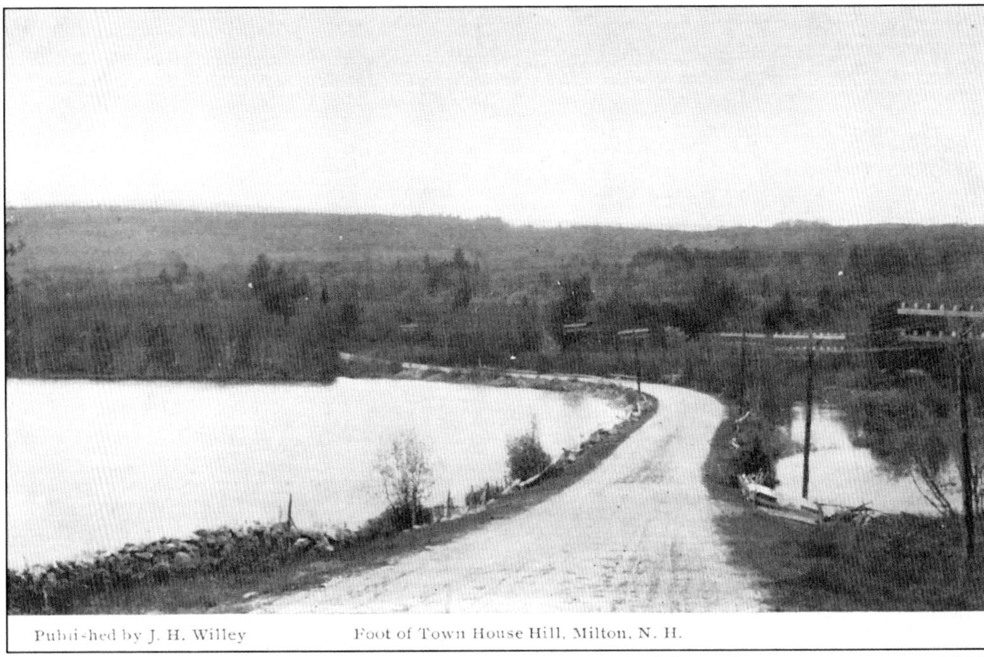

LOOKING FROM THE TOWN HOUSE. In this scene photographed from the Town House in 1912, the dirt road and part of Meeting House Pond is visible. The area of water on the right is still there. Telephone poles line the right side of the street.

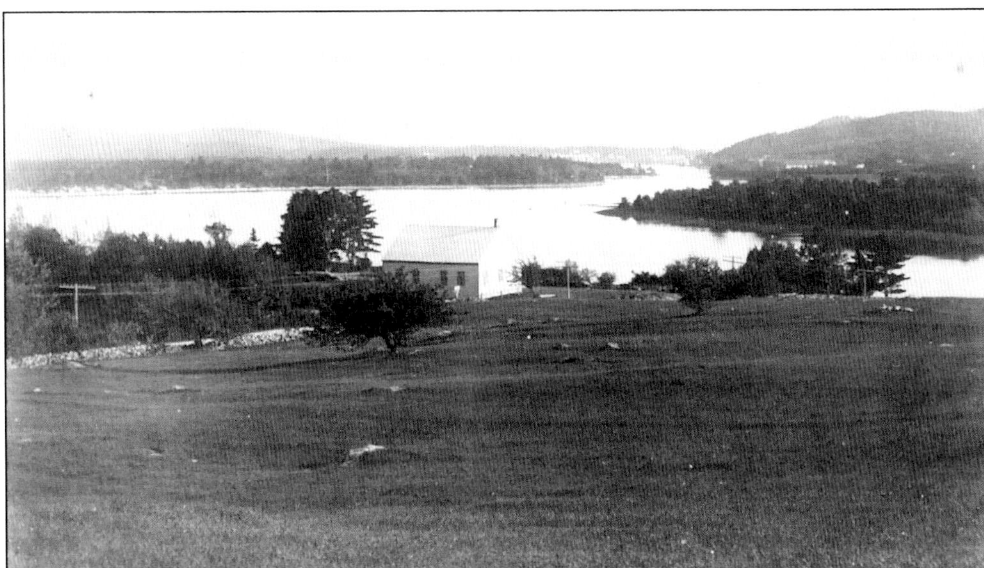

THE TOWN HOUSE. This is a beautiful view of the Milton Town House, with the Meeting House Pond behind it. Before the Town House was built, town meetings were held at the Jones Tavern, which is now the New Hampshire Farm Museum, farther up on the Ridge. This photograph was actually taken from the Town Pound. The Pound was the area where stray animals, such as cows, were brought when they were found wandering. When the owners came to retrieve their animal, they had to also pay a fine.

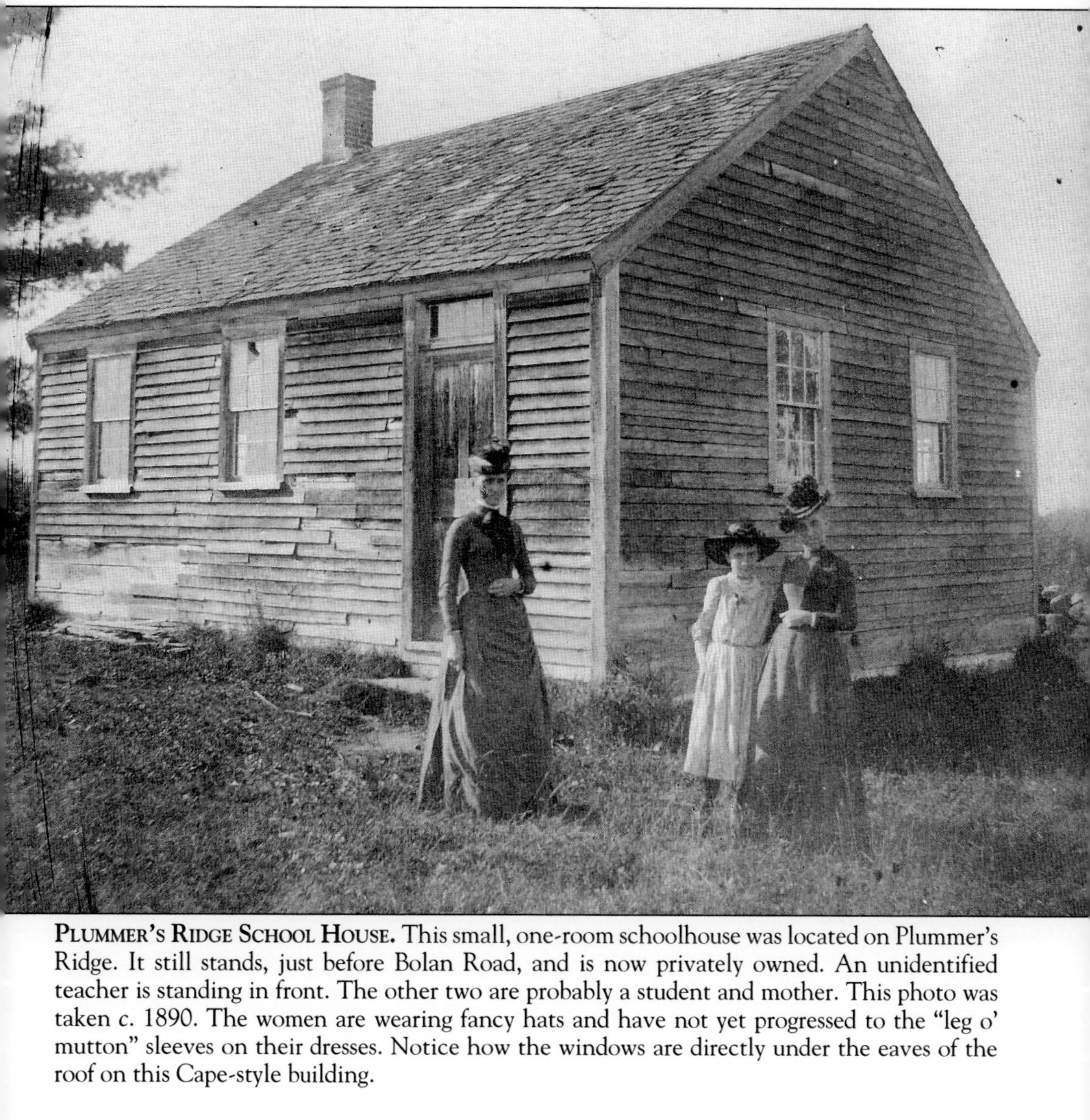

PLUMMER'S RIDGE SCHOOL HOUSE. This small, one-room schoolhouse was located on Plummer's Ridge. It still stands, just before Bolan Road, and is now privately owned. An unidentified teacher is standing in front. The other two are probably a student and mother. This photo was taken c. 1890. The women are wearing fancy hats and have not yet progressed to the "leg o' mutton" sleeves on their dresses. Notice how the windows are directly under the eaves of the roof on this Cape-style building.

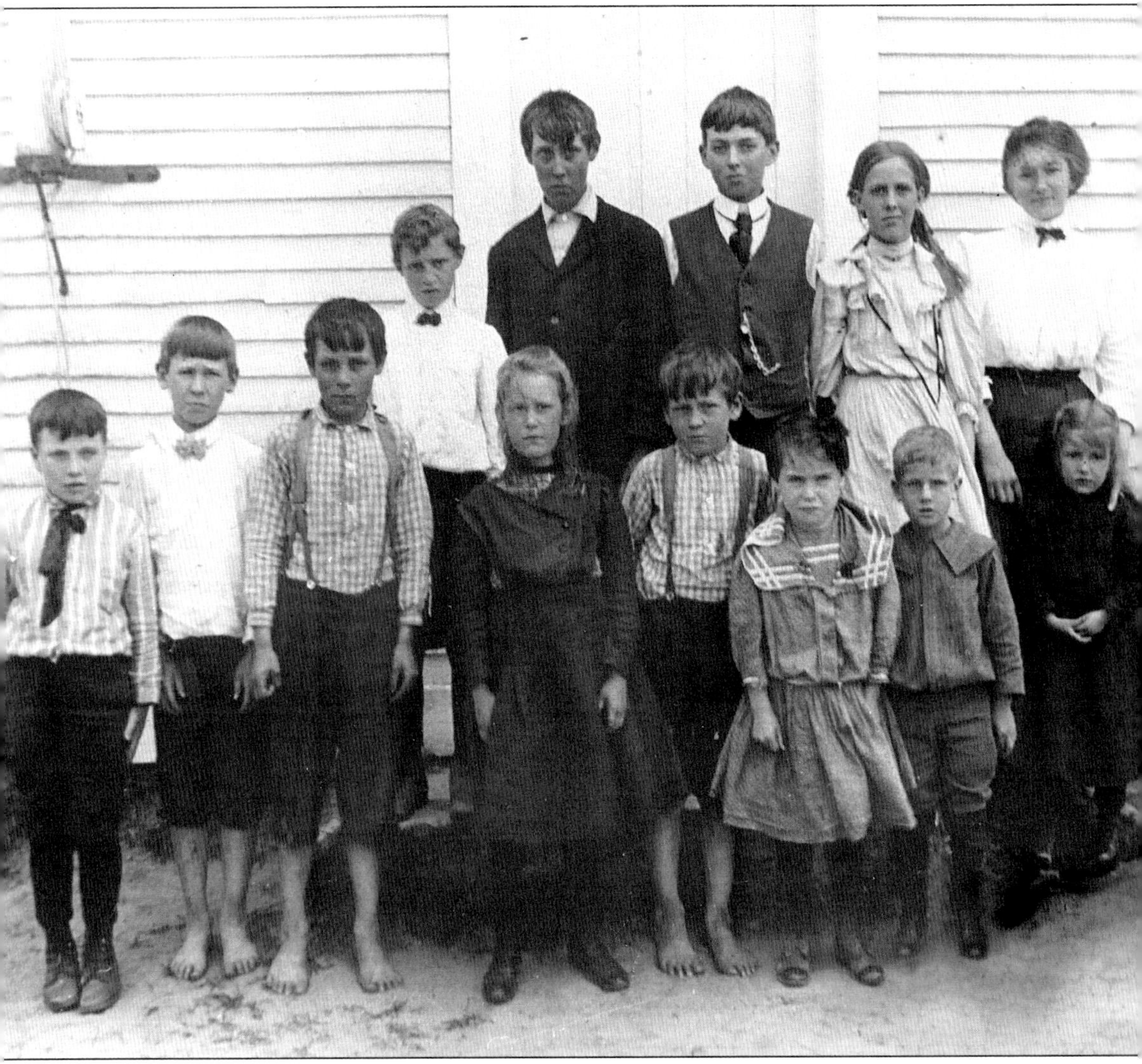

Plummer's Ridge School Children. From left to right are as follows: Milford Gaudette, Charles Twombly, Vane Nickerson, unidentified, Ailene Hayes, Willis Nickerson, Maurice Nickerson, Ralph Doe, Hilder Gaudette, unidentified, Jane Hayes, Edna Hayes, and Rosamond Piper (teacher). Notice that some of the students are not wearing any shoes, but they are wearing ties or suspenders. Miss Piper's shirt is in the "leg o' mutton" style, which was popular during this time, *c*. 1895.

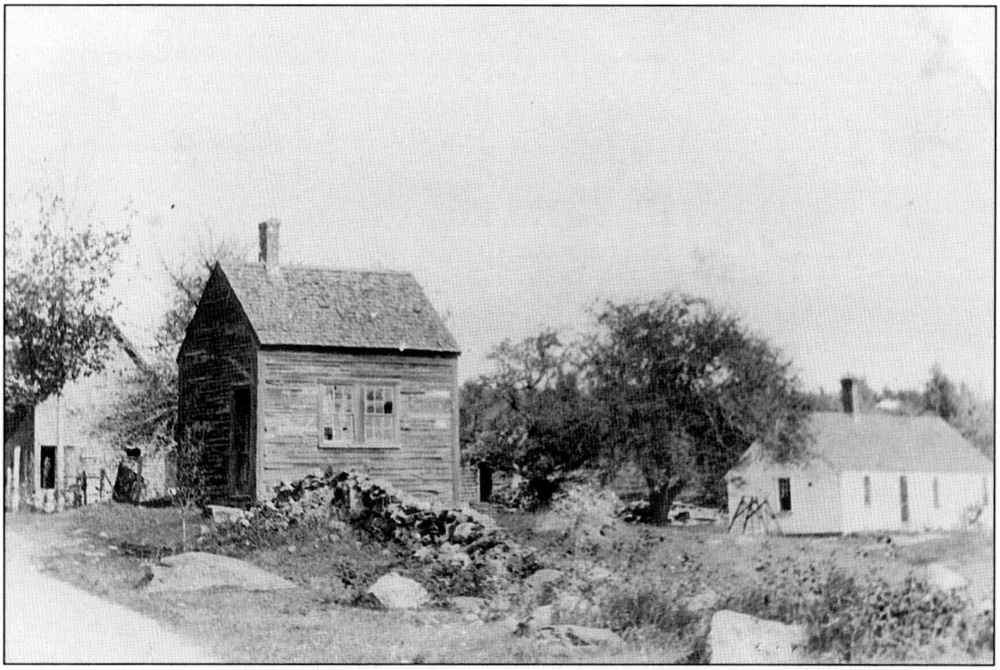

The Harvey Dorr Farm. This photograph was taken c. 1900. The small building in the foreground is a shoe shop. Since this picture was taken, the shoe shop has been moved. The Cape Cod house on the right has had a second-story addition and a porch added. The building behind the shoe shop is the barn.

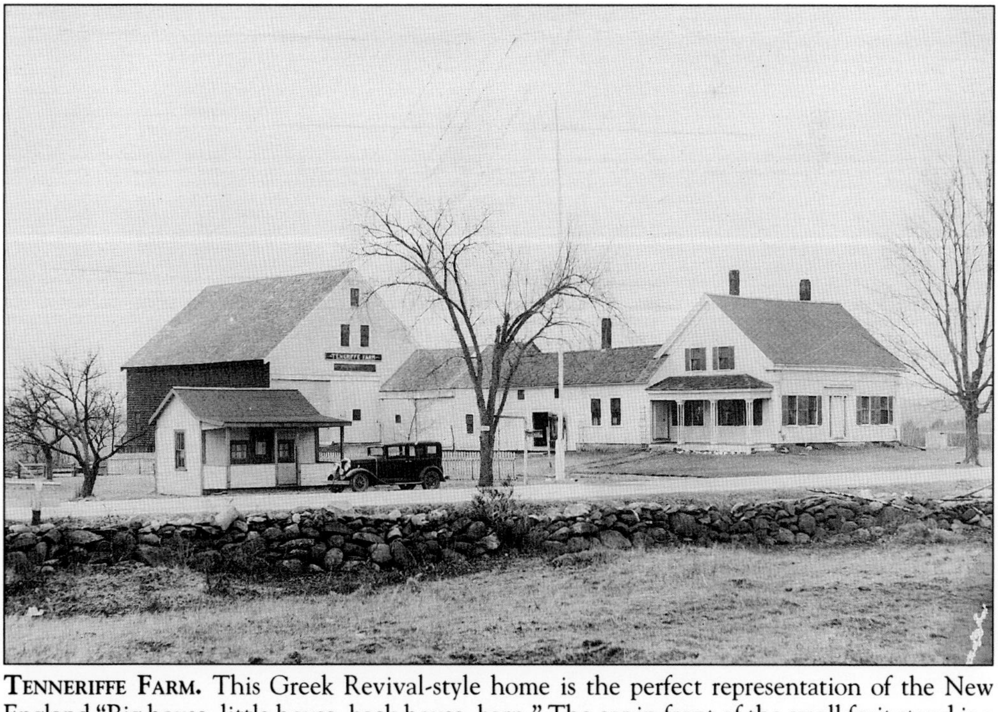

Tenneriffe Farm. This Greek Revival-style home is the perfect representation of the New England "Big house, little house, back house, barn." The car in front of the small fruit stand is a 1930 four-door Ford. The home is owned by Mrs. Wilfred Dawson.

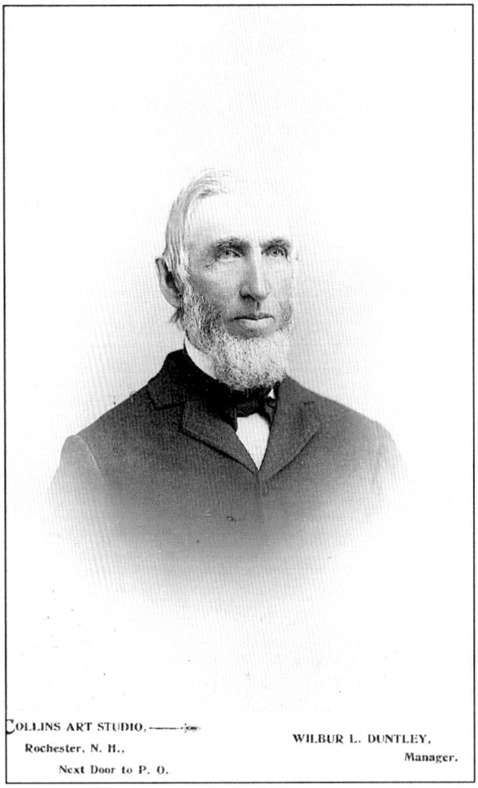

ENOCH W. PLUMMER. Enoch Plummer acquired his land *c.* 1895, around the same time he and his wife, Orinda, celebrated their 50th wedding anniversary. Enoch is wearing what the older men still considered proper at this time. Note the high collar on his shirt.

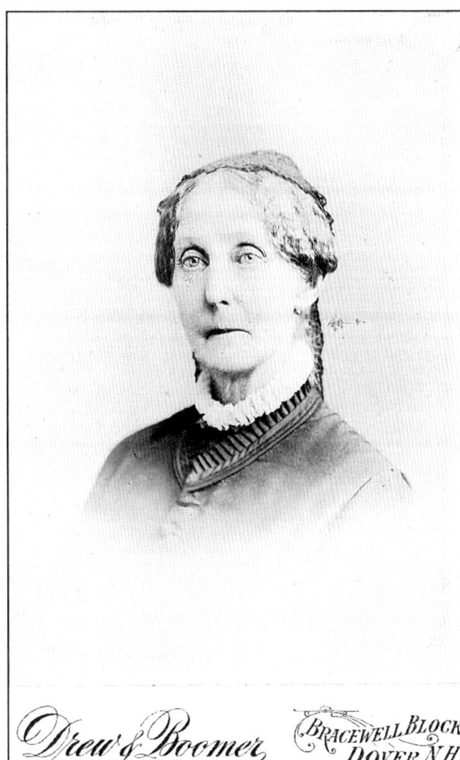

ORINDA PLUMMER. Orinda Plummer was the wife of Enoch Plummer and the mother of Bard B. Plummer. Notice how her hair was probably naturally curly, but with it pulled back, it is only wavy. She is also wearing earrings.

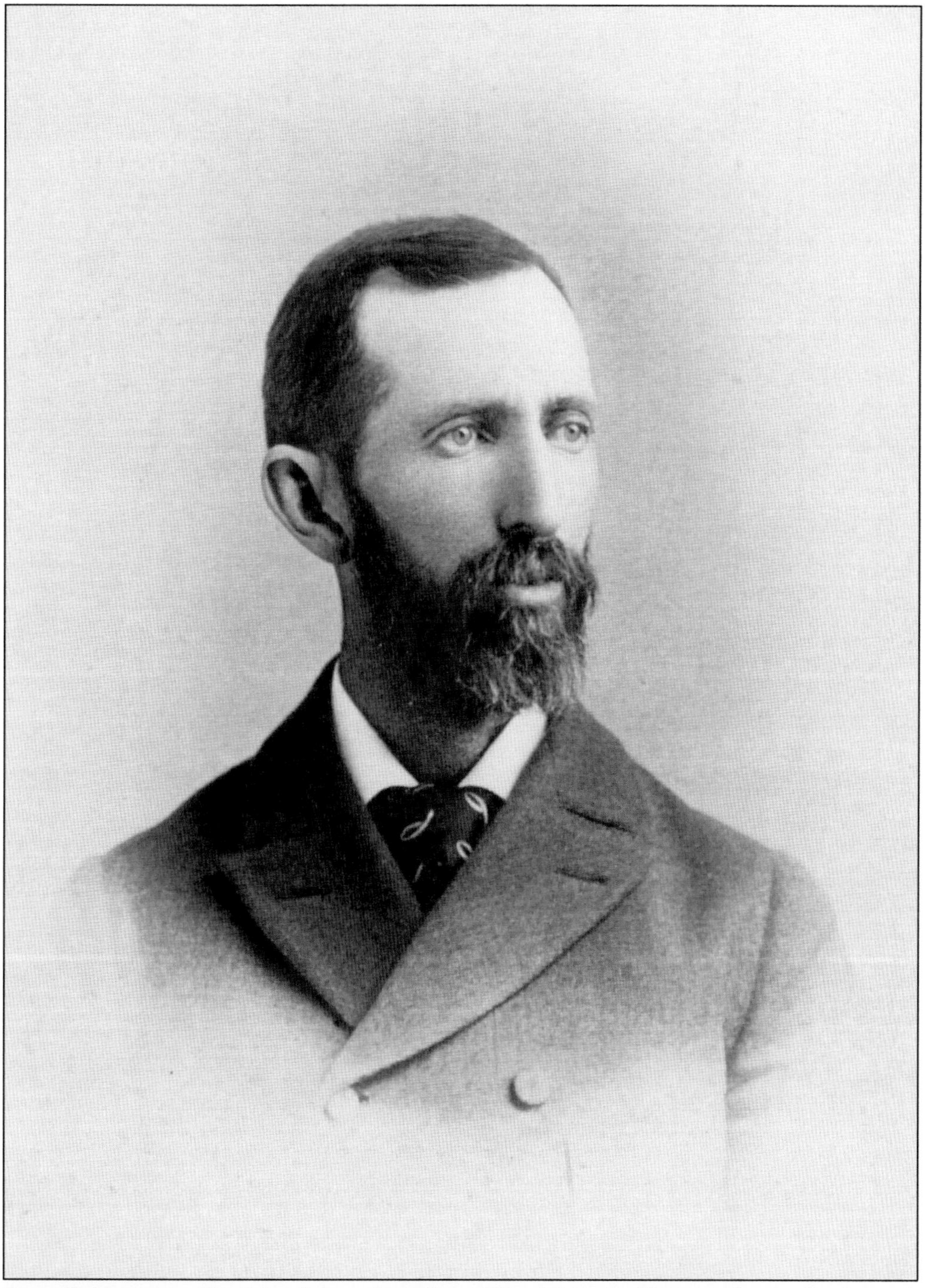

Bard B. Flummer. There has been a long line of "Bards" in the Plummer family. By the mid-20th century, the family had acquired about 800 acres of farmland. This photo was taken at the same time as the one of his father on page 92; the difference in age is apparent in the clothing style. Bard's collar is more like what is seen today, and the tie is no longer a bow.

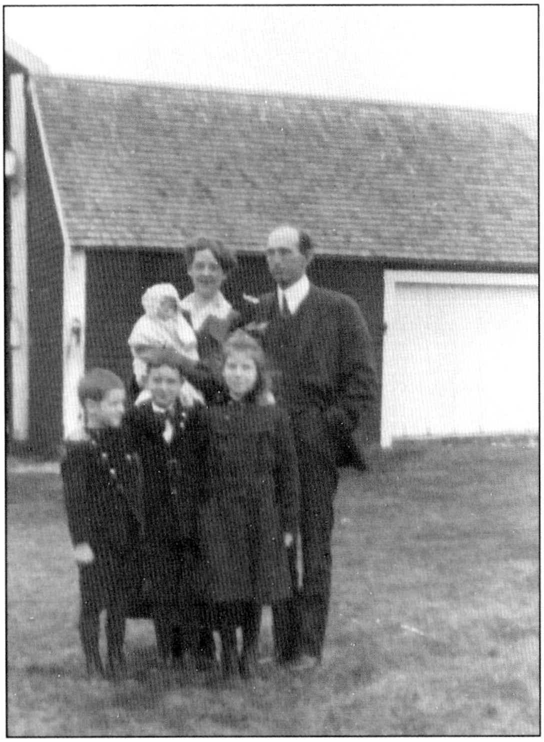

Bard B. Plummer and Family. This photograph of Bard B. Plummer and his family was taken in 1918. Mrs. Plummer is holding baby Dorothy in the back row and is standing beside her husband, Bard. Their other children, in the front row are Lyman, Bard, and Ruth.

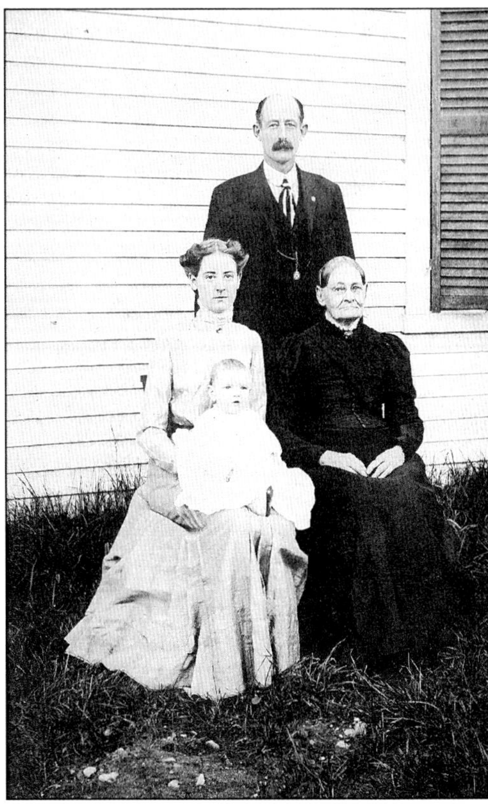

George Fall and Family. George Fall is pictured here with his mother and his daughter, Ruth Fall Plummer. The baby is George's granddaughter Elizabeth, who at this time was only one and a half years old. It's remarkable to see a picture with four generations of the same family together.

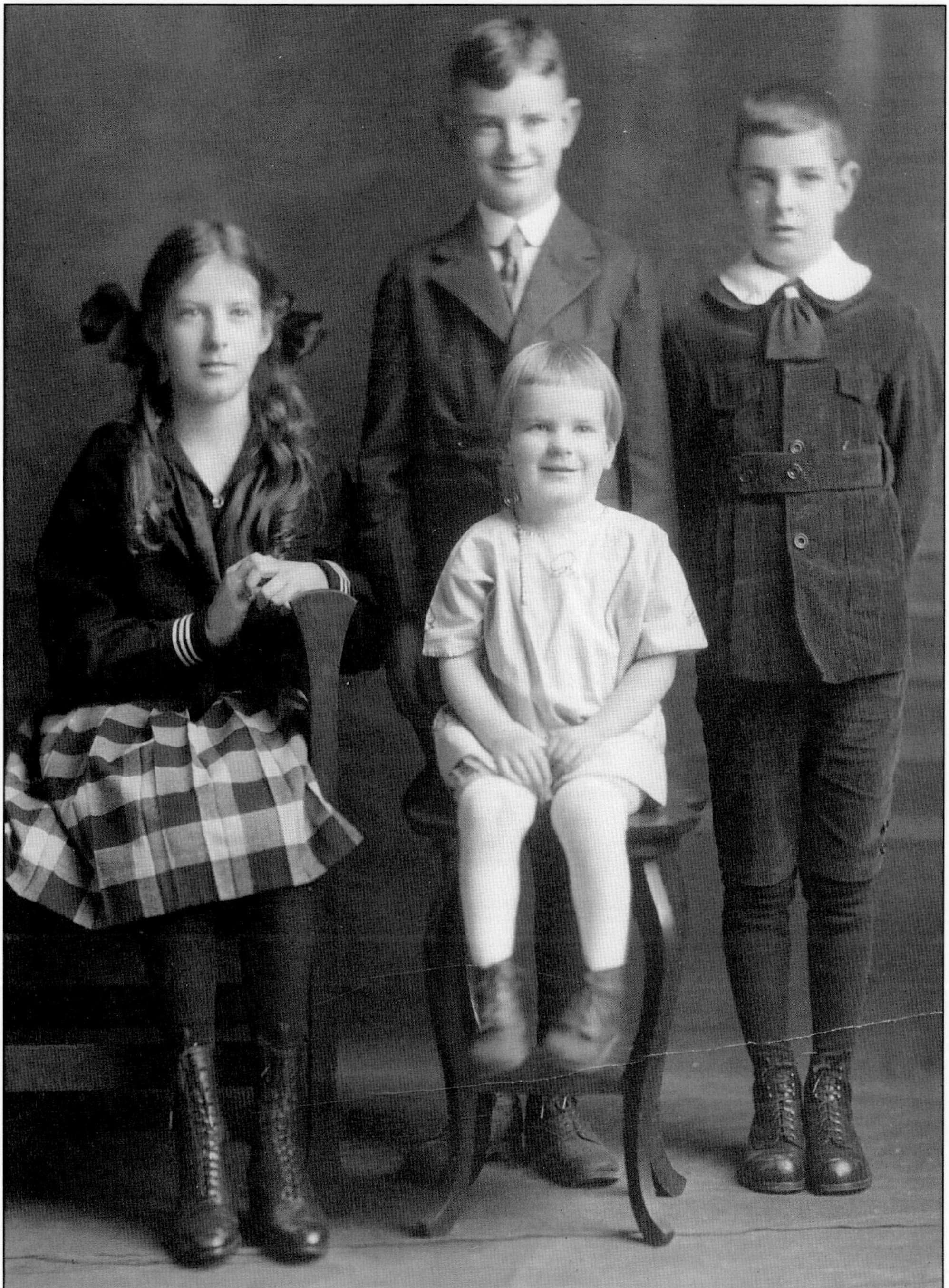

The Plummer Children. This photograph was taken in 1920 or 1921, according to the caption on the back. The children are Ruth, Bard, Lyman, and Dorothy. Note that the outfit Ruth is wearing resembles a sailor suit.

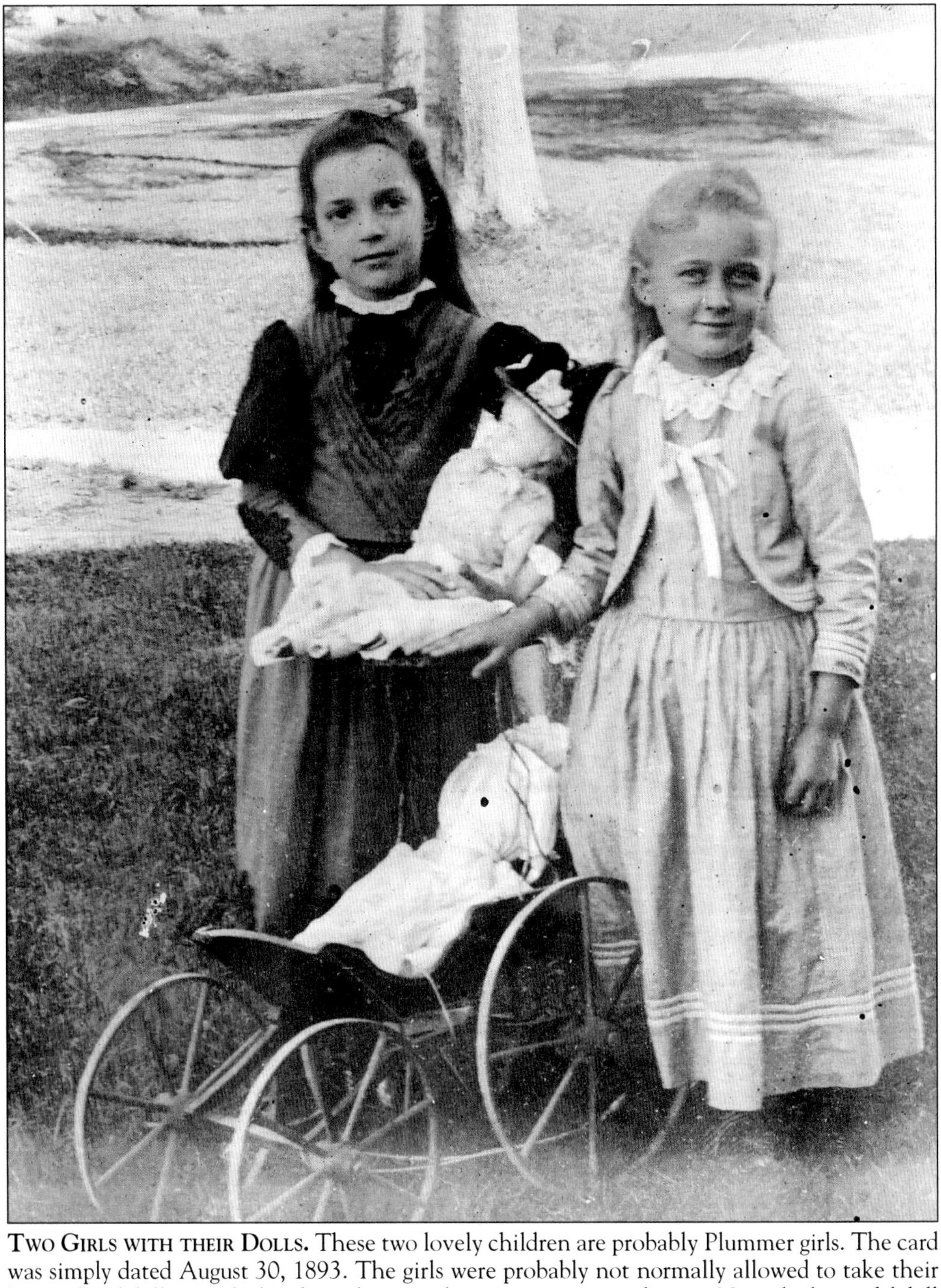

Two Girls with their Dolls. These two lovely children are probably Plummer girls. The card was simply dated August 30, 1893. The girls were probably not normally allowed to take their bisque-head dolls outside, but for a photograph, any props are good props. Note the beautiful doll carriage. Along with the dolls for the photo, they also seem to be dressed in their best clothes.

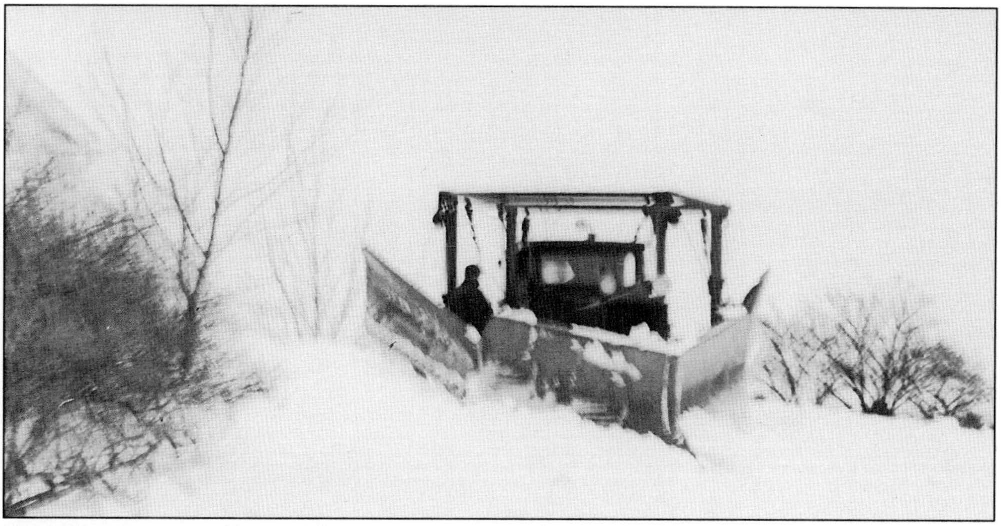

Snow Scene on the Ridge. This snow scene was taken at the Plummer Homestead in the early 1930s. Note the old snow plow and the height of the snow!

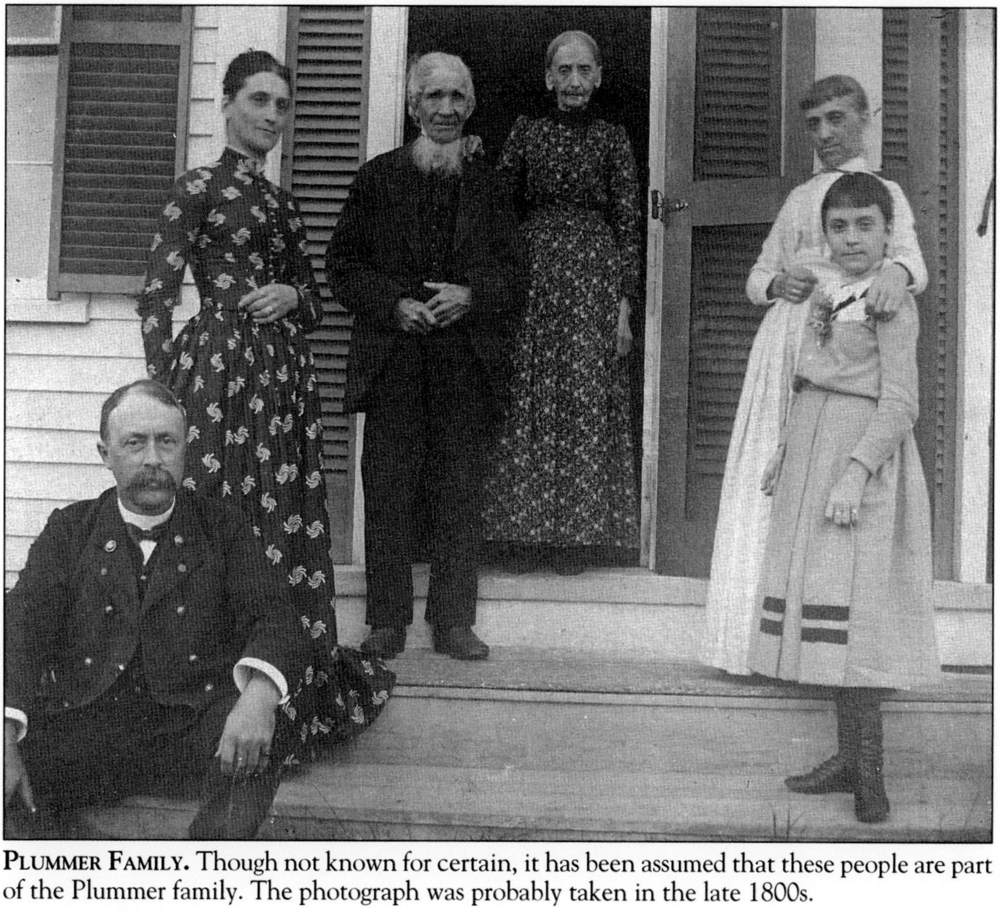

Plummer Family. Though not known for certain, it has been assumed that these people are part of the Plummer family. The photograph was probably taken in the late 1800s.

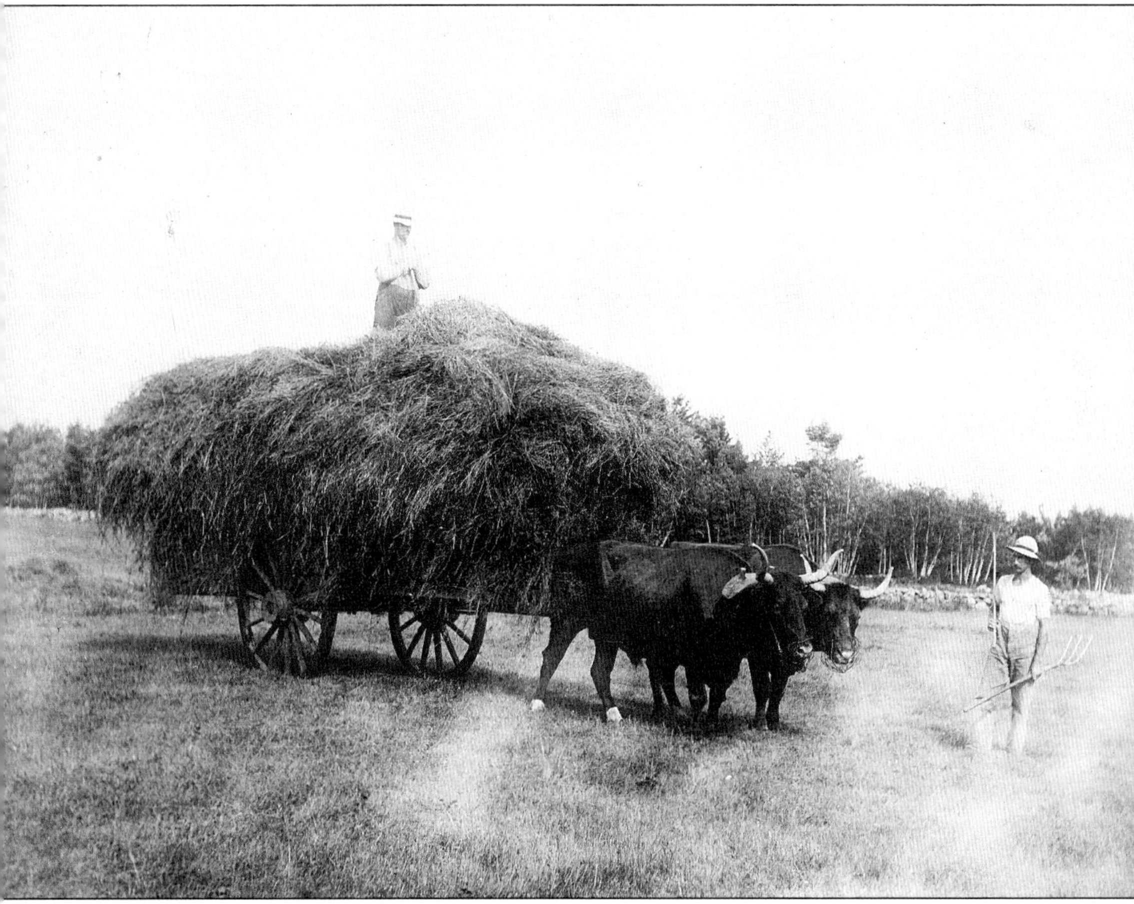

A SUMMER DAY IN THE FIELDS. This wagon, drawn by two oxen, is full of fresh hay, apparently gathered by the two men in the photograph. This hay will be taken back to the barn and stored for the winter months.

Seven

MILTON MILLS

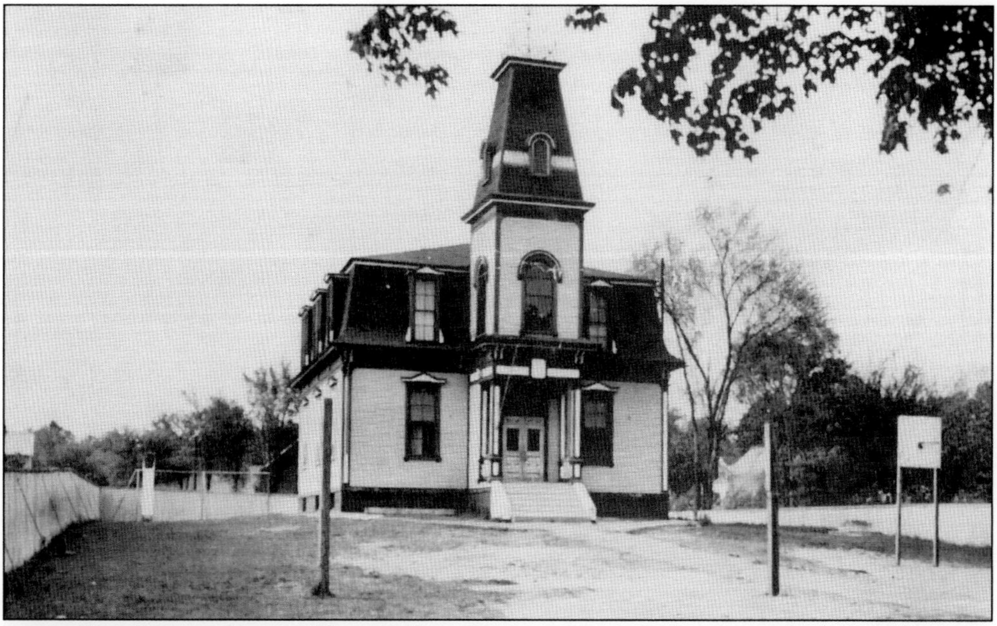

LITTLE RED SCHOOL HOUSE. Though this school was not red when it was built in 1875, many people now fondly refer to the small school as the "little red school house." Recently, this Second Empire-style building became the Milton Mills Library. This architectural style was very popular in the mid to late 1800s. The mansard roof allows a full second story (in some buildings a full third floor), which would usually not be able to be used because of the eaves.

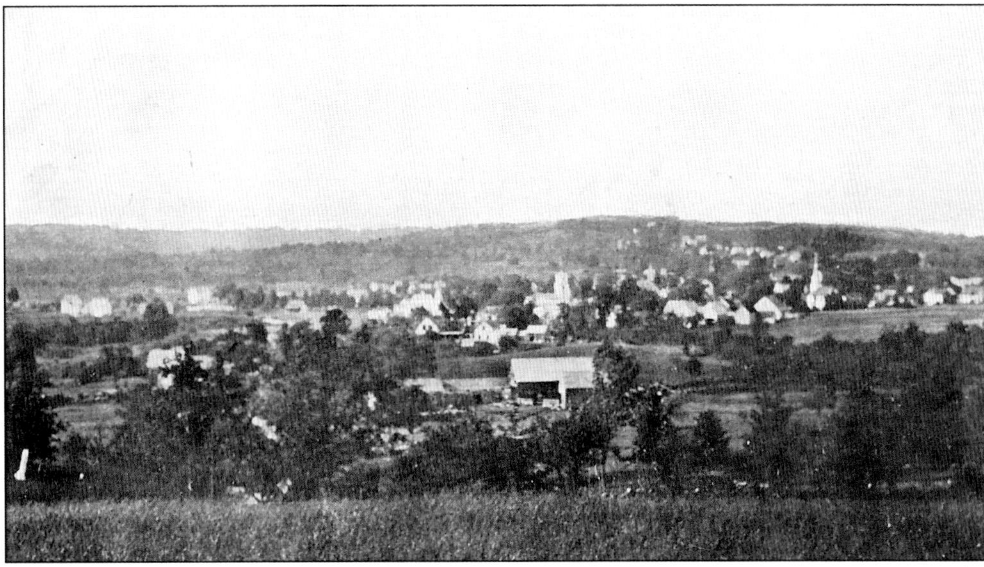

BIRD'S-EYE VIEW. Milton Mills is part of Milton, though sometimes that fact is forgotten. This picture, taken from Fox's Hill, shows just how big Milton Mills really is. On the right, in the distance, is the Methodist church. Also near the center of the picture is Miltonia Mills.

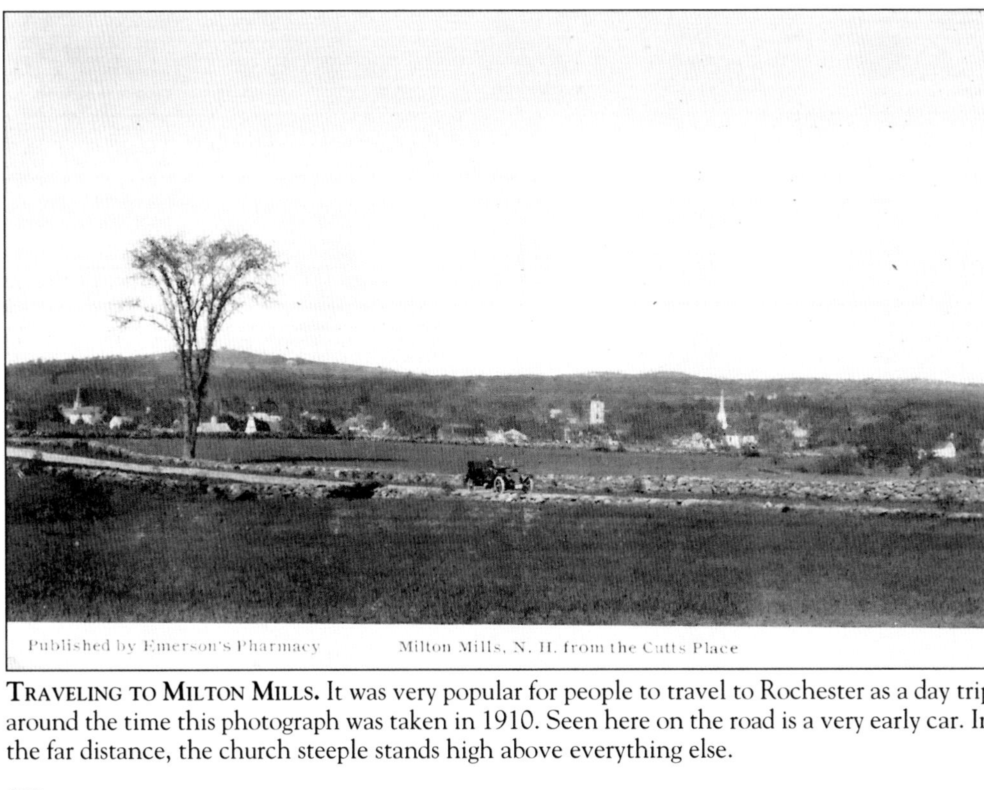

TRAVELING TO MILTON MILLS. It was very popular for people to travel to Rochester as a day trip around the time this photograph was taken in 1910. Seen here on the road is a very early car. In the far distance, the church steeple stands high above everything else.

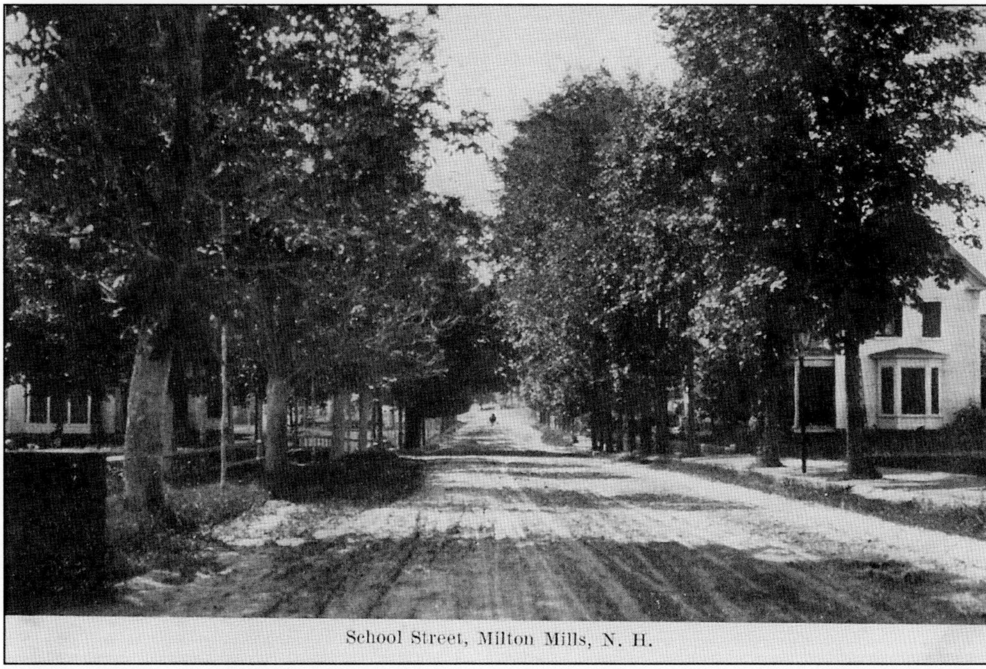

SCHOOL STREET. In the distance, on this beautiful sunny day, you can see a child playing. The trees shade the wide dirt street, making a tunnel for the child to play in. The house on the right was built in the Greek Revival style, with a bay window.

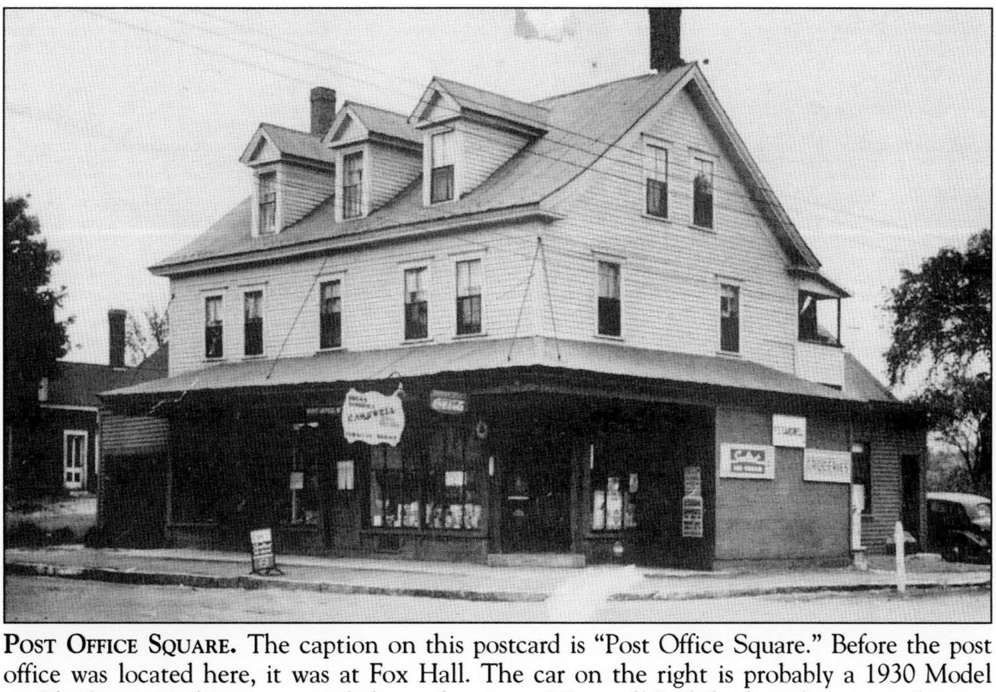

POST OFFICE SQUARE. The caption on this postcard is "Post Office Square." Before the post office was located here, it was at Fox Hall. The car on the right is probably a 1930 Model A. The large sign hanging outside bears the name, "Carswell," while the other signs advertise Coca-Cola, ice cream, and groceries.

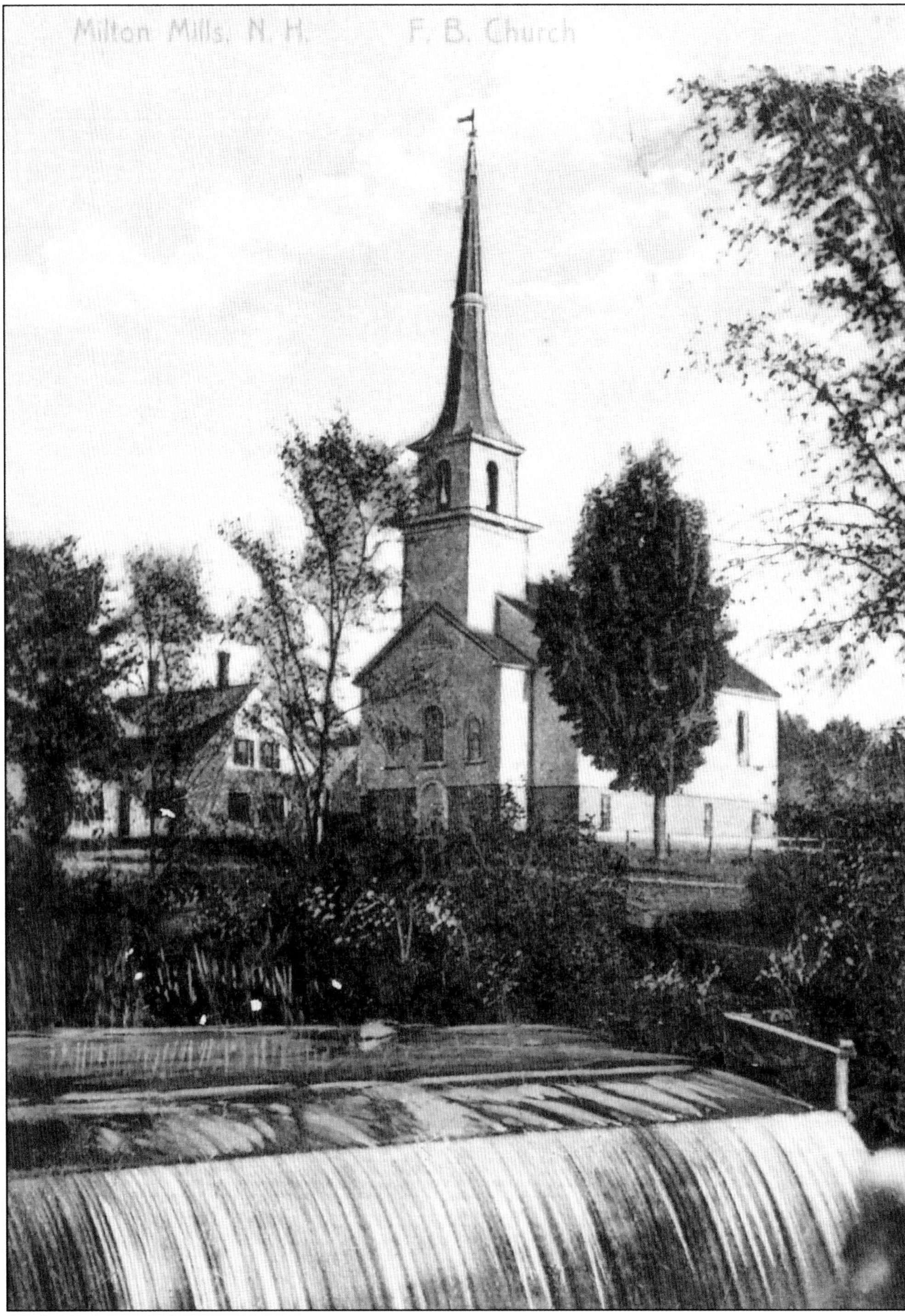

THE FIRST BAPTIST CHURCH. Located near the small dam, this photograph was taken in 1908. This church was built in 1840, but the original Baptist Church was first organized in 1780. This was the oldest continually operating church. In 1802, the Church consisted of eight members, and Gersham Lord was the first preacher.

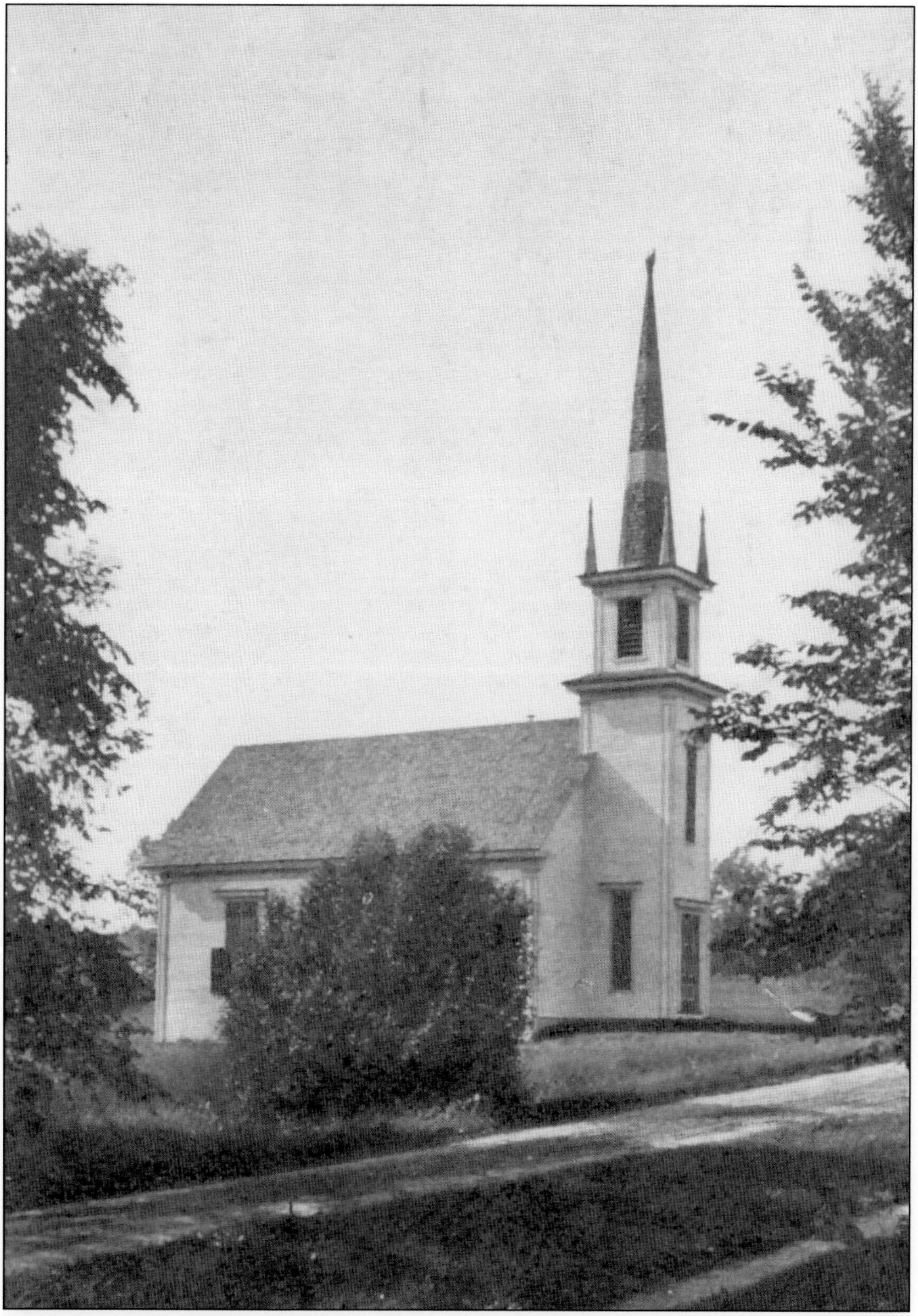

Methodist Church. The Methodist Church was organized in 1871 and built in 1872. The steeple is a "clenched fist" with the index finger pointing toward the sky. It was designed and molded by blacksmith Ratice Shaw. This church spire still attracts visitors, but it is now privately owned and kept preserved inside the church.

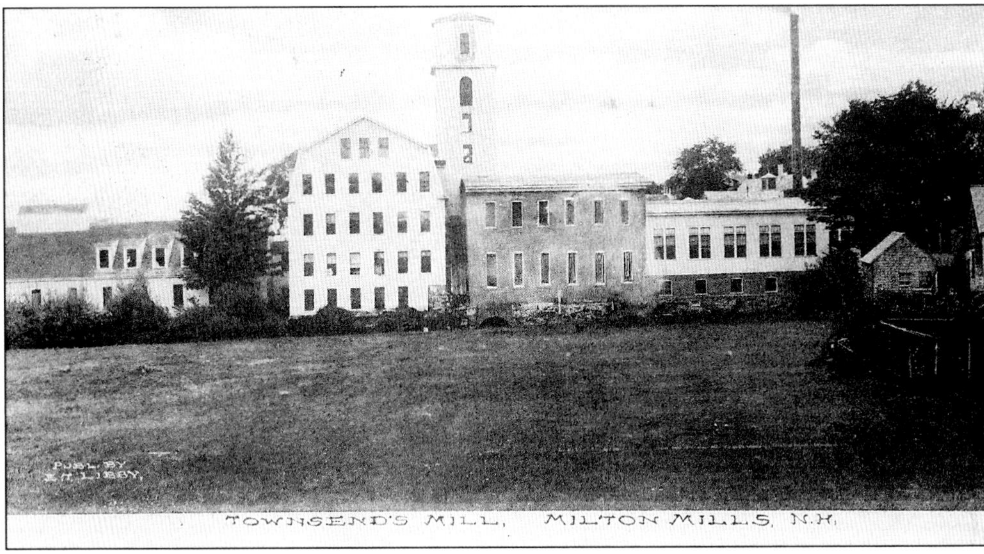

MILTONIA MILLS. This factory was one of the blanket mills for which Milton Mills was known. Many of the local people, especially young girls, worked here and at the other mills to help support their families. It was actually built in 1872 by Henry H. Townsend. Henry died in 1904 and was succeeded by his son, John. At one point, 65 people were employed here. Felt was the primary material made until 1881, when it was replaced with blankets. It was then that the name was changed from Townsend & Co. to Miltonia Mills. The wool blankets were used in the exploration of Admiral Peary, discoverer of the North Pole, and by Admiral Richard Byrd, who explored the Antarctic. Mrs. Calvin Coolidge used these blankets in the White House while her husband was in office.

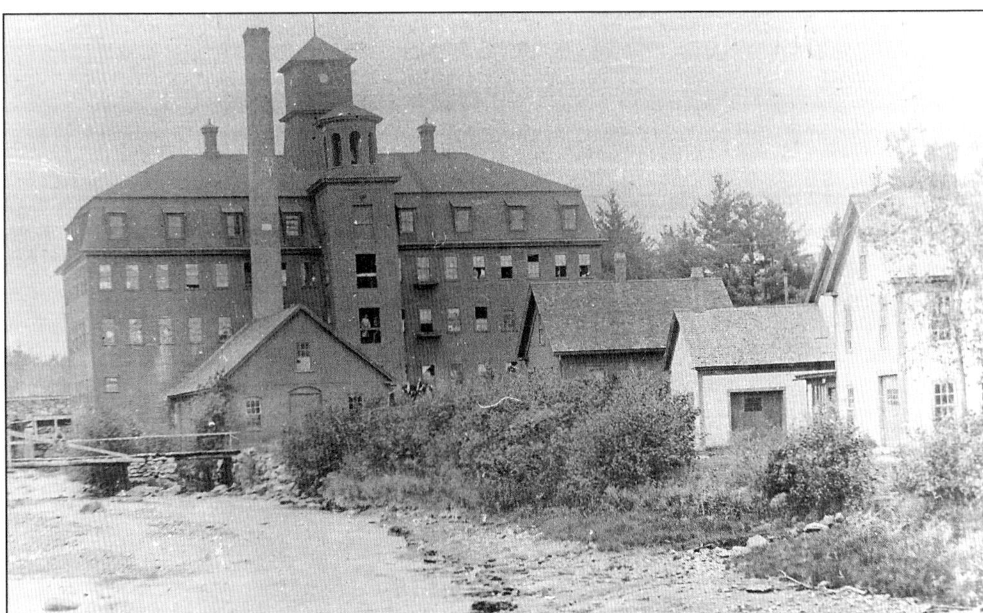

SHOE SHOP. The shoe factory was originally a felt mill in 1860, but it burned down in 1873. The mill was rebuilt and sold to Varney and Lane, who began manufacturing shoes.

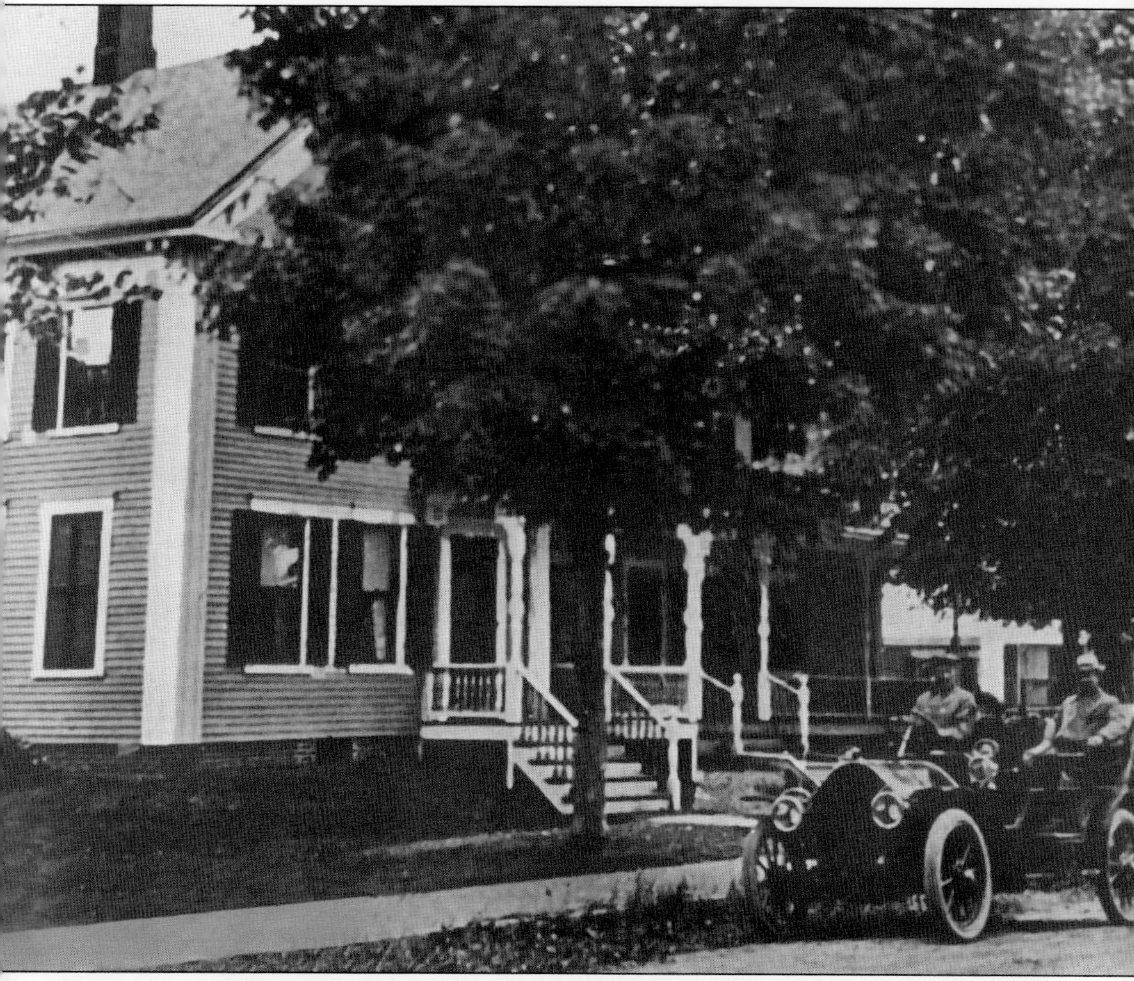

COULD IT BE A BUICK? This photograph is dated 1910. It was taken in front of this huge Greek Revival home. The building not only served as a home for Asa Fox and his family but also was the local general store. It is the longest-operating store in Milton's history. The two men in the car are obviously very proud of the house and the car.

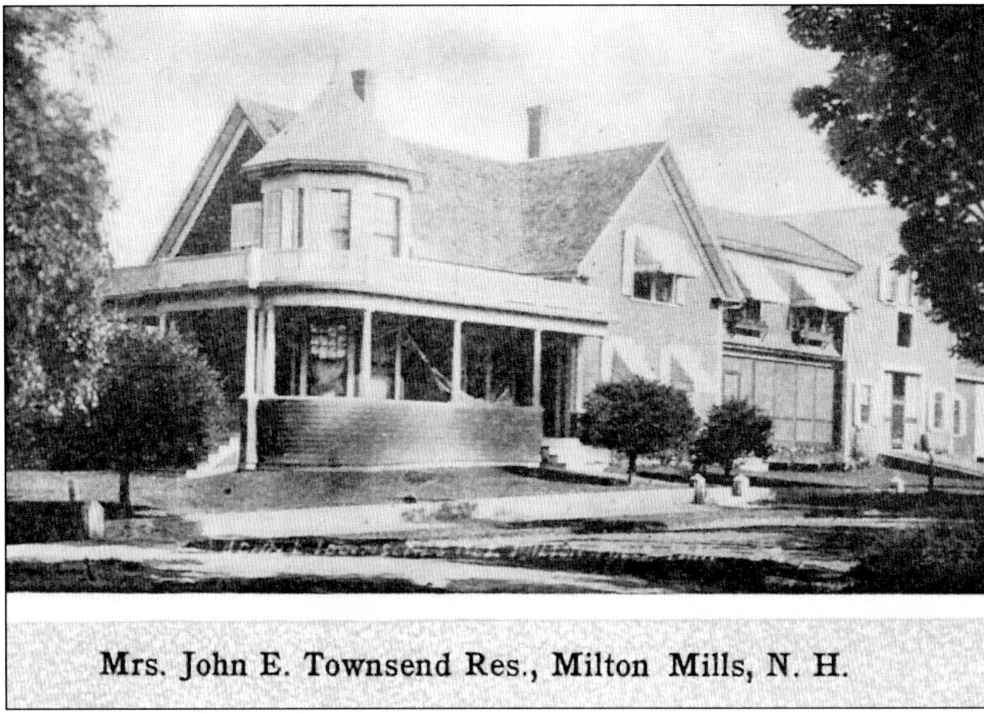

Mrs. John Townsend Residence. John Townsend was married to Eda Lowd of Acton, and was the son of Henry Townsend, the owner of the Blanket Mills. This house was built in the Victorian Shingle style, which was popular between 1880 and 1900. The large porch on the front of the house is one of the many features of the Shingle house.

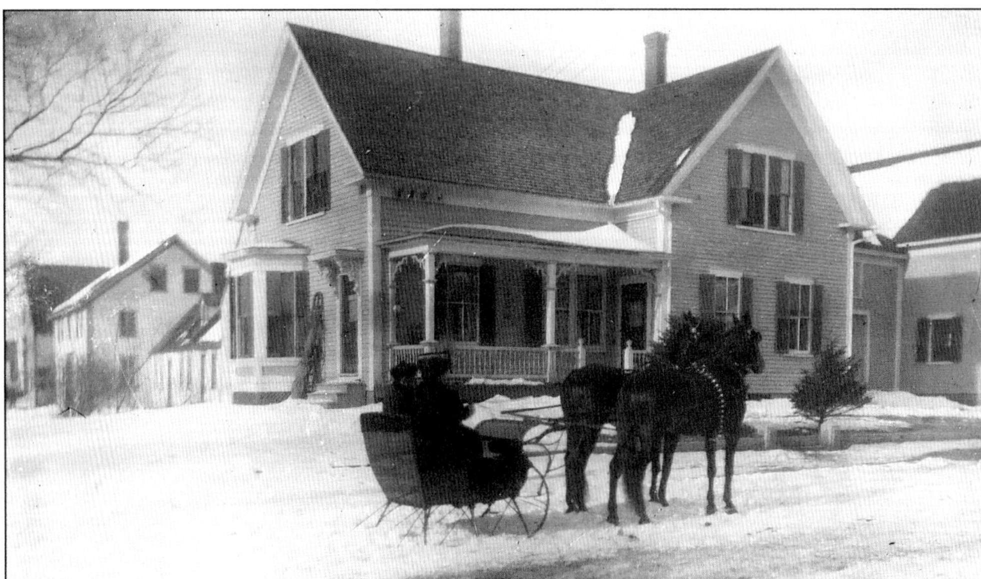

The Hayes Family Home. This Greek Revival-style house was a very popular style all over the country between 1825 and 1860. The horse-drawn sleigh brings forth images of a Christmas in New England. The house is located on the corner of Church and Western Avenues.

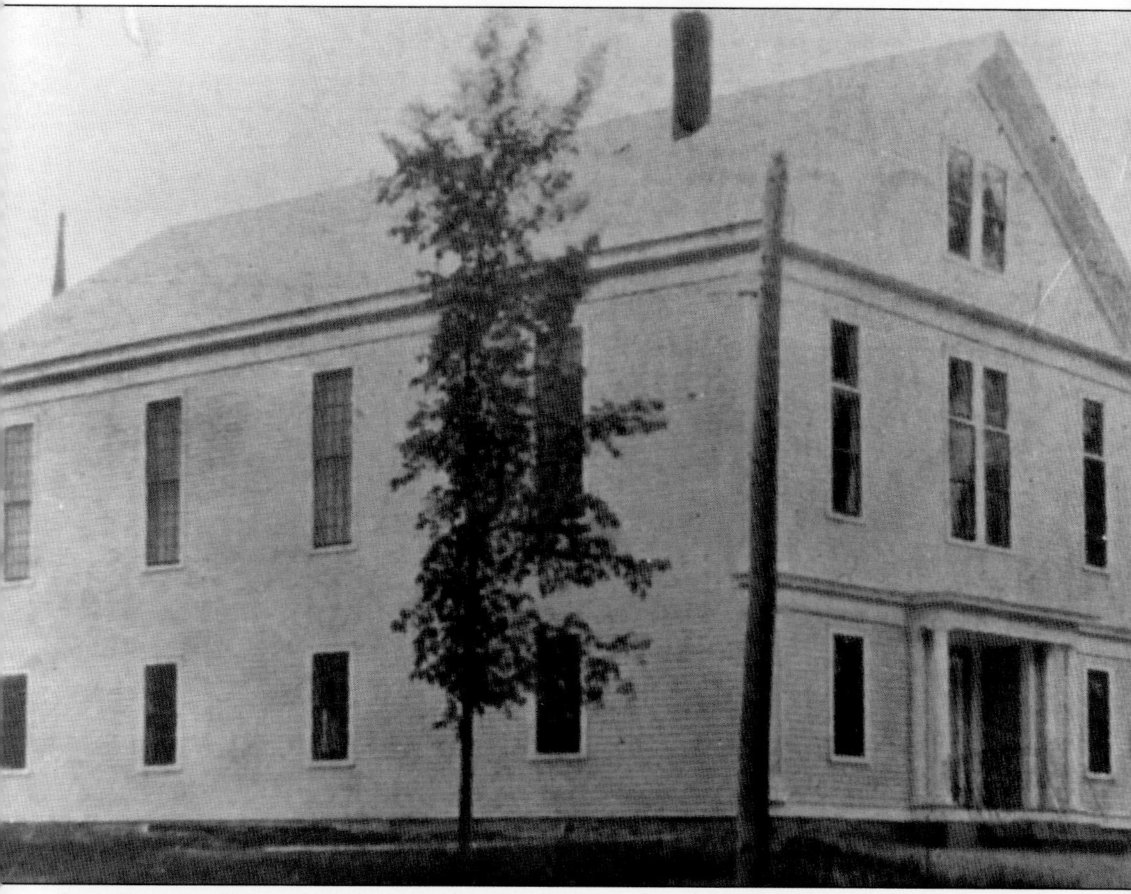

ODD FELLOWS HALL. At one time, this Greek Revival building housed the Congregational Church of Milton Mills. Later it went onto become the Odd Fellows Hall.

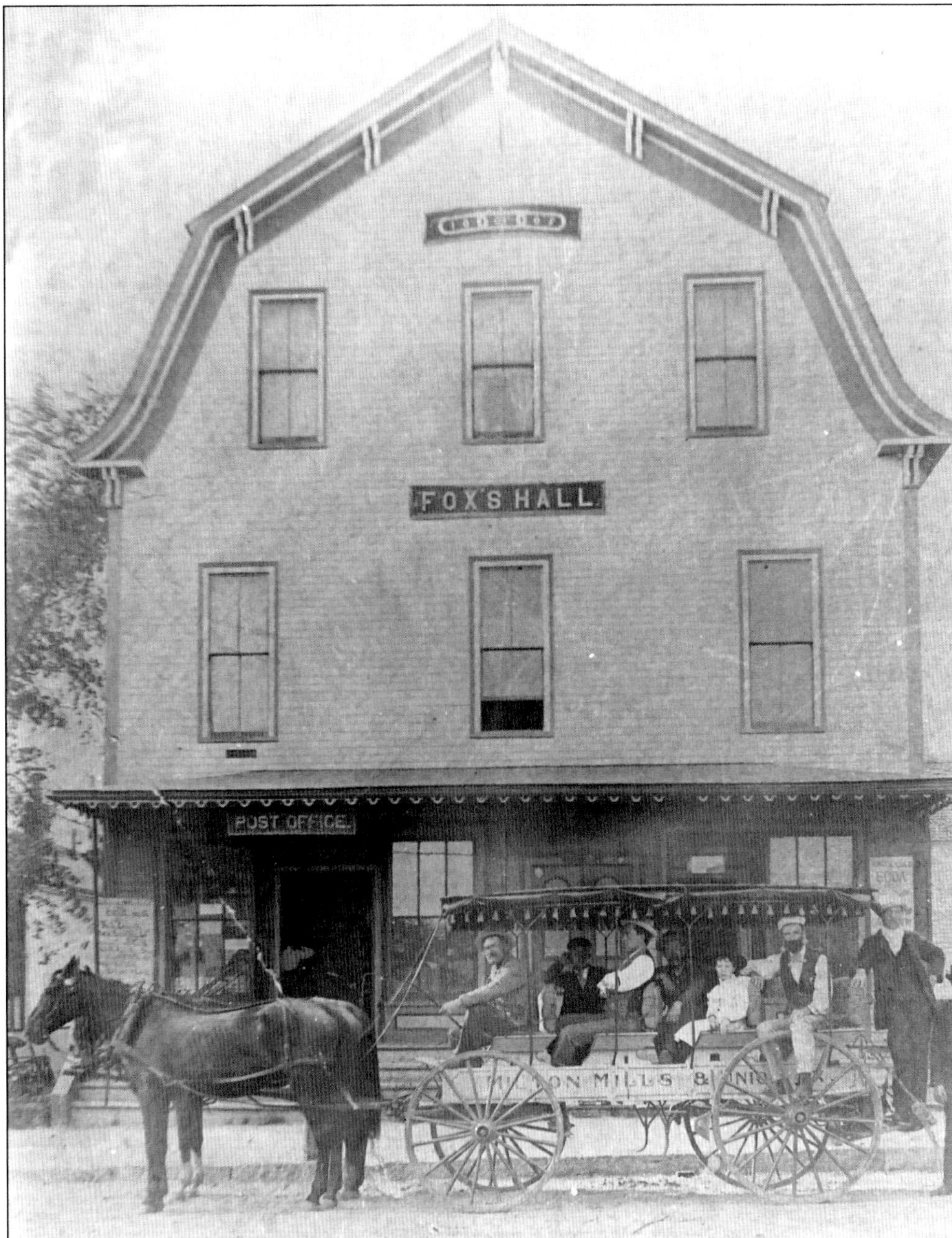

Stagecoach. This stagecoach went between Milton Mills and Union before 1900. The stage is actually marked with its destinations. Most residents of Milton Mills went to Union to buy supplies of flour and sugar, since it was much easier to get to than Milton Village. This photograph was taken in front of "Fox's Hall"; the building is constructed in the Dutch- Colonial style, with Italianate-influenced brackets under the eaves.

Eight

The New Hampshire Farm Museum

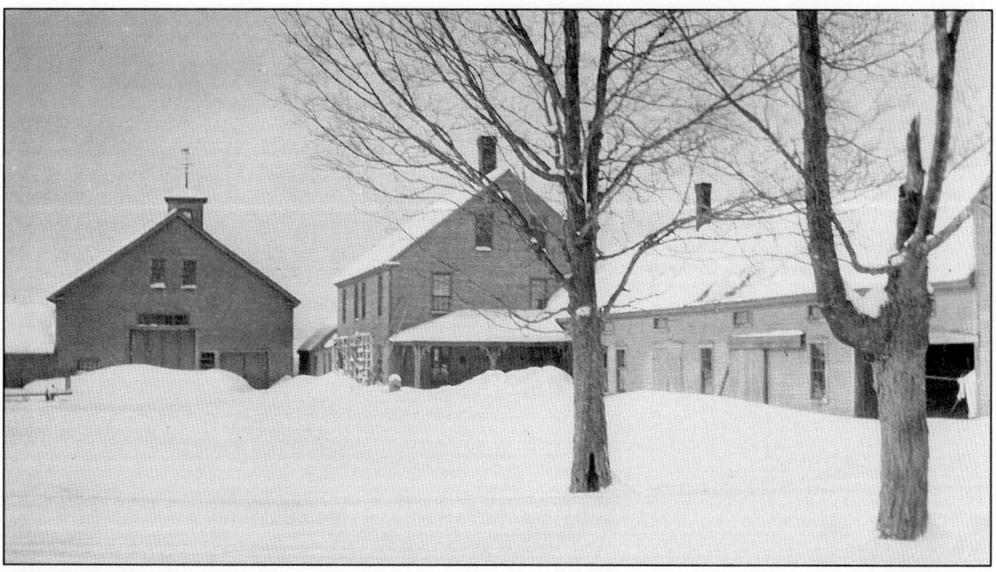

The Jones Farm. The farm is located on Route 125, on Plummer's Ridge between Milton and Milton Mills. It does not face the road like most houses, but "sprawls" lengthwise, starting with a large stable at the road, continuing through several sheds to the kitchens, and ending at the main two-story house. The main house, a Cape Cod-style structure, was Joseph Plummer's house in 1777. The two-story house was added in 1804.

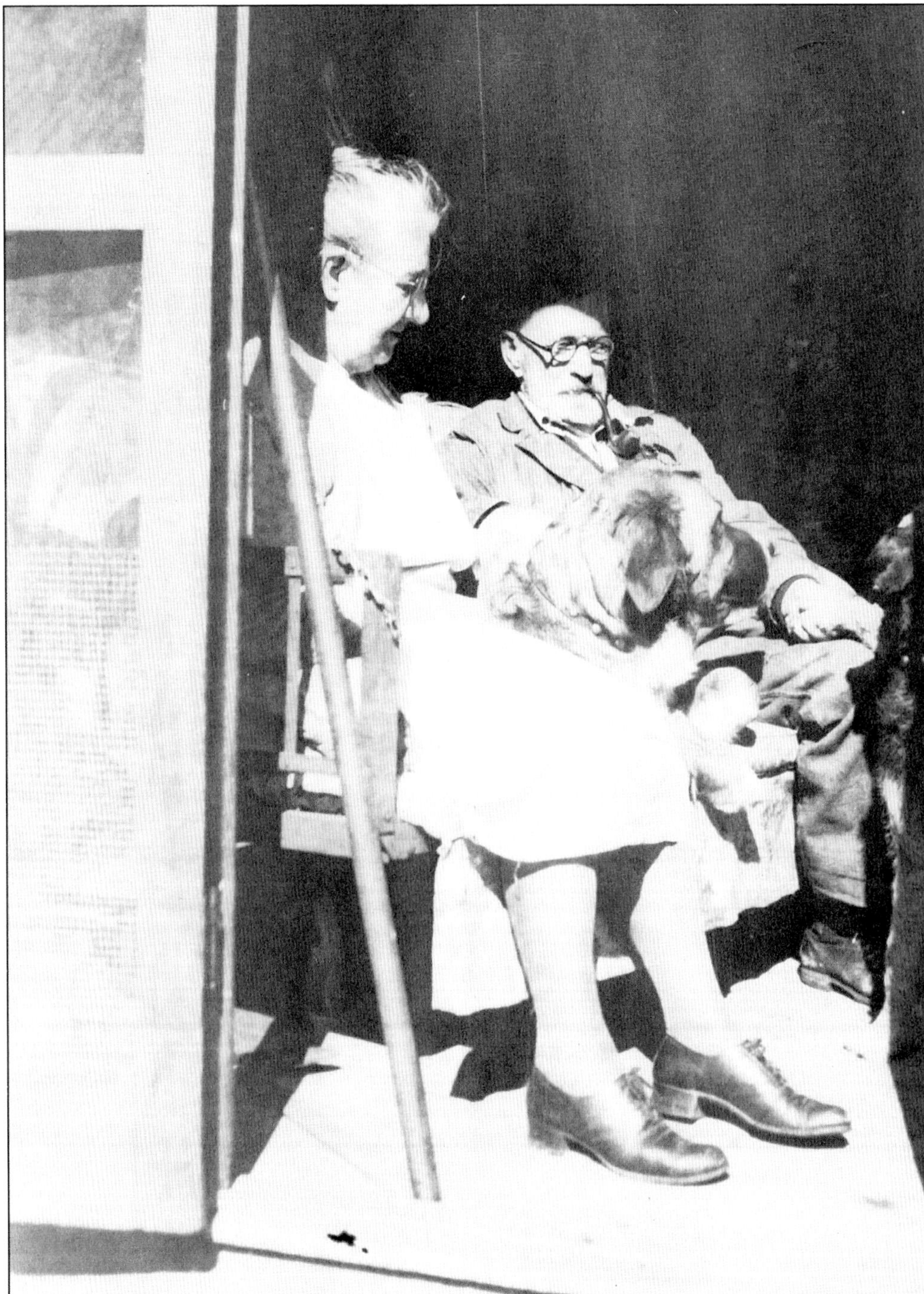

FRED AND EMMA JONES. Fred was born c. 1850 in the farmhouse. Fred and Emma raised five children on the Jones Farm. Here they are shown in their later years, seated on a swinging chair set up inside the barn. Their beloved saint bernard shares their space.

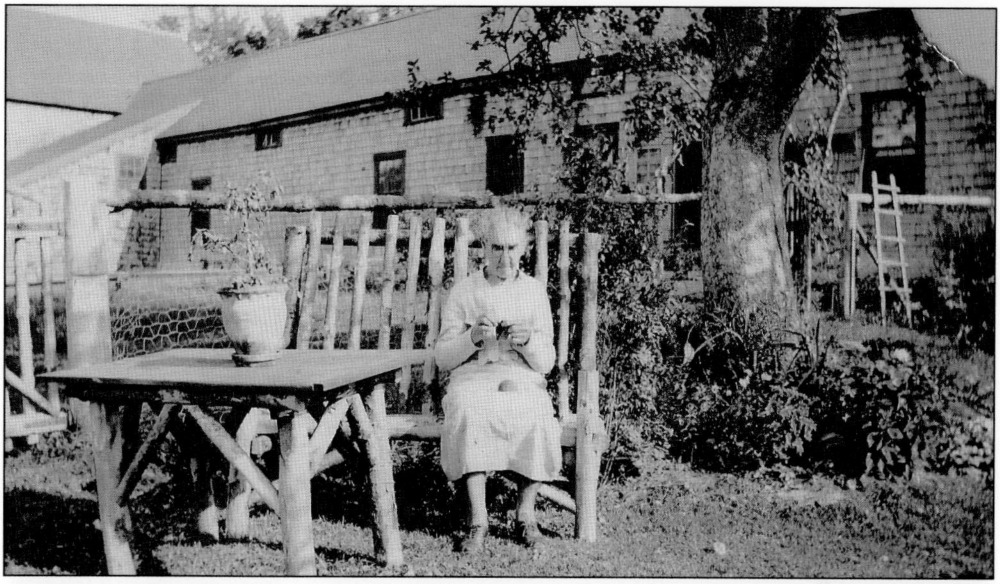

Emma in her Garden. Emma Cowell Jones was born in Lebanon, Maine. She attended Bradford Academy in Massachusetts, which was a private school for girls, and went on to study at the New England Conservatory of Music in Boston. Later in life, she gave private singing and piano lessons in her home. In this photo, she is seated on a hand-made bench. The table, too, appears to have been made at home. Emma took great pride in her garden and spent every possible moment there, either working or relaxing.

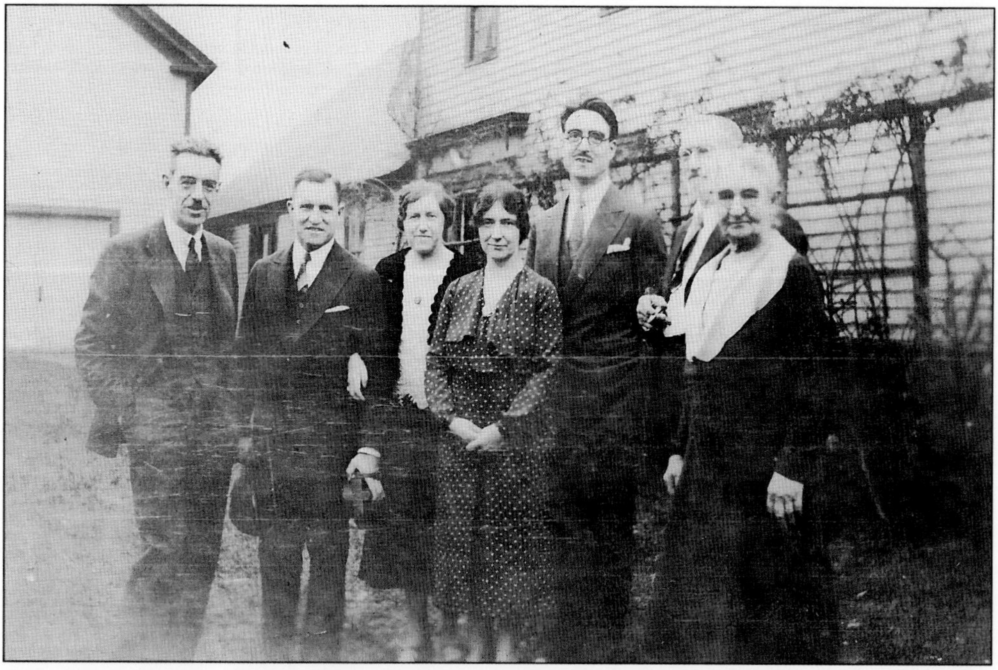

The Jones Family. Photographed in front of the farm, Fred and Emma pose with their five children. Members of the family, from left to right, are Charles (1885–1956), Philip (1886–1975), Alice (1896–1958), Elizabeth (1894–1975), Robert (1894–1954), Fred, and Emma.

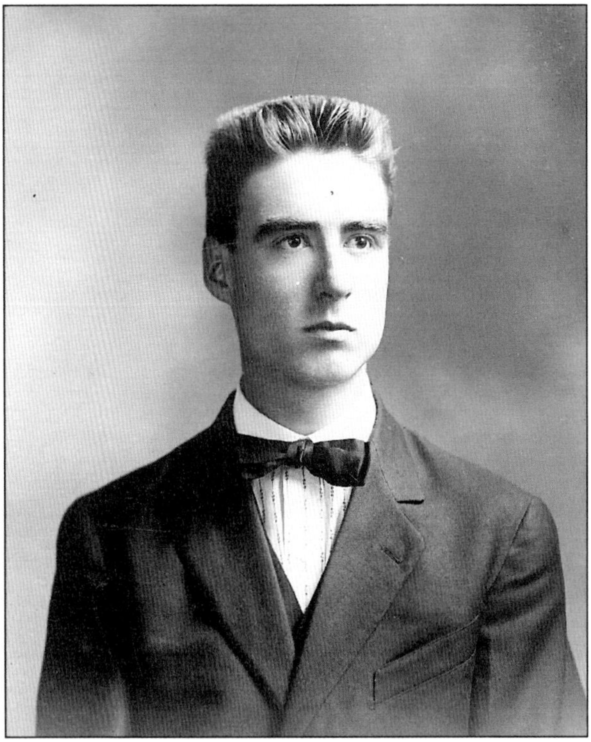

CHARLES JONES. Charles was the oldest of the Jones children, and this photo probably marks his high school graduation. Charles was an insurance agent. He and his wife Beulah never had children. They are both buried in the Plummer-Jones Cemetery in Milton.

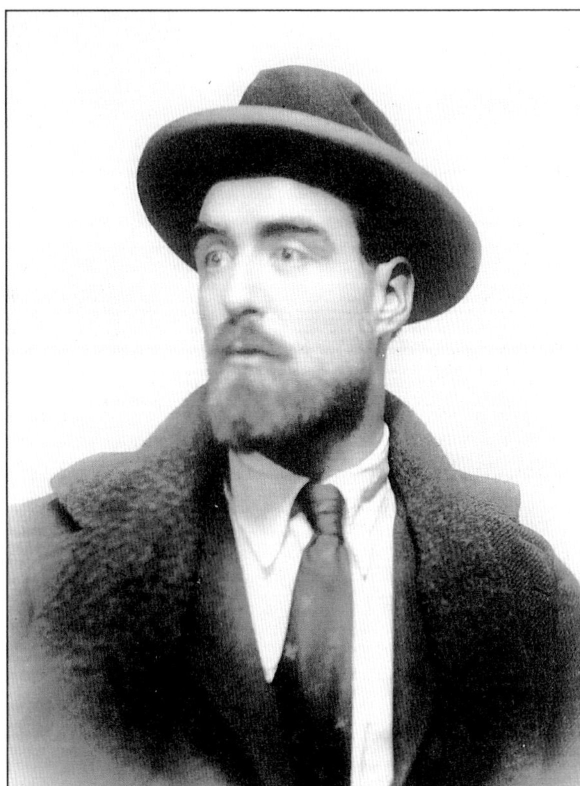

ROBERT EDMOND JONES. The second son, Robert, was the best-known member of the family. He was a movie pioneer who worked on the technical side. Robert is credited with perfecting the Technicolor process, though he was not the innovator of the technique. He was the first of the Jones children to pass away; he died in 1954 and was buried in the Plummer-Jones Cemetery.

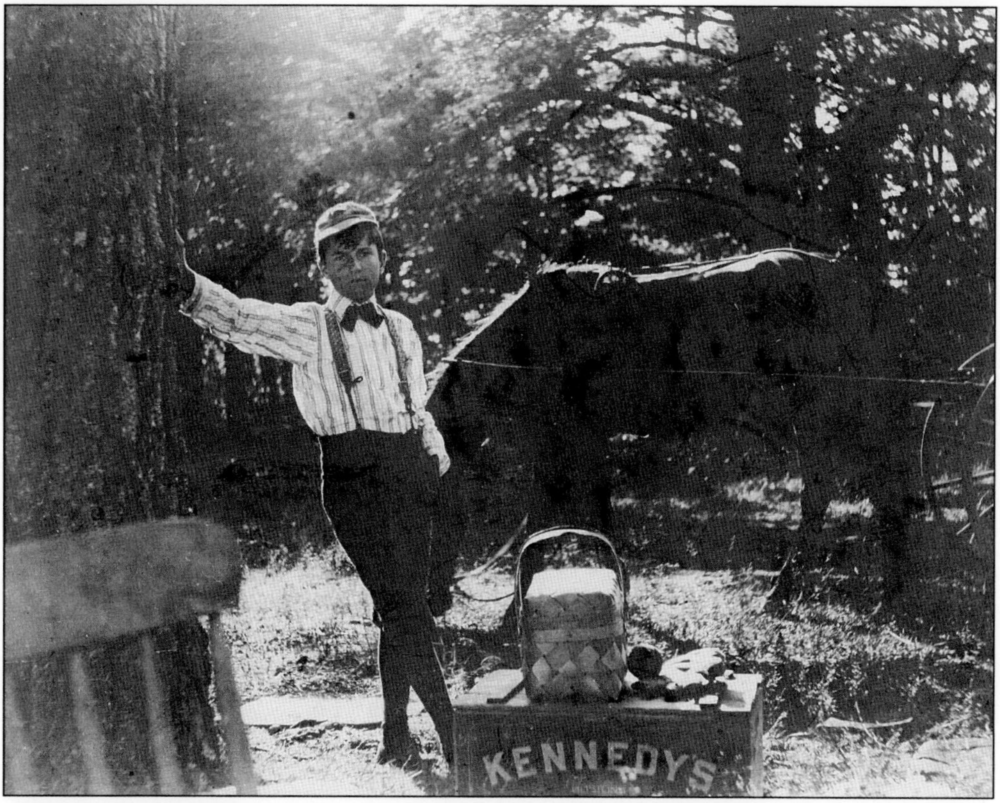

PHILIP JONES. The third child, Philip, was born in 1891. He is shown here at the age of nine, striking a casual pose. At his feet, a picnic basket is placed on top of a box from the Kennedy's Butter and Egg Store, a New England chain. He may be off to a picnic in the woods, but it is more likely that he is bringing a meal out to harvesters in the field.

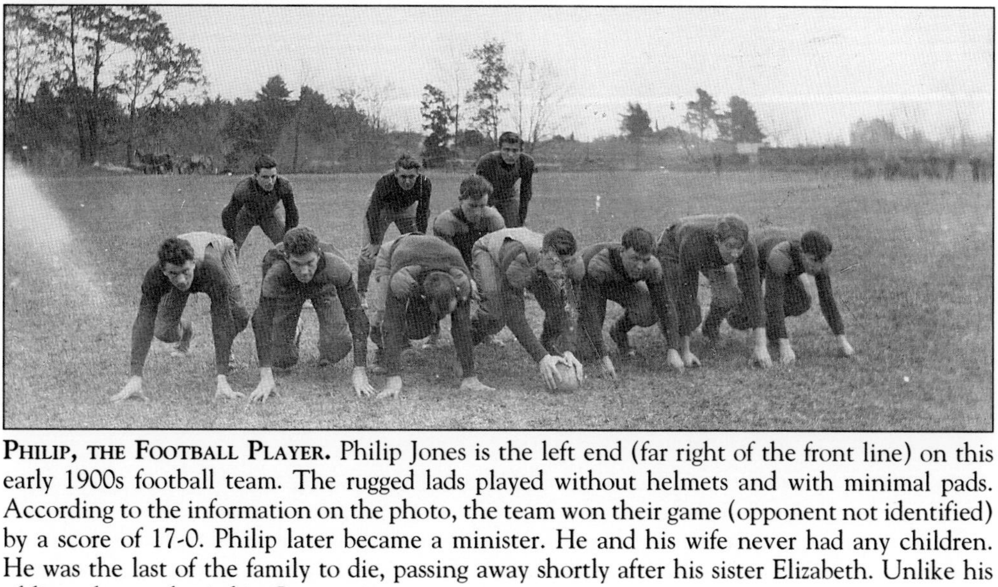

PHILIP, THE FOOTBALL PLAYER. Philip Jones is the left end (far right of the front line) on this early 1900s football team. The rugged lads played without helmets and with minimal pads. According to the information on the photo, the team won their game (opponent not identified) by a score of 17-0. Philip later became a minister. He and his wife never had any children. He was the last of the family to die, passing away shortly after his sister Elizabeth. Unlike his siblings, he was buried in Connecticut.

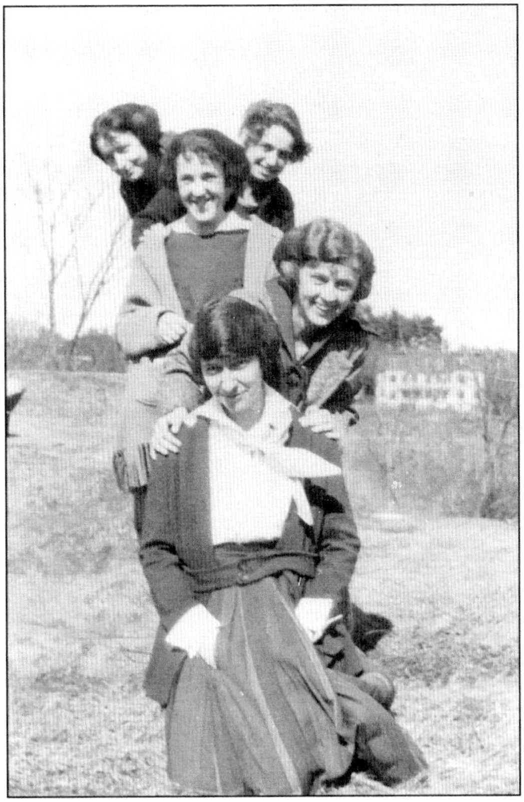

Elizabeth "Lib" Jones. Lib, born in 1894, remained single and stayed on the farm with her parents. She added chickens to the farm's livestock and took them on as her responsibility. Lib was one of the last of the family to die, and with her passing went the last of the Jones family to live on the farm. She is shown here in front of a group of friends. The photo dates from the late teens to the early 1920s.

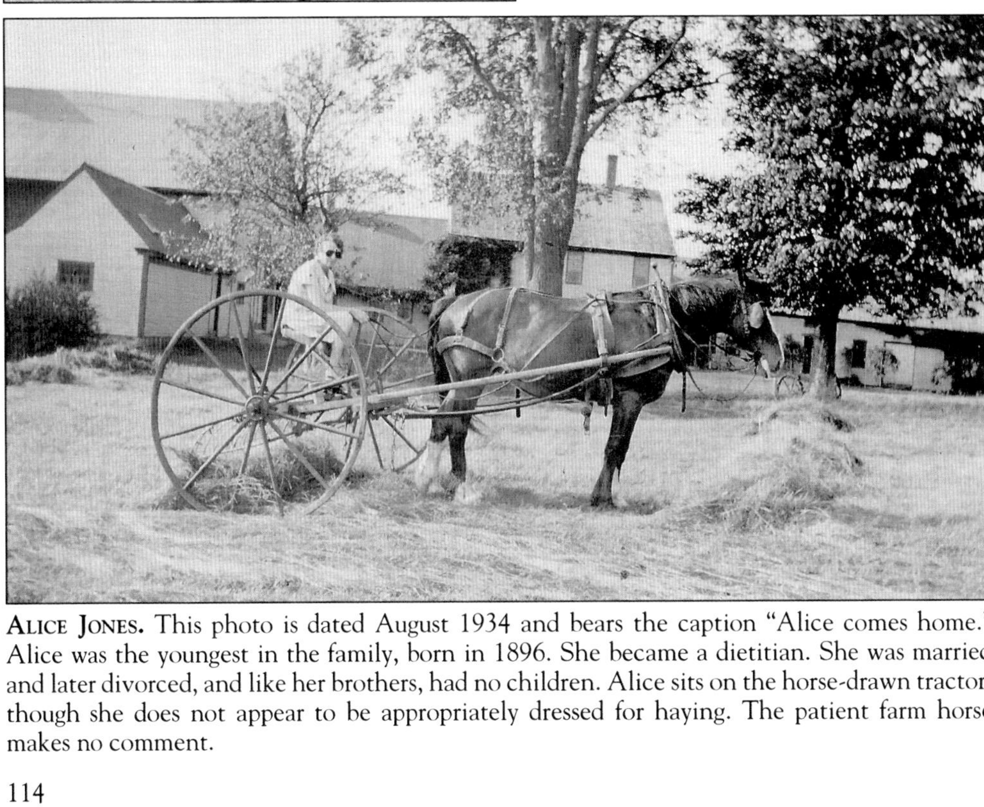

Alice Jones. This photo is dated August 1934 and bears the caption "Alice comes home." Alice was the youngest in the family, born in 1896. She became a dietitian. She was married and later divorced, and like her brothers, had no children. Alice sits on the horse-drawn tractor, though she does not appear to be appropriately dressed for haying. The patient farm horse makes no comment.

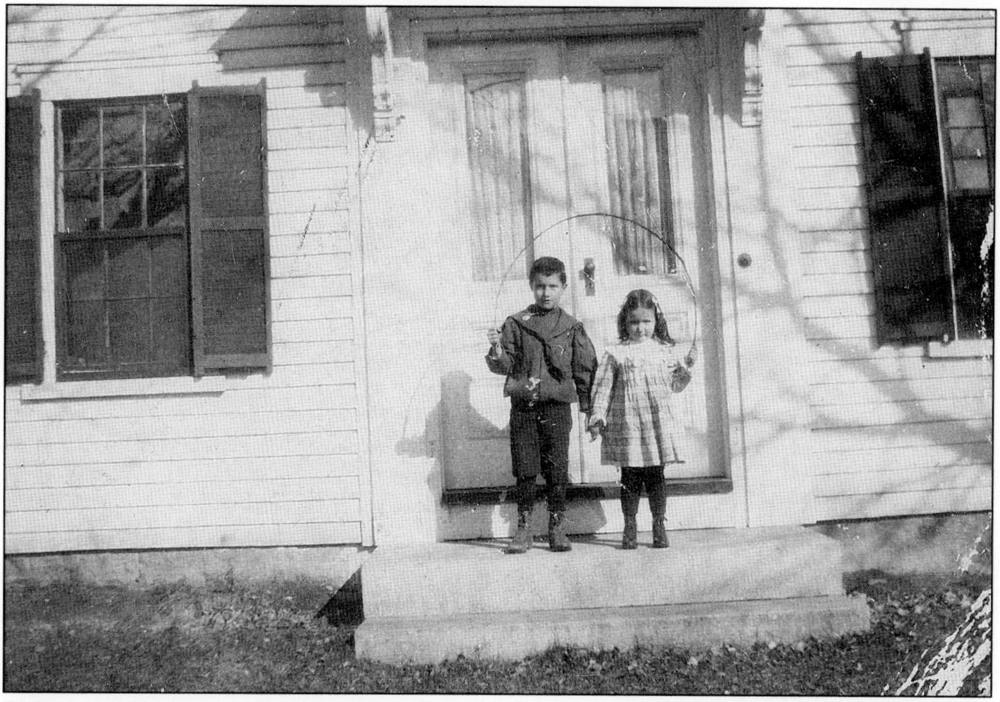

PHILIP AND ELIZABETH. Philip and Elizabeth, the two youngest Jones children, are standing on the front steps of Grandmother Cowell's home, presumably in Lebanon, Maine. Note Philip's clothing, with the sailor-type shirt and knickers.

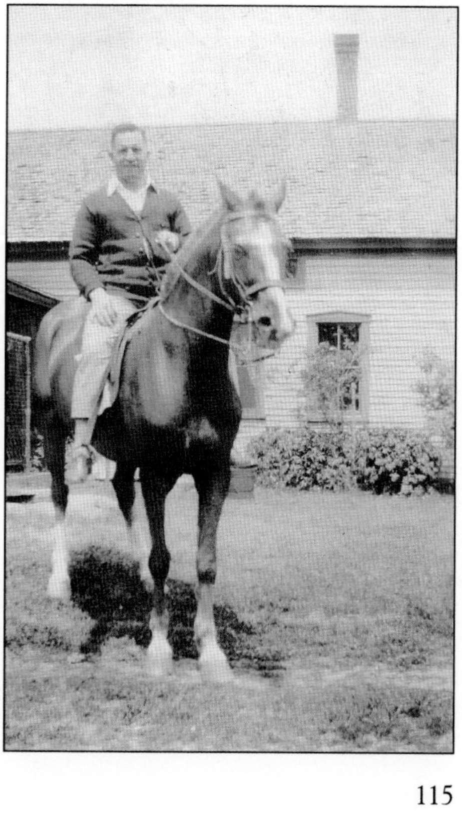

PHILIP. Philip is shown posing in front of the Cape Cod section of the farm. He is riding Elizabeth's beloved horse, Duke.

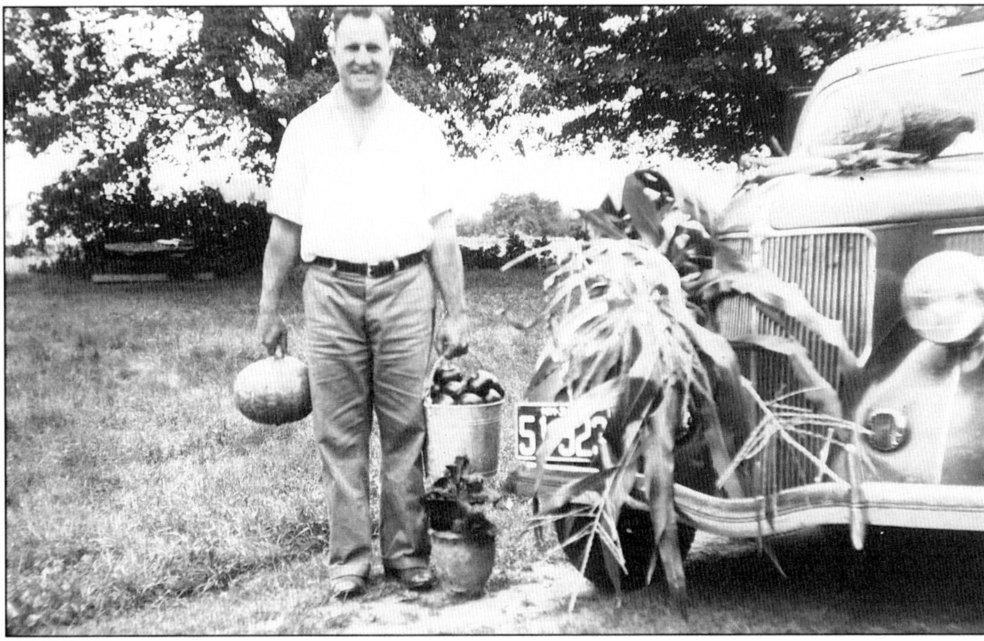

Philip in Later Years. Here, Philip poses in front of what may be his car. It appears to be harvest time, judging from the look of the corn stalks and the bucket of apples he's holding.

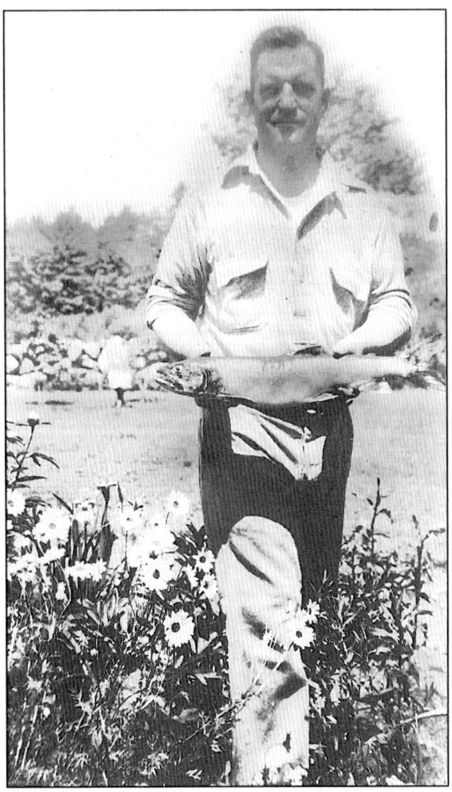

Philip with His Catch. Philip was an avid fisherman. He enjoyed having a picnic lunch down at the Jones River while trying to catch a fish. The size of the trout in the picture suggests that the luck of the river was with him on this day.

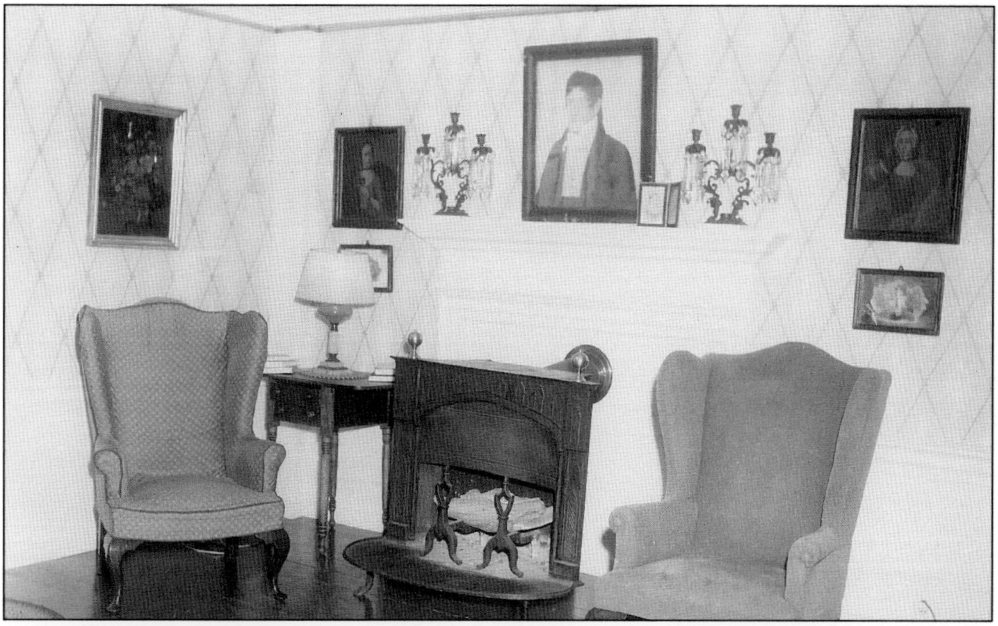

LIVING ROOM, JONES FARM. The original part of the house was built in the mid-1700s and was in the Cape Cod style. These photographs are the property of the New Hampshire Farm Museum. A portrait of Levi Jones (1771–1847) over the Federal mantelpiece dominates the living room of the Jones Farm. Wainscoting of wide pine boards and boxed corner beams indicate the age of the room. A pair of Queen Anne-style wing chairs flank the combination fireplace/stove that has replaced the original fireplace.

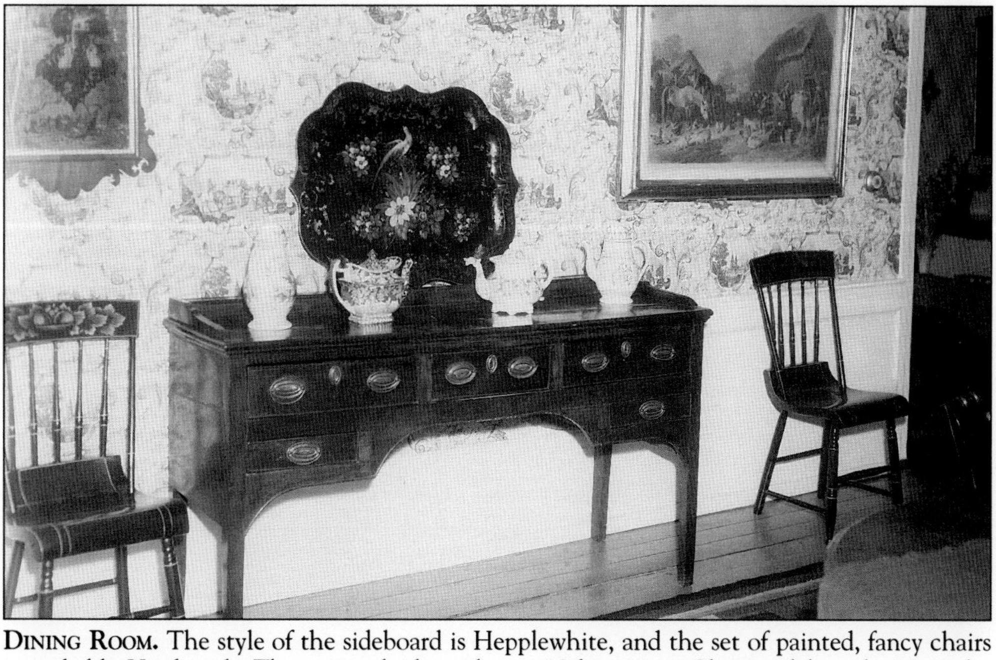

DINING ROOM. The style of the sideboard is Hepplewhite, and the set of painted, fancy chairs is probably Hitchcock. The mirror looks to be an 18th-century Chippendale style. Note the wainscoting is continued only part way along the wall. Please note the lovely pieces of porcelain on the sideboard.

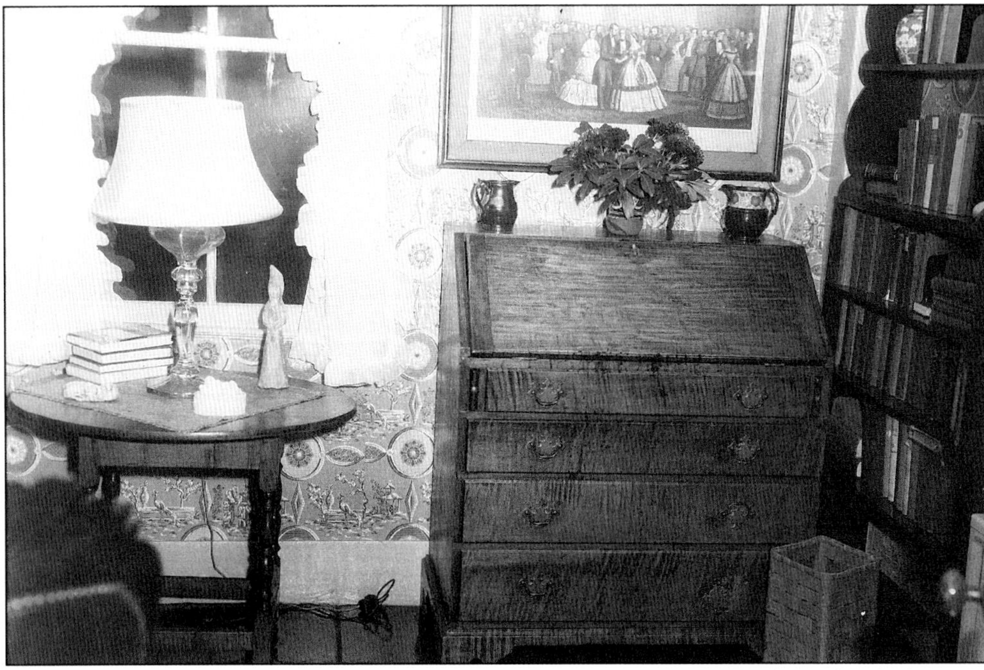

LIBRARY. In 1974, while Elizabeth was living in a nursing home, she had the family furniture auctioned. The slant-top desk sold at auction for $3,300; at the time, this was a very good price. The engraving over the desk looks to be Abraham and Mary Todd Lincoln, perhaps at an inaugural ball. Please note what appears to be a Chinese-style figurine on the table.

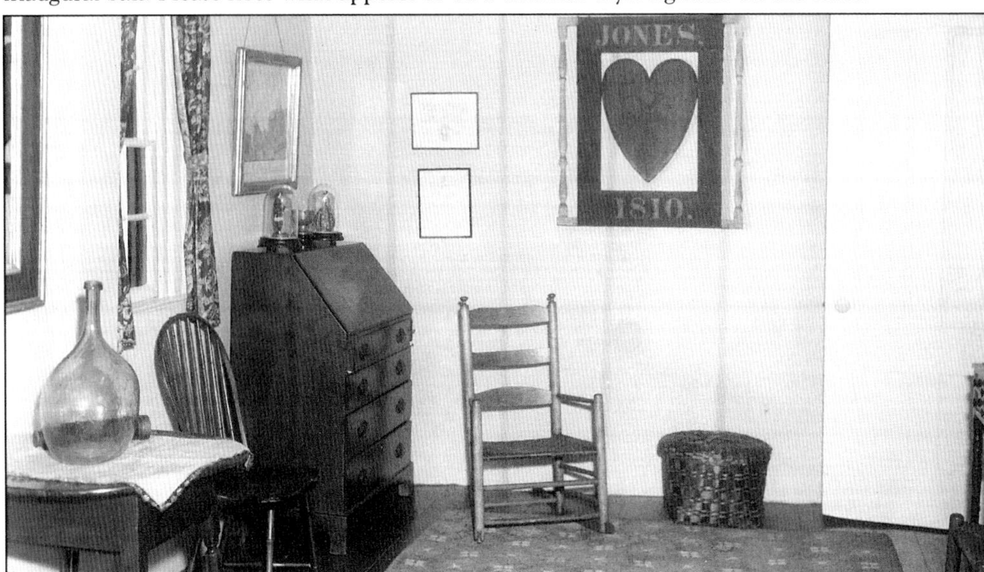

OLD KITCHEN. The old kitchen was part of the Cape Cod-style addition to the main house. Note the tavern sign, which was hung out at the road. Milton was the half-way point between Boston and the White Mountains, and the tavern was the perfect place for travelers to stop and rest. Note the slant-top desk and the Windsor chair. The other chair is probably an 18th-century-style piece. Also note the beautiful basket on the floor and the piece of blown glass on the table. This room shows how long the family had been adding furniture to their collection.

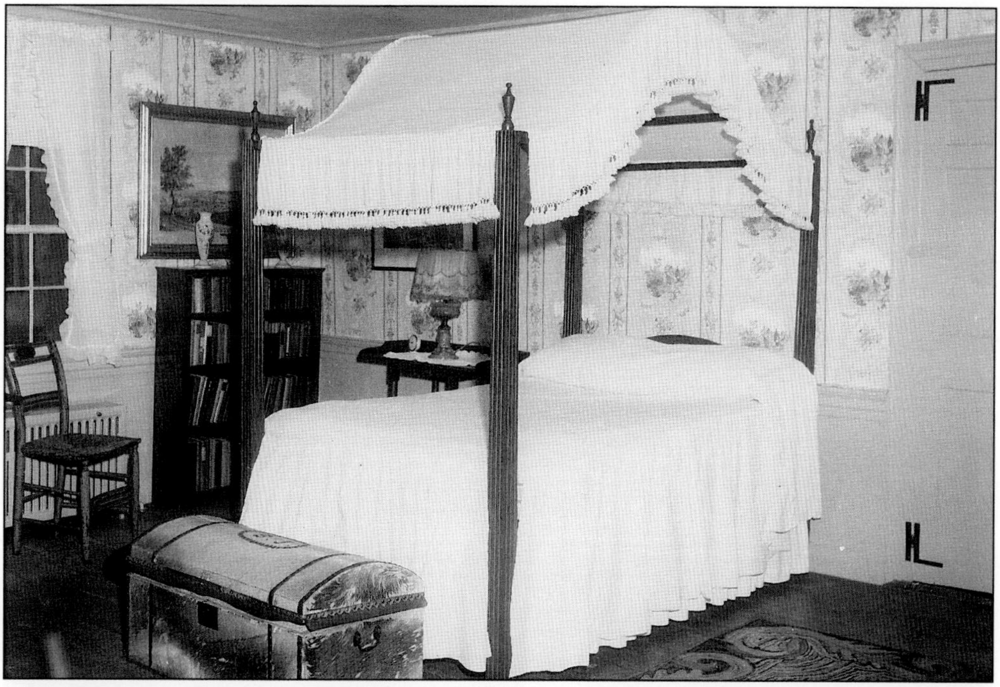

Lib's Bedroom. This four-poster canopy bed with classical motifs was sold at auction for \$175. The wainscoting indicates the age of the room. There appears to be a radiator under the window.

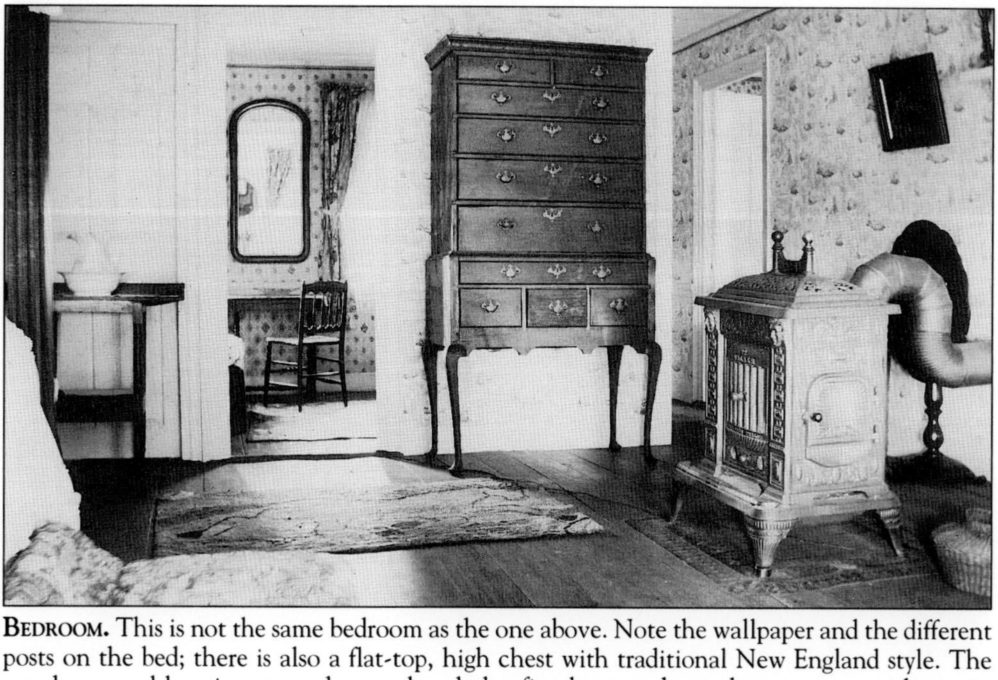

Bedroom. This is not the same bedroom as the one above. Note the wallpaper and the different posts on the bed; there is also a flat-top, high chest with traditional New England style. The wood- or coal-burning stove has replaced the fireplace; perhaps there was no radiator in this room.

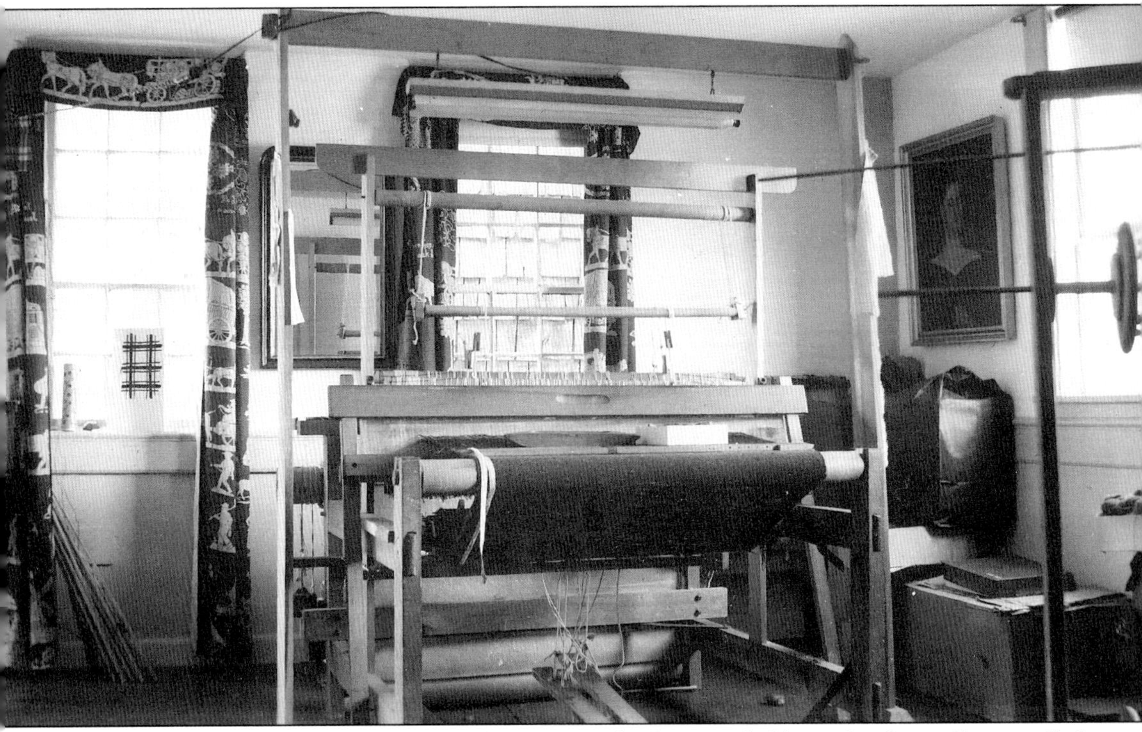

The "Shop." Pictured is Alice's headquarters at the farm, probably in the Cape. She installed this handloom and took up weaving. The wool may have come from local sheep.

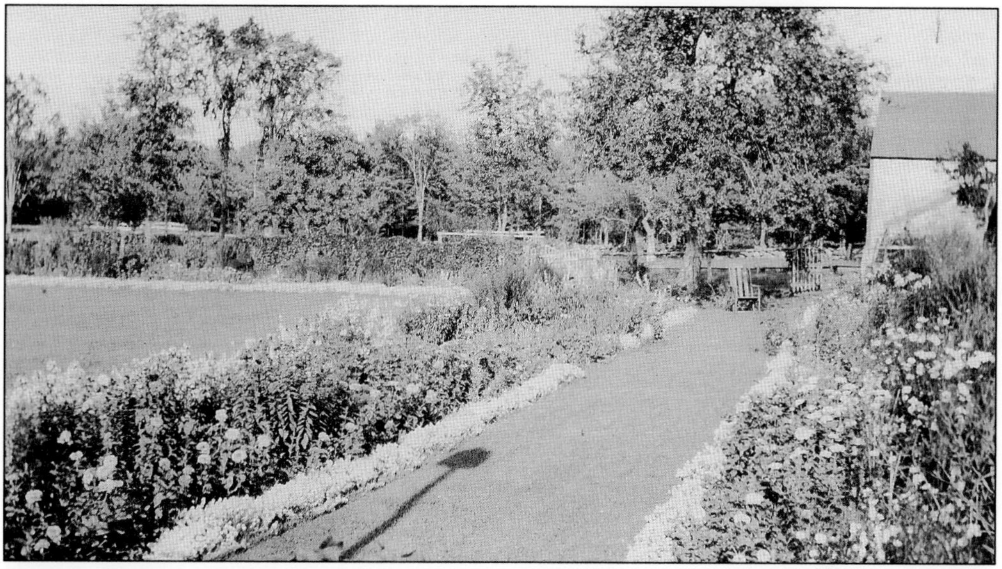

Emma's Garden. Emma Jones had numerous gardens and flowering boarders alongside well-maintained lawns. This is where friends and family preferred to gather when visiting or during reunions.

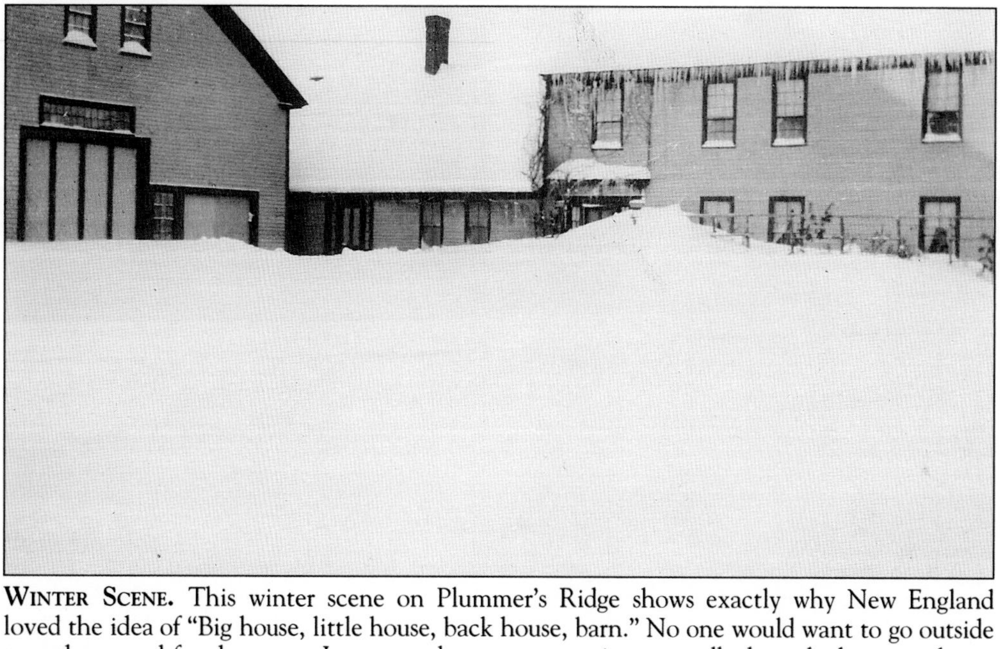

Winter Scene. This winter scene on Plummer's Ridge shows exactly why New England loved the idea of "Big house, little house, back house, barn." No one would want to go outside to gather wood for the stove. It was much more convenient to walk through the many barns and sheds.

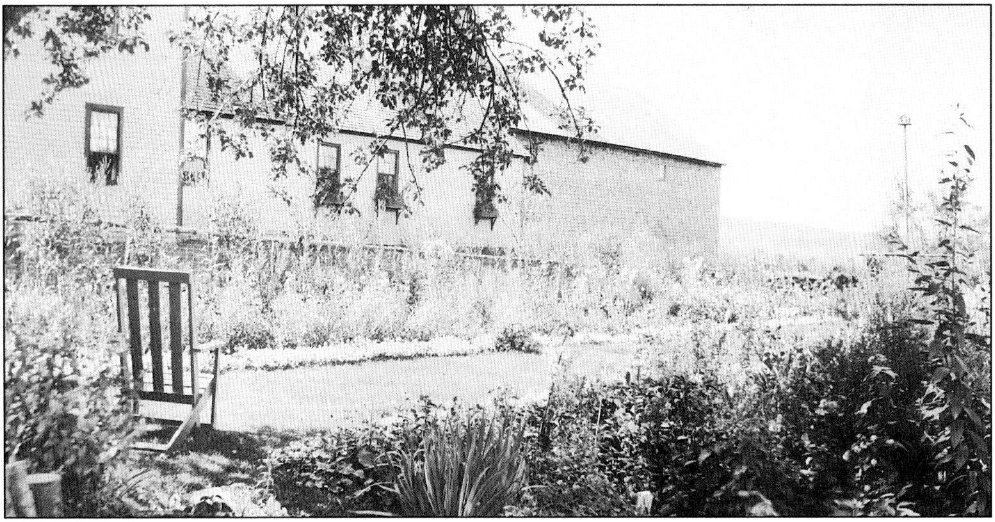

The Vista from the Side Lawn. The Jones family had a wonderful panoramic view of the surrounding hills from their spacious side lawn. A lawn chair invites guests to linger a while under the tree.

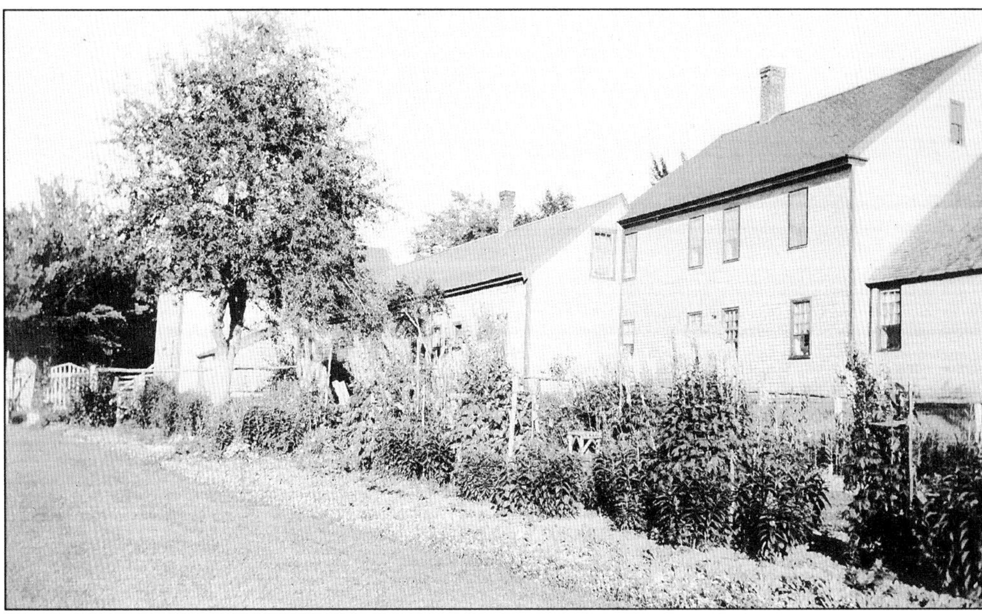

Big House, Little House, Back House, Barn. This unbroken line of continuous buildings is a New England concept. It permitted the farmer to move from house to barn without having to face mid-winter blasts of wind and snow or summer downpours. The main or "big" house is on the right of a one-story ell. Next is the "little" house, where the kitchen was located. Then comes the "back" house, or storage and workrooms. Last of all comes the barn. This is the longest, continuous running domestic building in all of New England.

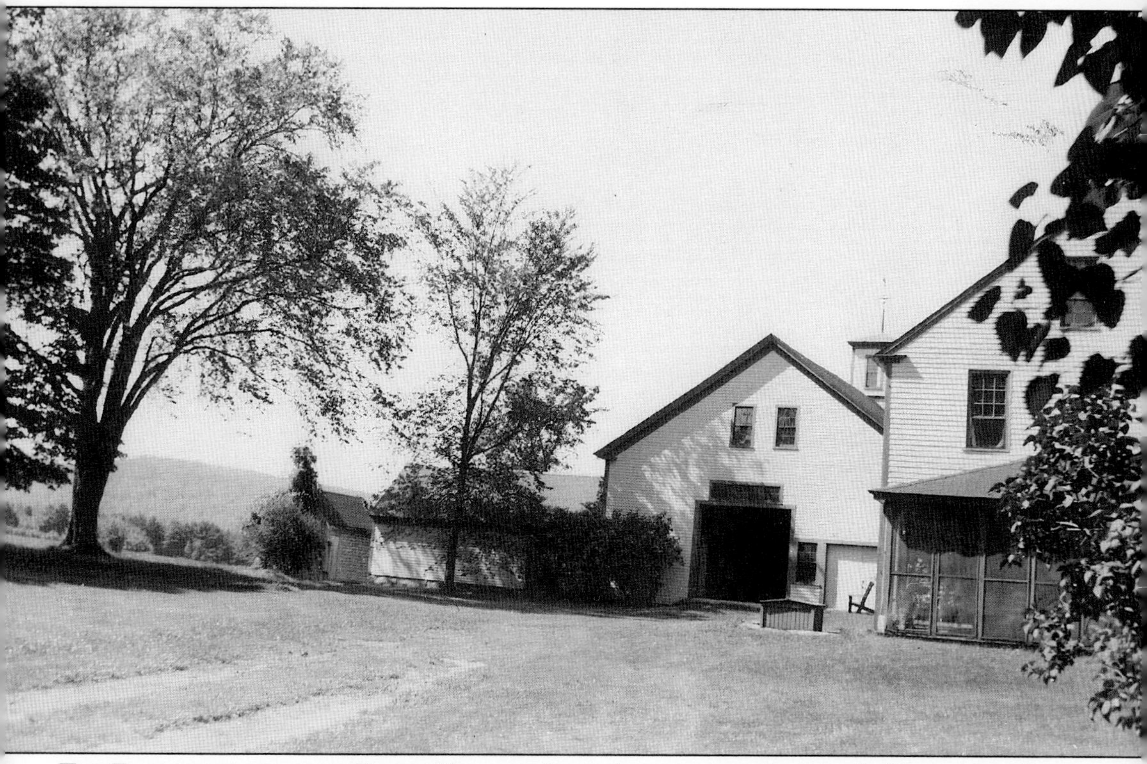

THE FARMSTEAD FROM THE ROAD. The main house has a screened-in porch. Please note the additional buildings that are attached to the barn.

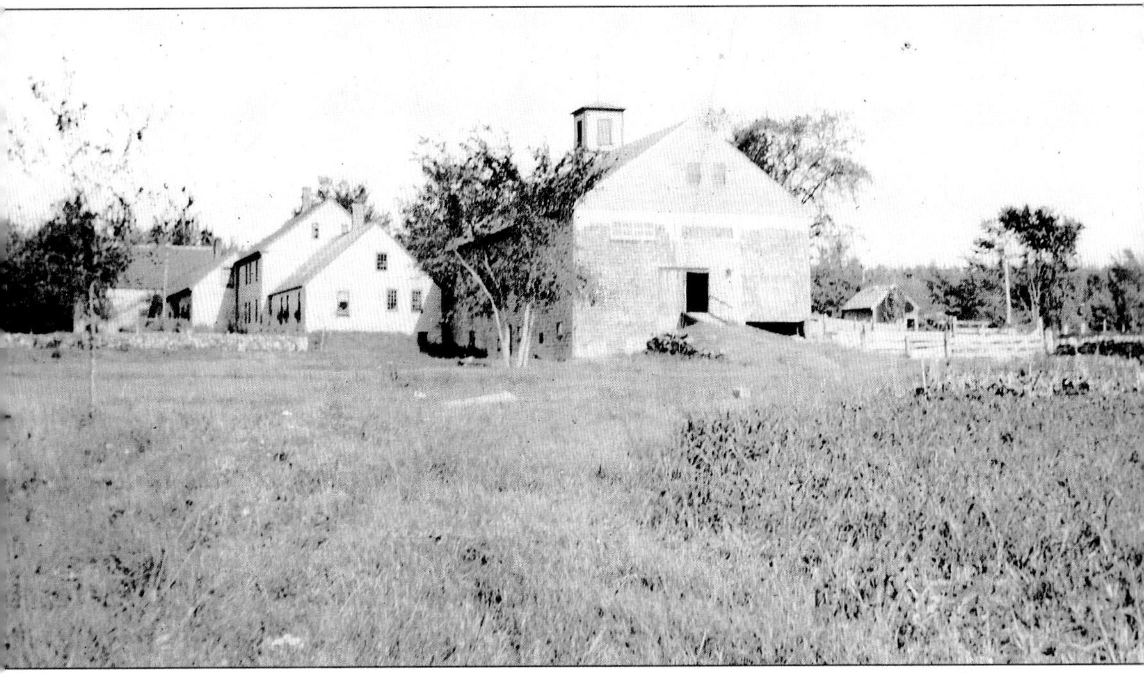

The Working End of the Barn. There was more than one barn on the property; this is a view of the back end, where the wagons and animals go up the ramp to enter.

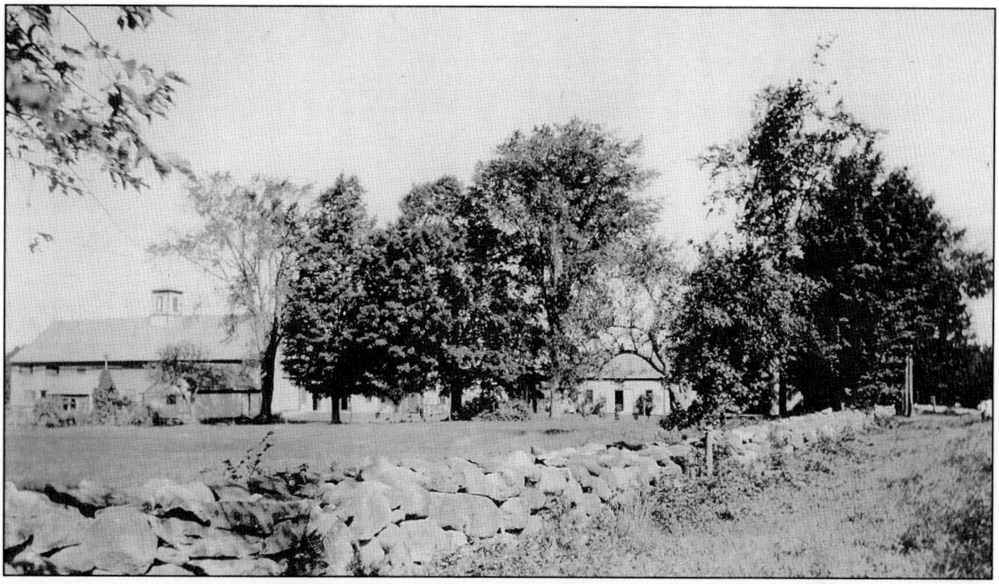

Elizabeth's Chicken Business. Lib had her father add multiple windows to the barn, and she turned it into a chicken coop after she went into the poultry business.

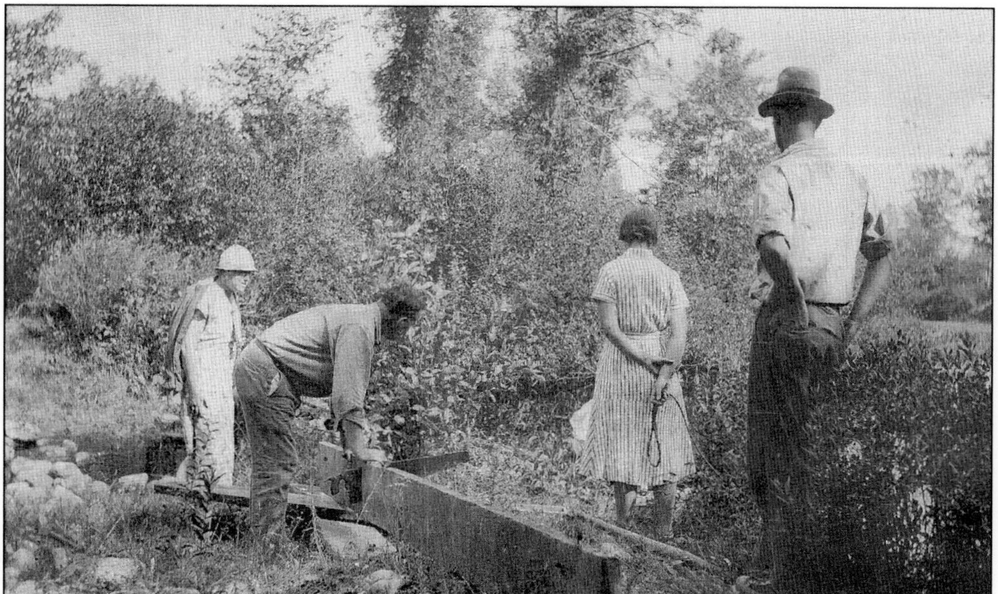

Jones River Bridge. A bridge was built over the Jones River in August 1934. Here, Elizabeth, accompanied as always by one of her dogs, "supervises" the construction.

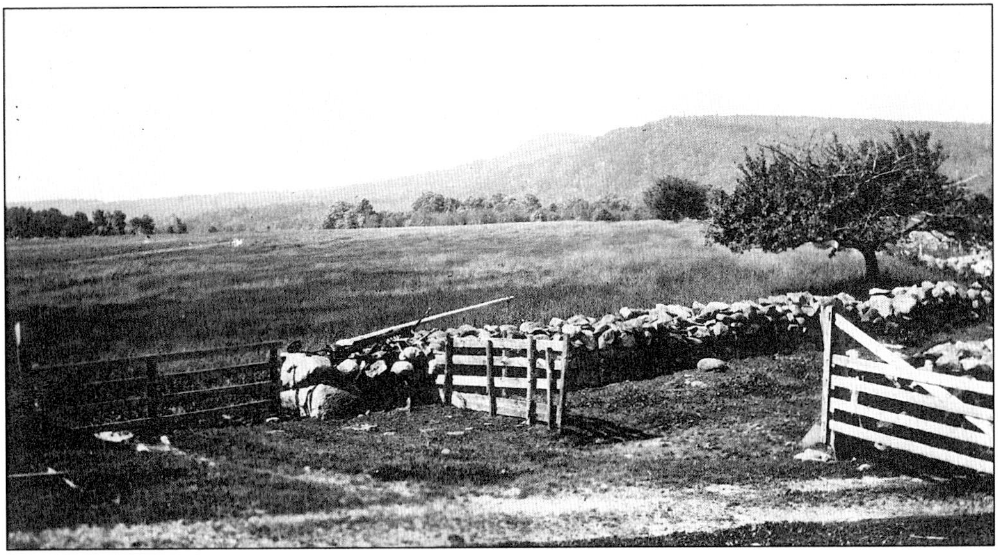

Jones Field. The Jones family had many acres of field and woodland. This photograph was taken in the back of the farm. All of this farmland belonged to the Jones family.

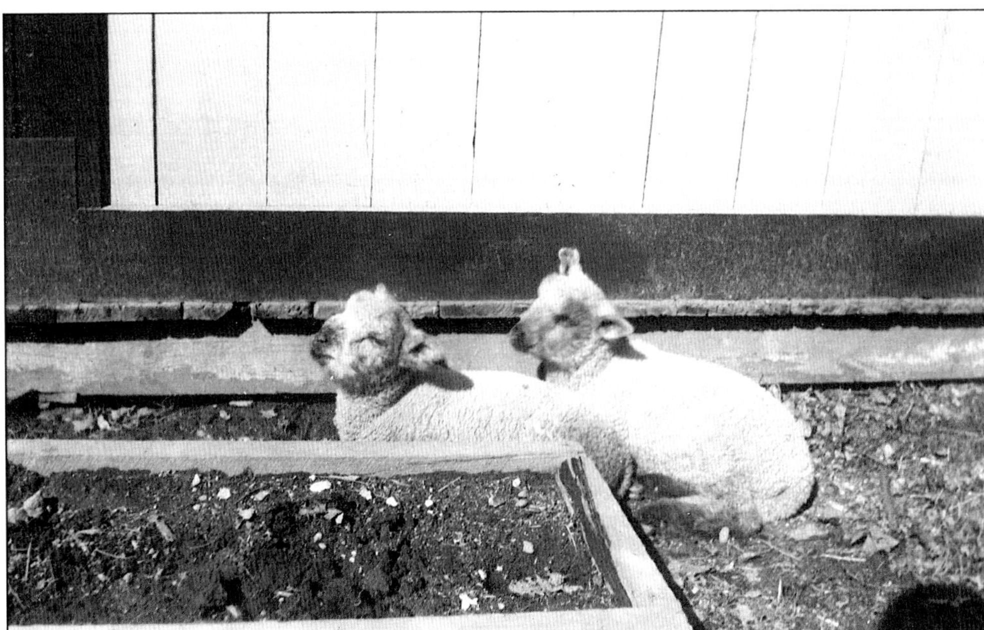

Lambs. All animals that lived on the Jones Farm were considered pets. These two new lambs were no exception. Elizabeth inherited her great love of animals from her mother, Emma, who always had some pet by her side. Until Elizabeth moved into the nursing home, she still had animals surrounding her.

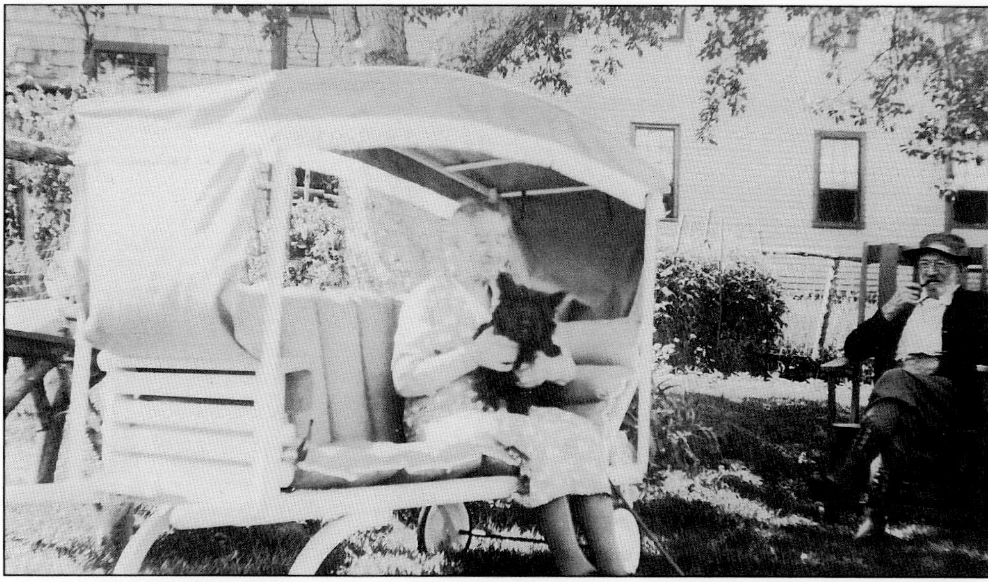

EMMA AND FRED. Here, Emma and Fred are relaxing in the garden. Once again, Emma is holding her dog, who was never far from her side, while Fred looks on.

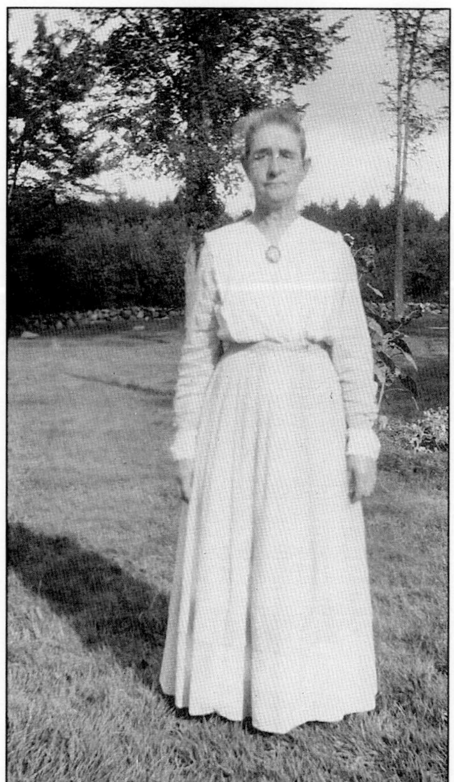

EMMA. Here is a wonderful close-up of Emma standing outside near her garden. Her garden was her pride and joy. She spent as much time as possible there, and it was very evident that she had a "green thumb."

VERY IMPORTANT AUCTION

EARLY AMERICAN ANTIQUES

MILTON, NEW HAMPSHIRE

TUESDAY & WEDNESDAY, AUGUST 20 & 21, 1974
Commencing each day at 10:00 a.m.

Richard W. Withington, Inc.

Auctioneer & Appraiser — Hillsboro, N. H. — Telephone 603-464-3232

THE END OF THE JONES FAMILY FARM. Elizabeth was the last of the Jones family to live in the farmhouse. In 1974, she was living in a nursing home. The furniture was auctioned to help pay medical bills. She died just short of a year after the auction. Because she and her brothers and sister never had children, there were no heirs to the property and house. Fearing the house would be turned into apartments, Elizabeth willed the house to be torn down upon her death. Fortunately, the Farm Museum was able to get the will reversed, with the blessing of Elizabeth's closest friends.